THE SCHOOL ON THE HILL

THE SCHOOL ON THE HILL

A history of the Hitchin Girls' (Grammar) School
1889–1989

by

Priscilla M. Douglas

with invaluable assistance from
Joyce Donald and Elizabeth Duignan

Published September 1988

ISBN 0 9513728 0 7

Printed by The Lavenham Press Ltd., Lavenham, Suffolk.

Contents

Dedication

When I first joined the staff of the Hitchin Girls' School, in 1973, I was intrigued by the two coats of arms, depicted as stained glass windows.

In trying to research their source and significance, it soon became apparent that there was little documentation of the school's history and I resolved to discover all that I could reveal, for myself.

Little did I think, in those early days, that my quest would result in this book.

In exploring all the avenues, I have been particularly impressed by recollections of the old pupils, some of whom are now over ninety. One common theme ran through all the memories of their school days: it was a privilege to have been at Hitchin Girls' Grammar School where they were happy and proud to be its pupils.

To them all I dedicate this book.

March, 1988   P. M. Douglas

vi

Acknowledgements

My grateful thanks are due to Joyce Donald who, at short notice, has collated my notes, done some original research and written most of the text. Without her full-time dedication to the task, over several months, this book would not have been completed.

My appreciation also to Elizabeth Duignan, a teacher at the school, for early assistance and for writing the chapters dealing with Mrs. Warwick's years at the school.

I am indebted to Hilary Cannon who has collated the subscribers' list, acted as accountant and banker, and who visited some old pupils.

Amanda Birkinshaw, ex-pupil and now studying engineering product design, has offered invaluable advice and ideas; has designed the dust jacket, redrawn and 'cleaned up' most of the maps, done some drawings and transcribed tapes; Amanda Richardson and Elizabeth Wells, both still pupils, have contributed their skill in the artistic line drawings and in copying the coats of arms. To all three, I offer my thanks and admiration.

Without the encouragement, help and interest of Terry Knight and Bill Smith of the North Herts. Gazette, when I first sought their help, I should have lacked the enthusiasm to continue and I owe them a debt of gratitude; also to Pat Gadd and members of the Hitchin Historical Society for their enthusiasm in my project.

To the staff of both the North Herts. Gazette and the Hitchin Comet I am grateful for their unfailing patience in exploring the photographic libraries and to Ian Walters for his copying of so many photographs.

To the Hertfordshire County Council Planning Department and Records Office I am indebted for their time and assistance, and for the many building plans.

My thanks too, to Mrs. Warwick for her cooperation in allowing the use of school records and to her staff for their patience with my queries and investigations; to Alan Fleck for his help with the Hitchin museum archives and to John Coxall for access to the property documents.

The Garter King of Arms and Mrs. Rita Chapple, of his staff at The College of Arms, have been most helpful and unstinting in giving their time pursuing my queries. I am most grateful to them.

The Hon. Victoria Glendinning gave time and help, and loaned photographs for my chapter on her family 'The Seebohms'. I appreciated her help.

I am greatly indebted to Gordon Donald, for his assistance, encouragement and 'refreshing' interest.

The many contributors to the school magazine may never know how invaluable have been their records of events, long gone, in compiling the school calendar for the past hundred years. To them my thanks.

To the staff and pupils, governors and friends of the school, both past and present, I am greatly indebted for their encouragement, unstinting time, marvellous memories and the loan of their photographs and memorabilia.

Dr. James Robertson, Terry Knight, Maureen O'Connell, Joan Williams and Isabel Blackman gave time and care in correcting the draft copy for which I am most grateful. Lastly, my thanks to my family for their long-suffering tolerance of my four-year obsession with 'The School on the Hill'.

P.M.D.

Diary of the Main Events in The History of Hitchin Girls' (Grammar) School

School
Roll

7   1889   1st May, H.G.G.S. (Independent Private School) opened in Bancroft, under Head Mistress **Miss Janet E. Gosnell**.

1891   The Girls took over the whole of the main building, Hitchin Boys' Grammar School (H.B.G.S.) having moved into their new, adjacent building in Grammar School Walk.

1892   Cookery School built.

1895   First Prizegiving.

1896   Kindergarten Dept. opened with three pupils – the youngest 3½ yrs. old. Closed in 1950.

New Assembly Hall and classrooms added.

121   1906   Building in progress 'on the hill'.

1908   Move to new buildings on top of Windmill Hill, Highbury Road, on land given by Frederic Seebohm. Officially opened – 25th July.

1914   First Gymnastics Competition.

1916   March. Old Girls' Association established (disbanded 1976). Fellowship Fund started in 1921.

1919   Spring. Formation of the 1st Hitchin (School) Company of Guides and Brownies. (Discontinued and restarted several times. Finally disbanded in 1986.)

1919   **Miss Annie Muriel Chambers** became Head Mistress.

First Deportment Girdles awarded (discontinued 1986).

Choir and Games Club formed.

1920   Three temporary classrooms and cloakrooms built on site of kitchen garden. Remained until 1939.

School Orchestra formed. Form Running introduced.

311   1922   October. Joined the Union of Girls' Schools Mission (U.G.S.) to support some of the Settlements in London. Continued until 1975.

1927   Summer uniform introduced – the 'butcher blue slips'.

The Misses Seebohm presented the Wood and Lower Field.

1929   The levelling of the new field was completed ready for hockey.

1929   The West Wing was built giving Rooms 11–16, and the West Cloakrooms.

1932   25th July. First Founder's Day Service at St. Mary's Church, attended, jointly, by H.G.G.S. and H.B.G.S.

1933   On 7th July, the new Swimming Bath was formally opened on the Lower Field.

408   1938   Summer. First meeting of the School Council.

1939   New Hall, Art Room and 3 Laboratories built and officially opened by Lady Elphinstone.

447   1940   Autumn. Eastbourne High School evacuated to Hitchin and shared the school until Easter 1943.

1945   **Miss Mary Alice Badland** became Headmistress.

510   1950   Last seven pupils left the Kindergarten which then closed.

1951   Archways on to corridor by Rooms 9 and 10 were filled in, thus enclosing the gymnasium (Drama Room).

450	1952	Building completed on what had been Miss Badland's garden, providing new Domestic Science room and two new Form Rooms. October. First Harvest Festival.
	1953 ⎱ 1954 ⎰	Construction of First Floor on top of Junior Building completed, giving three First Forms and Va a classroom each. Senior VI moved to the old dormitory, now converted into a series of private studies.
	1955	Senior VI moved again into the old Library (Staff Room) and the former dormitory was converted to the Library.
	1956	May. Christian Union Group formed.
499	1958	Dining Room extended to more than double its size. December. Miss Badland joined the Boarders living at Highbury House. Main Entrance Hall enclosed.
	1960	The last five Boarders left.
	1962	**Miss Gladys Margaret Harrison** became Headmistress.
510	1964	75 years' Anniversary Celebrations. VI allowed privilege of wearing any suitable blue or yellow dress and could wear discreet make-up.
	1965	Marriage of Miss Harrison – now Mrs. G. Margaret Warwick.
590	1966	School supports Save the Children Fund as well as the Mission.
	1968	Introduction of Athletics in Sport.
	1969	Luncheon in honour of Girton College Centenary.
	1972	Science and Gymnasium Block completed.
608	1973	Four Form entry begins.
	1974	H.G.G.S. becomes 'Hitchin Girls' School'. Swimming pool heated.
740	1975	Mobile classrooms arrive. Junior block demolished and new building commences. Five form intake. H.G.S. withdraws from supporting U.G.S. and the Mission.
	1978	Lower School and Domestic Science Rooms completed.
900	1981	Footbridge built over Highbury Road to provide safe access to Highbury House for Music lessons.
	1982	April. Music Block completed. Introduction of Duke of Edinburgh Award scheme.
	1983	September. Introduction of Whole Food Health Bar in Lower School.
884	1988	Centenary Celebration planning begins.

THE FOUNDATION

A measure of the wealth of the Mattock family can be seen at St. Mary's Church, in Hitchin, where Nicholas Mattock donated the magnificent South Porch and was granted his Arms in 1494.

In 1639, his descendant, John Mattock, a true philanthropist, wished to benefit mankind in ensuring the education of the young. To this end, he gave the rents and profits from nine acres of land for 'the maintenance of an able and learned schoolmaster for instructing the children of the inhabitants of Hitchin in good literature and virtuous education for the avoiding of idleness, the mother of all vice and wickedness'. It is not known whether, in using the word 'children', John Mattock was a man before his time in considering the education of girls or whether he followed the popular assumption that only boys required schooling. Whatever his intention, the wording was strictly interpreted in the school that opened in Bancroft Street, a hundred and fifty years later. The full text now appears above the main entrance to both the Boys' and the Girls' Schools which grew out of his Foundation.

John Mattock first appointed eleven of his friends and fellow townsmen to administer the Trust, appoint a schoolmaster and supervise the good running of the establishment. This did not, of course, cover the cost of the building, but friends, by financial assistance, allowed him to buy an ancient house, at the top of Tilehouse Street, which had been used as a school for at least a hundred years. Thus began the Free School.

The first master, Thomas Hayndy, had the great misfortune, soon after his appointment, of the Civil War coming to Hitchin in the shape of three thousand Parliamentary troops, quartered in the town and drilling daily in the Market place. This understandable distraction meant that school work suffered, and it is to his credit that the school did not founder almost at birth. However, from the 1660s onward, there was increasing conflict between the wishes of the townspeople and the Trustees over what should be taught. The Trustees favoured the Classics and Latin so as to develop a 'whole personality', while the locals would be content with the 'three Rs' so as to equip a boy to earn his living.

In the eighteenth century there were further problems, with bad debts and a series of incompetent, unsuitable schoolmasters. Standards rallied under Joseph Niblock, but when the health of the fifteenth master failed in 1876, it was decided that the school must close. The Education Act of 1870 had made elementary education compulsory for all children and the provision of other newer and more modern schools in the town threatened a further decline in numbers. John Mattock's original Foundation had lasted for 236 years.

*   *   *   *   *

One Trustee, at the time of the closing of the Tilehouse Free School, was the Quaker, Frederic Seebohm, partner in the banking house – Sharples, Tuke, Lucas and Seebohm, later to become Barclay's Bank. A man of wealth, influence and vision, he now turned his thoughts to secondary education. 'If the Foundation could no longer support a Free School, why not open a fee paying Grammar School with some scholarship places for the children of the poor and include both boys and girls?' This proposal was so strongly opposed by some of the Trustees, as being outside the parameters of their Trust, that a petition was taken to Parliament. An

3

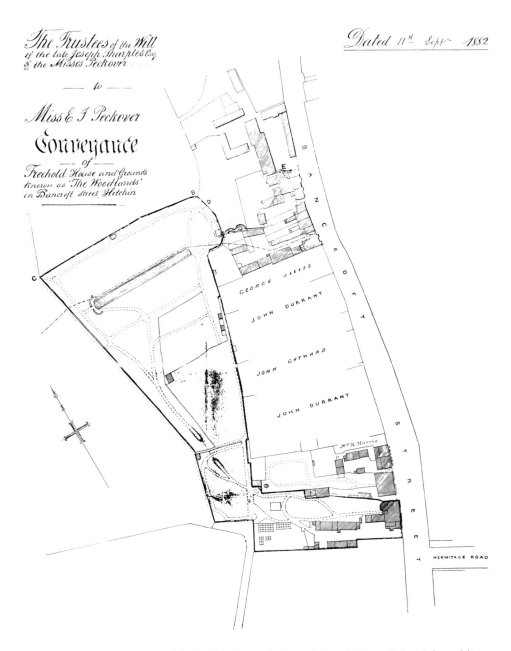

The Trustees of the Will
of the late Joseph Sharples Esq
& the Misses Peckover

— to — —

Miss E J Peckover

Conveyance

of

Freehold House and Grounds
known as 'The Woodlands'
in Bancroft Street, Hitchin

Dated 11ᵗʰ Septᵣ 1882

inspection by the Endowed Schools' Commission of the old Free School found it to be quite inadequate and the petition failed.

In the meantime, a search for suitable premises had not been really necessary, for 'The Woodlands' was across Bancroft Street opposite Mr. Seebohm's home. It was a house familiar to him, having been the family home of the Sharples family for three generations and the home of his partner, Joseph Sharples, until his death in 1871. Joseph's only surviving daughter, Eliza, had married Alexander Peckover of Wisbech in 1858 – later Lord Peckover with Arms granted in 1880. These and the Arms of the Mattock family appear as stained glass windows in the present girls' school building. Under the terms of their grandfather's will, the three Misses

4

Left: The arms of Nicholas Mattock of Hitchin in the County of Hertford granted 23rd July, 1494.
The blazon: *Shield:* Azure a chevron quarterly or and argent between three fleur de lys of the second. *Crest:* Bear per bend argent and sable muzzled gold sitting within a chaplet ermine.

Drawn by Elizabeth Wells 1983–

Right: The arms of Algernon Peckover of Wisbech in the County of Cambridge granted 27th December 1880.
The blazon, or heraldic description, given by Garter King of Arms is as follows:
    'Per pale Gules (Red) and Sable (Black) a Garb Or (Gold) on a chief nebuly of the last three lions rampant Azure (blue) and for the Crest On a wreath of the Colours a Lion Rampant Azure holding in the dexter paw a Sprig of Oak fructed and slipped proper and resting the sinister forepaw on an Escutcheon charged with the Arms.'
It should be noted that in the stained glass in question, part of the field of the Shield on which the Garb is placed is shown as checky Argent and Sable, looking like a draught board, this being an error, the background tincture being all Sable, as the 1880 grant makes clear, rather than checky Argent and Sable.

were 'to sell the property or postpone such conversions and sale and to hold all monies and investments, in trust'. In 1882, when the youngest sister came of age, the house was technically put up for sale and 'sold' to the oldest Miss Peckover for £2,500 – 'the freehold house and grounds in Bancroft Street . . . The School and classrooms; outbuildings, summer houses, vinery and hot houses, yard, gardens, pleasure grounds, shrubberies and paddock – all the piece of land containing five acres and eight perches . . . "The Woodlands" reserved for Alfred Ransom.'
Peckover – Elizabeth Josephine aged 12, Alexandrina aged 11 and Anna Jane aged 10 – inherited 'The Woodlands', to be held in trust for them by Alfred and William Ransom.

After the death of Joseph Sharples the house had been let to two school masters, Messrs. Woodhead and Sharp, and had already been used as a school before attracting the attention of Mr. Seebohm. Under Joseph Sharples' will, the trustees

Reginald Hine claims, in 'History of Hitchin Grammar School', that the purchase price was £3,150, a misconception which has appeared in subsequent works. The original documents are quite clear as to the price of the building; the remainder of the money was probably used to equip the new school.

In December 1889, exactly seven months after the school opened, the Indenture was signed 'In consideration of £2,500, the land, together with the buildings which were, for many years, in the occupation of Joseph Sharples and afterwards Messrs. Woodhead and Sharp and now the Governors of the Hitchin Grammar School. . . . As described in the map and plan drawn in September 1882 . . . To the use of Rev. Lewis Hensley and Frederic Seebohm, in trust for the Governors of the charity called The Hitchin Grammar School . . . Foundation as regulated by a scheme made under the Endowed Schools Act on the 3rd May 1888.'

The John Mattock Foundation had risen, like a phoenix, from the ashes.

FURTHER DEVELOPMENT OF THE FOUNDATION

In 1902, the County Councils, by Act of Parliament, were obliged to take responsibility for secondary education in their areas, which meant that some financial support would be forthcoming from central funds. Later, in 1945, all fee paid places were abolished and the County became solely responsible for the standards of education within the schools. Nevertheless, the Foundation Trustees were outraged when, in 1950, the Hertfordshire County Council planned to take to itself all charity trusts and endowments with the intention of spreading the proceeds more evenly. The trustees maintained that the funds were specifically intended for the children of Hitchin and that individual needs would be better assessed nearer home. At County level, the argument reached stalemate so it was taken to the Ministry of Education. Eventually a compromise was reached and the Foundation was required to pay an annual sum to central funds, but thereafter, the County took a lively interest in the disposal of the remaining money.

In the 1960s a system of joint governing bodies was set up so as to have liaison between the schools in one area. Those for Hitchin remained the Foundation Trustees and it was proposed to include the two secondary modern schools in the benefits accruing from the Trust. The Education Ministry decreed that these establishments had no historical connection with the Foundation and turned it down. Ten years later there was still dispute as to what could, and what could not, be properly paid for by the Foundation. It was not until the early 1980s that the Charity Commissioners decided that permission need not be sought for spending of funds on anything not normally covered by the County.

In 1974 when secondary schools became all-ability, each school had its own governing body and the Foundation, for the first time, became independent. We now have the Hitchin Education Foundation, which, in Mrs. Beryl Wearmouth, coincidentally shares its Chairman with Hitchin Girls' School. It still administers their properties in the town, collects the rents and invests wisely. The original Foundation is still very much alive and helping in the education of the children of Hitchin.

6

HITCHIN GRAMMAR SCHOOL FOUNDATION.

LIST OF GOVERNORS.

REPRESENTATIVE GOVERNORS (for five years).

	BY WHOM APPOINTED.
REV. LEWIS HENSLEY,	TRINITY COLLEGE, CAMBRIDGE.
MR. ROBERT LONG,	
„ THOMAS PRIEST,	RAND'S FOUNDATION.
MR. JAMES H. TUKE,	
„ FREDERIC SEEBOHM,	
„ THOMAS PERKINS,	HITCHIN CHARITY TRUSTEES.
„ GEORGE A. PASSINGHAM,	
„ THOMAS A. DASHWOOD,	
MR. WILLIAM RANSOM,	
„ WILLIAM SEYMOUR.	DONORS AND SUBSCRIBERS.

CO-OPTATIVE GOVERNORS (for eight years).

MR. W. ALDIS WRIGHT,	MISS EMILY DAVIES,
„ MARLBOROUGH R. PRYOR,	MRS. L. HENSLEY,
	MRS. J. H. TUKE.

The Governors intend to open the Grammar Schools for Boys and Girls on MAY 1ST, 1889.

ADMISSION.

The Schools will be open to pupils between the ages of eight and seventeen years.

Applications for the admission of Boys and Girls should be addressed to the Head Master and Mistress respectively, or till they come into residence, to F. SEEBOHM, Esq., Hon. Sec., Hitchin.

All candidates must be provided with a certificate of good conduct and must pass an entrance examination consisting of (at least) Reading, Writing from dictation, Sums in the first four simple rules of Arithmetic, with the Multiplication Table.

GRAMMAR SCHOOL FOR GIRLS.

Under the Scheme of the Charity Commissioners, 1883.

HEAD MISTRESS :

Miss J. E. GOSNELL, B.A., LOND., late Assistant Mistress at the Ladies' College, Jersey.

Besides Religious instruction the following subjects will be taught in the School :—

Reading, Writing and Arithmetic ;	Algebra ;
Geography and History ;	Geometry ;
English Grammar, Composition, and	Domestic Economy and Laws of Health ;
Literature ;	Drawing, Drill, and Vocal Music ;
Latin, French, and German ;	Needlework ;
One or more branches of Natural Science ;	Instrumental Music optional, at an extra fee.

The Course of Instruction will be according to the classification and arrangements made by the Head Mistress.

SCHOLARSHIPS.

Four Foundation Scholarships for Girls will be open for competition before the opening of the School. Two of these will be in the form of partial exemption and two of total exemption from the payment of fees. One of the latter will be for girls who have been for not less than three years scholars in any of the Public Elementary Schools in Hitchin, and one under similar conditions for the Schools in Holwell, Ickleford, Pirton, and Lower Stondon, with a preference to Holwell.

Particulars of these and of other future Scholarships will be duly announced.

REGULATIONS.

The following regulations apply to both Schools :—

DIVISION OF SCHOOL YEAR.—There will be three Terms in the year, each Term being about thirteen weeks.

FEES.—For pupils up to 12 years of age, £2 10s. per term.
„ above 12 „ £3 10s. per term.

The fees are to be paid in advance to the Head Master and Head Mistress respectively, and are due on the first day of each Term.

Stationery and Drawing Material will be provided at a charge of 3s. 6d. per term. The School Books in use can be purchased at the Schools or at the Booksellers.

REMOVAL.—A Term's notice in writing, addressed to the Head Master or Head Mistress, will be required previous to the removal of a pupil.

The above Regulations have been framed in accordance with the requirements of the Scheme for the Administration of the Hitchin Grammar School Foundation, copies of which may be obtained from Messrs. PATERNOSTER & HALES, Hitchin, price 6d.

Further regulations will be made from time to time, as required.

Prospectuses may be had gratis of Messrs. PATERNOSTER & HALES.

THE GOVERNORS

There were fifteen governors when the Grammar Schools opened in 1889, though the Foundation governing body had been formed at the planning stage, a year earlier. The governors were responsible for raising the money for the running of the school, for the upkeep of the school fabric and for deciding the priorities in school spending. They also controlled the curriculum of subjects taught and were responsible for the appointment of teaching staff. With the exception of raising the money, the school governors still have much the same responsibilities today. The Rev. Canon Lewis Hensley was elected the first Chairman in 1888 and remained so until his death in 1905. Mr. Tuke, a banker, was appropriately the Hon. Treasurer, and remained so for the next eight years. Mr. Seebohm took on the duties of Hon. Secretary and later was Hon. Treasurer from 1896 until 1912. The first Clerk to the Governors was Francis Shillitoe, succeeded in 1911 by his son, Francis Rickman Shillitoe and in 1949 by his grandson, Francis George Shillitoe. The Clerk to the Governors is now John Coxall.

In 1902, the Local Authority became responsible for secondary education and therefore paid a considerable sum towards the building of the School on the Hill. Henceforth, the Governing Body would be radically altered and five governors would be appointed by both the County Council and the Urban District Council. For the first time, there was a political element in the make-up of the Board. In addition to these ten, there were still five co-optative governors plus two each from the Trustees of the Hitchin Charity and of the Rand's Foundation and one each from Trinity, Girton and Newnham Colleges. The last two reflect the rise in girls' opportunities for further education.

The co-opted governors no longer appeared after the 1930s, but the structure and function remained fairly constant until, in 1944, the two schools joined with Bessemer Boys' and Hitchin High School for Girls. With four schools to supervise, the governors had a heavy work load, reflected all round the country, and this scheme was abandoned with the setting up of all-ability schools. Once more, each school had its own governing body. These now had non-voting parents and staff representatives. More recently the teachers and parents have chosen their own representatives with full voting rights and senior students have joined in a non-voting capacity. Representatives of industry and commerce have been co-opted to share their experience in the wider world. Yet still there lingered the last remnants of the old structure, with one governor appointed by the Rand Charity to each of the former grammar schools and the vicar of Hitchin representing Trinity College at the boys' school. In 1988, under yet more reorganisation, these last links with the original Trustees and Governors of the Grammar Schools passed into history.

The Chairmen of the Governors

The Rev. Canon Lewis Hensley	1888–1905
W. Aldis Wright	1906–1913
Marlborough R. Pryor	1913–1914
The Rev. Canon R. St. John Parry	1915–1931
Hugh Exton Seebohm	1931–1946
C. J. Widdows	1946–1954
W. A. Hill	1954–1973
Mrs. Beryl Wearmouth	1973–

The Rev. Canon Lewis Hensley,
M.A.
1888–1905

Mrs. Beryl Wearmouth
1973–

Hugh Exton Seebohm, J.P.
1931–1946

Charles J. Widdows, J.P.
1946–1954

Walter (Jimmy) Hill, O.B.E., J.P.
1954–1973

The Chairman of the Governors not only conducts Governors' meetings but has a special part to play in the school. The primary role is that of support in tackling and solving problems with the Head, especially when these involve the suspension of a pupil. The position of the Chairman should be one of impartial arbitration. A school is only a building unless the pupils are there and so it is important to see and be seen around the school premises, to support school functions and to know, and be known by, the pupils.

Both Mr. Hill and Mrs. Wearmouth are well known in the town as hard-working, dedicated public figures. Both have been Chairman of the North Hertfordshire District Council and of untold other committees, spreading their time between political and philanthropic causes and yet each, in their own way, has left a mark on the history of the Girls' (Grammar) School, and fulfilled their duties to it. In her very busy life Mrs. Wearmouth can still say: 'It is quite a time-consuming job as you can appreciate. There are so many things to attend, not only from a sense of duty but also out of pure enjoyment. I am determined not to be the chairman of a remote body of people. That is why I am always delighted to be recognised and spoken to by the girls when I am out and about in Hitchin. My one regret is that I

9

always know the intellectually able and the girls who transgress – I rarely get to know the average pupil as well as I would wish to.' With sentiments like these, the chairmanship of the governors is still in safe hands.

THE SEEBOHM FAMILY

Frederic Seebohm

The Quakers, in Hitchin, developed a tradition of bringing education to the masses and as early as 1810, the Hitchin Friends set up an evening school for boys, to be followed by another for girls and still later, adults. Among other prominent schools started by Quakers were those of Mary Exton, who founded and ran a school in Walsworth, and of Joseph Sharples, run by his daughter, Eliza, at Sunnyside. Hitchin Girls' Grammar School was the special concern and interest of the Seebohm family.

Frederic Seebohm was the son of a wealthy Bradford wool merchant. When he was called to the Bar he practised in London, and chose to live in his mother's home town, Hitchin, where he had both relatives and friends. He married Mary Ann Exton, in 1857, and two years later became a junior partner in the bank which her father had started with Sharples and Bassett. This later became Sharples, Tuke, Lucas and Seebohm. (William Exton's other daughter married into the Barclay family which later took over the bank which remains on the same premises as in Frederic Seebohm's day.)

On the death of his father-in-law, Frederic Seebohm inherited the family home,

'The Hermitage', in Bancroft Street. It was a substantial, rambling house with gardens and grounds which extended up to and included Windmill Hill in the east and Highbury Road in the north; tunnels ran under the road to provide private access to the more remote parts of the property. He later sacrificed the southern edge of his garden to provide Hermitage Road, a direct connection to Walsworth Road and the railway station.

Frederic Seebohm was the driving force behind the concept of adapting the John Mattock Foundation to provide the Grammar Schools in 1889. The list of donors and benefactors is ample evidence of his powers of persuasion amongst his family, friends and fellow townsmen. He gave £500, a sum which was only the start of his generosity, for he was soon to provide a laundry room where the girls could perfect the housewifely skills.

When the Girls' Grammar School outgrew its Bancroft premises, Frederic Seebohm gave not only the new site on Windmill Hill but also £1,000 towards the building. The rest of Hitchin Hill was a gift to the town and therefore provided a route to school which is still used by the girls today.

He became, over the years, a well respected, self-taught historian and was honoured for his writings by Oxford, Cambridge and Edinburgh Universities; it was therefore not surprising that he greatly valued books and for the rest of his life gave regular sums of money for their purchase and for furnishing the school library.

Frederic and Mary Ann had a son and five daughters who comprised a totally devoted, Victorian household, where father was adored and his word was law. Three of the children were also destined to benefit the school: Esther, the second daughter, Hugh Exton, the fifth child, and Hilda, the youngest.

After Frederic's death in 1912, Esther and Hilda, the two sisters still at home, remained until after the war and then moved from 'The Hermitage' to a smaller

c.1890. *L. to R.:* Esther, Freda, Hilda and Juliet in the Hermitage Garden.

[Hon. Victoria Glendinning]

home, 'Fairfield', which they renamed 'Little Benslow Hills'. Both sisters were governors of the school which they loved and which played such a large part in their lives. The Misses Esther and Hilda were regular visitors at the 'School on the Hill' and encouraged the pupils to visit them in their home. Following the family tradition of generosity they were constantly providing gifts and prizes for the school, the most notable of which were further grants of land: in 1920 they gave a strip of land running along the southern boundary of the school and later, in 1927, another grant of land, including woodland. Here Hugh stepped in and gave £500, half the sum needed to level part of it for use as playing fields.

Miss Hilda died in 1931 but her sister survived a further twenty years before dying at the age of ninety. Even in death she gave to others and left 'Little Benslow Hills' for the founding of the Hitchin Rural Music School.

In addition to a great deal of financial help, Hugh Exton Seebohm also gave generously of his time as a governor of the school and later as Chairman of the Governors for fifteen years.

In 1964, Mrs. Derrick Seebohm J.P. followed her father-in-law and became a governor of the school, thus carrying on the family tradition of interest and involvement started by Frederic Seebohm seventy-five years earlier.

THE BENEFACTORS AND FOUNDER'S DAY

The Benefactors

In 1932 Miss Chambers, who was a devout Anglican, conceived the idea of a regular Founder's Day service to be held at St. Mary's Church, Hitchin, in conjunction with the Boys' Grammar School. There is no record, other than the order of service, to mark this historic occasion. The following year she enlisted the help of Reginald Hine to draw up a list of the benefactors and his reply is still preserved.

The names he suggested were: **John Mattock** who founded the original school in 1632; **Joseph Kempe** who, in 1654, willed his friend the endowment of a house in Tilehouse Street 'for the better maintenance of his school and instruction of six poor children of Hitchin'; **Thomas Kidner** – vicar of Hitchin who in 1667 left the bequest of sixteen acres at Higham Gobion for teaching ten poor children; **Ralph Skynner** – his trustee, empowered to choose the deserving children and who was also a benefactor; **Sir Ralph Radcliffe** and **Dame Mary Radcliffe**, husband and wife, who 'gave money for many years to clothe twenty poor children at Mattock's school'; **Mark Hildesley** – vicar of Hitchin 1730–1755. For his first two years in Hitchin he lived in the Free School in Tilehouse Street, and taught the boys daily. After his marriage he encouraged the boys to visit his home and meet the six gentlemen's sons whom he taught there; **John Margetts Pierson** and **William Wilshere** were senior trustees in 1750 when there was a dispute involving the

Attorney General – both made substantial bequests; **Lord Dacre**, one of the new trustees in 1825, was required 'to frame laws and ordinances for the good and well ordering of the school' after it had suffered a decline in both numbers and standards. These are the last named in connection with the old Free School.

Trinity College, Cambridge made a donation to the new school in 1889 and by tradition, has been represented on the governing body of the Boys' Grammar School ever since. **Frederic Seebohm, James Hack Tuke, William Ransom, Thomas Perkins, Marlborough R. Pryor** and **Thomas Priest** were members of the first governing body of the new school in Bancroft. Some of these men gave substantial sums of money for the new building and in 1895, with the addition of **Alexander Peckover** and **Joseph Gurney Barclay**, four of them provided almost £1,000 to write off the deficit in the school's account. When the new school on the hill was to be built some of them, yet again, dug deep into their own pockets for funds and **Thomas Fenwick Harrison** made a generous donation. **Hilda Seebohm** and **George E. Spurr** had both been governors of the school, had devoted time to it and had given generous gifts. He also included **The Rand Charity** – mentioned elsewhere as a constant charitable support to the school. These twenty-three names were those suggested by Reginald Hine, though it was not until 1935 that they were printed on the service sheet.

Down the years, other names have been added. **Edward Radcliffe** and **John Skynner** have been added from the 17th Century; **William Dawes** from the 18th; **Henry Seebohm** and **Francis Lucas** from the 19th Century and **Sir Frederick Macmillan, Francis Ransom** and **Lewis Hensley** from the 20th.

In addition to these, friends and benefactors who died after 1932 have been included: **Hugh Exton Seebohm** and his sister, **Esther Margaret Seebohm**; **Charlotte Lyndon** and **Charles John Widdows**, ex-Chairman of the Governors.

There seem to be some inconsistencies in the choice of names honoured and of those overlooked in this list, which would bear further investigation.

Founder's Day

The first Founder's Day service for both Grammar Schools took place in St. Mary's Church on the 25th July 1932. The date was chosen because John Mattock signed his deed of donation on 25th July 1639. It would have been fitting had it celebrated the tercentenary – but seven years is a long time to wait!

There is no report of that first service, but this photograph shows a very wet day indeed with a few umbrellas and a lot of wet girls. The next year was much kinder and the girls are shown, walking single file with a lone kindergarten boy in their midst, sporting an enormous panama hat!

For over thirty years, the girls walked in an orderly 'crocodile' down first the hill and later Hollow Lane to the church for a morning service. This was later changed to the afternoon, but the girls still walk in procession down to St. Mary's. Appearance is of great importance – clean shoes, tidy hair and the uniform of the day must be worn. Some concessions were made in war time but were later revoked.

In the 1970s the Sixth formers were allowed to wear 'mufti' to school but were still expected to attend Founder's Day in a suitable dress, in colour as near as possible to the school uniform blue.

When the service was in the morning, the afternoon was usually occupied with field sports or swimming, though 'A Midsummer Night's Dream' was staged in the evening one year and the Sixth Form had a 'Flannel Dance' another. In 1956 there was an Open Day for parents to visit the school. Between 1960 and 1966 the school was closed for the afternoon and the girls returned in the evening. The registers were marked to highlight the defaulters and there were open school concerts, exhibitions and Parents' Open Days.

By 1967, both schools had outgrown the seating capacity of the church and until 1978, the service was changed to the afternoon with only the senior school going to St. Mary's, the First Forms to the Non-Conformist churches and the middle school remaining at school. They occupied themselves with dancing and gym displays. In

1932.   On their way to the First Founder's Day Service.   [The Pictorial at Hitchin Museum]

1977 they went to the Boys' School for a drama production and the next year, the boys visited for songs, dance and drama.

Communion was taken for the first time in 1973 and breakfast provided afterwards, in school, at a cost of 10p. In 1980, this rose to 32p.

In 1979 the service once more reverted to the morning with only the Fifth and Sixth Form pupils attending St. Mary's. The pupils left behind were entertained in various ways. One year there was a visit by the Ballet Minerva; a popular singer, Julie Felix, came on another occasion and a third year a film was shown. In 1984, the morning entertainments were discontinued and the school returned to normal lessons. Since 1979, the afternoon has been taken up by Summer Fairs, games and competitions, sports day and stalls.

The Founder's Day, now having taken place for more than fifty years, has become an important part of the school's history.

1939.   This photograph was taken from the church gallery during the Founder's Day service – the year of the Tercentenary of the Foundation and the fiftieth year of the school.   [Pictorial, Hitchin Museum]

1939.   [Pictorial, Hitchin Museum]

1968. This photograph was the first time that the whole school did not attend St. Mary's.

[North Herts Gazette, Hitchin Museum]

July 1982. *L. to R.:* Mr. I. Miskelly, by pillar; Miss H. Bond, disguised as a bottle of silver nitrate; Mrs. G. M. Warwick; Mrs. B. Wearmouth, Chairman of Governors; Miss. I. Blackman, Deputy Head.

[Miss E. Duignan]

HEADMISTRESSES
and their Deputies

Miss Chambers, Miss Gosnell and Miss Badland at the Old Girls' Reunion in 1948.

1963.   Miss M. Harrison.

Miss Janet Elizabeth Gosnell 1889–1919	:	B.A.(London).
Miss Annie Muriel Chambers 1919–1945	:	Final Hons. School of Modern History, Oxford, F.R.Hist.Soc.
Miss Mary Alice Badland 1945–1962	:	B.A.(Manchester).
Mrs. Gladys Margaret Warwick (née Harrison) 1962–	:	B.A. Hons.(London); G.R.S.M.

Second Mistresses

1902–1909 Miss M. S. Ward
1910–1917 Miss E. Parker
1917–1920 Miss M. A. Button

1920–1945 Miss M. A. Flinn
1945–1946 Miss D. E. Wright

Senior Mistresses

1946–1948 Miss J. Wells
1948–1950 Miss E. D. Allright
1950–1952 Miss A. K. Stanier
1952–1954 Miss A. Lamb

1954–1956 Miss M. Chrystal
1956–1958 Miss J. Williams
1958–1960 Miss K. Britton
1960–1962 Miss E. M. Bolton

Deputy Heads

1963–1965 Miss E. D. Allright (Acting
    Head, Sept.–Nov. '62)
1965–1971 Miss K. Britton
1971–1981 Miss I. M. Blackman

1973–1984 Miss P. E. Fletcher
1981–   Mr. J. N. McCutcheon
1984–   Miss E. M. Beddard

Head of Lower School

1978–1984 Miss E. M. Beddard   1985–   Mrs. M. Mead
(Mrs. G. Jones, Acting Head of Lower School – September to October 1986.)

JANET ELIZABETH GOSNELL
1858–1949
Head Mistress 1889–1919

Janet Elizabeth Gosnell was just thirty-one years old when she was appointed by the Governors to be the first Head Mistress of the new Hitchin Girls' Grammar School. It must have presented an exciting challenge which required much faith and

18

Miss Janet Elizabeth Gosnell, B.A.(London), Head Mistress 1889–1919.

courage though she was academically well suited to the post. A Batchelor of Arts graduate of the University of London, she had already been headmistress in Cheltenham as well as holding three junior teaching positions.

It is clear that she had a very real affection for the school which was her home in Bancroft for nearly twenty years and, in 1939, wrote of 'that old house, with its large and lovely garden behind, linking our grounds with the plantation where so many happy evenings were spent. We were a happy family party, having indoor games in the winter between tea and preparation'.

Miss Gosnell's philosophy was that schooling is not so much about learning as in fitting oneself for life. Ethel Widdows wrote: 'She had very high ideals about the standard of work and considered that girls should work for the love of it and not for the marks gained'. She disapproved of individual prizes for achievement but gave way to pressure, around the turn of the century, and prizes were introduced. Ten years later, they quietly disappeared again in favour of 'team effort' awards in inter-form competitions.

It is interesting that many of her earliest pupils remembered her as a rather remote, strict figure; always fair and kind. Aillie Latchmore summed up the general opinion when she wrote: 'Miss Gosnell was a wonderful headmistress. She was very strict but extremely just and those of us who were at school under her guidance can only respect her for the great influence she wielded on her pupils.'

One punishment, when still in the Bancroft School, still causes amusement. After some misdemeanour, the girls were forbidden to be together in the town but must walk singly. The unfortunate result of the edict was to have long 'crocodiles' of girls winding in and out of the streets. The rule was quickly amended to allow the girls to walk in pairs!

It was with regret that Miss Gosnell left her home in Bancroft; 'The new school on the hill seemed, by contrast, almost "institutional"', she admitted years later.

The Head Mistress was physically a very small woman, privately known to her pupils as 'Little Miss Gosnell'. She had five nieces in the school; Dora (called 'Doe') and Gladys Pennefather and their three cousins, Phyllis, Joan and Enid Gosnell. All called the Head Mistress 'Auntie Janet', as did the rest of the school when not in her hearing!

Pupils in Bancroft remembered her high-piled hair, high-necked blouse and a rustling black skirt, which with her jangling keys always betrayed her approach. In the new school she was a familiar sight in her long black dress, academic gown and mortar board when she made her daily inspection of the school. Vera Davis remembered that, when in the Kindergarten, she lived in Pirton and was unable to go home for lunch as did her friends. Of Miss Gosnell, she said, 'If she found me sitting alone in the cloakroom, she would take me by the hand and the two of us would continue the tour. . . . I could never understand why the other girls found her so frightening.'

On the matter of dress, Miss Gosnell had very strict rules. When Aillie Latchmore returned, in 1911, as a pupil teacher she was quietly chided and asked to lengthen her skirt because it showed her ankles, which was 'not a good example to the children'. Another incident, about the same time, involved Leslie Carlisle and three of her friends. On a lovely summer Saturday the girls had been for a country ramble and had collected branches, flowers and fungi. Turning into Hermitage Road, they came face to face with Miss Gosnell whose admonition, 'No gloves on! Put them on', reduced them to blushing fumblings to find the missing apparel.

The outbreak of the Great War in 1914 presented Miss Gosnell with a dilemma since she had intended to retire that year. She now, typically, felt that she could not desert her pupils in the face of the uncertain future and remained at her post until the summer of 1919.

During this time she made an uncharacteristic error. She had great enthusiasm for supporting the war effort in any way possible and, in the face of food shortages,

Surname *Gosnell* Christian Names *Janet Elizabeth* Style { Mr. / Mrs. / Miss }

1. Date of Birth.	2. Date of appointment on probation.	3. Date of definitive appointment.	4. Date of leaving.
11th June 1858		Feb: 6th 1889	29 July 1919.

5. Schools and Colleges at which educated, with dates. State names and types of institutions.	6. Particulars of Public and University Examinations taken, and certificates and degrees obtained, with dates.
Private Schools. Private Tutor - 1877-1880 University College, Bristol Ap: 1884 . July 1884 Jan: 1886 -- July 1887	London Matriculation 1880 Jan London Inter. B.A. Cl. I 1884 July London B.A. Div: I 1887. Oct.

7. List of teaching posts held, with dates.	8. Particulars of training in teaching, if any, and certificates or diplomas obtained, with dates.
Mathematical Mistress (Temporary) Oxford High School. Sept - Dec: 1880 Private Coaching. Jan: 1881- July 1881 Jersey Ladies' College Sept: 1881-Dec 1883 " " Sept: 1884 - Dec: 1885 Head Mistress Cheltenham High School Jan: 1885 - Dec: 1888 Head Mistress - Hitchin from 1889. May 1st	9. State external teaching or official work undertaken, if any, in addition to duties in the School.

10. Special subject or subjects.	11. State principal duties assigned, and subjects taken. (Any subsequent changes and their dates to be indicated in red ink.)
Classics Mathematics French	Subjects taken - Scripture throughout School - French The duties of Head Mistress

12. Total annual emoluments.	13. Particulars of retiring allowance, if any.
Salary, with scale, if any. £100 Capitation Fees, £3 for first 50 girls if any. £2 after. Altered in 1910 to £2 for each girl in the school. Estimated value of board and lodging if given as part of emoluments.	Pension under S.J. (5) Act 1918 payable from. 1. 8. 19.
	14. Post, if any, taken up after leaving the School.

267070—W. & S. Ltd.—G680—30,000—3-08.

From Staff Register, Book I.

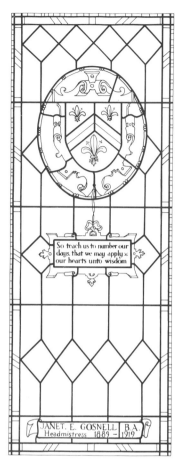

JANET. E. GOSNELL B.A.
Headmistress 1889 – 1919

Drawing by Amanda Birkinshaw 1980–87.

caused boiled rhubarb leaves to be served for lunch. Since these are highly toxic it was fortunate that the result was only some very ill schoolgirls!

Miss Gosnell remembered 'cowering', all wearing dressing-gowns, with the boarders in the lower corridors, while the murmuring of the Zeppelins passed overhead. She was greatly affected by the tragic loss of the many young men from Hitchin, and Bernard Sanders, who was in the Kindergarten, remembers: 'Miss Gosnell stood up there crying, saying one of Mr. Spurr's sons had been killed in the war.' (Mr. Spurr lost three sons.)

On her retirement, Miss Gosnell moved to Bexhill-on-Sea, but she retained a great interest in the school and returned for the Tercentenary and the opening of the new Large Hall and New Wing in 1939.

Just after the end of the Second World War, Miss Gosnell returned to Hertfordshire and spent the rest of her life in Letchworth. It is appropriate that her declining years should have been spent in the area, close to the school she had loved and to which she had devoted her life's work.

She died in 1949 at the age of ninety-one. Obituaries to her in the school magazine, by a member of staff and an ex-Head Girl summed up Miss Gosnell's influence on Hitchin Girls' Grammar School:

[From Miss Read, member of staff] – 'We were able to go to her for help, knowing that she would deal with matters in a just way and with a sense of humour.'

22

[From Gwendoline Bryant, ex Head Girl] – 'We all respected her and loved her: respected her because she was such a lady in the truest sense of the word, and loved her when we realised what a personal interest she took in us all.'

A memorial window to Miss Gosnell was installed in the library – at that time situated above the main entrance – bearing the text 'So teach us to number our days, that we may apply our hearts unto wisdom'. A fitting tribute to a remarkable lady.

MISTRESSES APPOINTED DURING MISS GOSNELL'S TIME 1889–1919

1889–1919	Janet E. Gosnell	Scripture, French
	Head Mistress	
1889–?	Edith Arblaster	First Assistant to Headmistress
1890s	Other teachers mentioned at this time:–	
	Miss Widdows	
	Miss Finlayson	Kindergarten
	Miss Bingham	Kindergarten
	Miss Paine	?
	Miss Owbridge Ward	Geography
–1902	Miss Withers	
1902–1908	Edith E. Johnson	Gymnastics, Games, Dancing, Elocution
1902–1909	Mabel S. Ward	English Literature, French, German,
	Second Mistress	Geography
?	A. D. F. Salmond	English, Modern Languages
?	A. Rutter	Drawing, Needlework
?	A. Berridge	Music, Singing
?	Miss Bussell	Cookery
?	Miss M. Lucas	Preparatory School
–1910	J. C. Glen-Bott	Science, Mathematics
1905–1911	Mary B. Cox	History
1905–1912	Jessie E. Wigfull	French, English Literature, Latin, Librarian,
		Magazine Editor
1905–1919	Katherine A. Johnson	Drawing, Painting, Needlework, Magazine
1906–1913	Mabel Underwood	Music – full charge
1907–1909	Clare Coley	All Science – Chemistry, Physics, Botany
1907–1911	Margaret A. Kelly	French, English, Geography
1907–1915	Dora Wilkins	All subjects in Preparatory Dept.
1908–1909	Evelyn M. Norris	Gymnastics, Games, Dancing, Elocution
1908–1910	Gertrude Bott	Mathematics
1908–1914	M. Ada Scrivener	Solo and Class Singing
1909–1909	Mary B. Mathews	English Language and Literature
1909–1911	Edith M. Vobes	Science – Chemistry, Physics, Botany
1910–1911	Katherine M. Byles	English Language and Literature
1910–1913	Alice E. Graves	Gymnastics, Dancing, Games
1910–1917	Elizabeth Parker	Mathematics and Arithmetic
	Second Mistress	
1911–1912	Edith Tisdall	German, English, Arithmetic
1911–?	E. Aillie Latchmore	Student Teacher – Kindergarten (pupil at
		Bancroft)
1911–?	? Brydie	Music Assistant
1911–?	? Chapman	Assistant to Miss Wilkins in Prep. Dept.
1911–?	? Grieve	Assistant to Miss Wilkins in Prep. Dept.
1911–1914	Grace Nicholls	History, English Language, Librarian
1911–1914	Dorothy R. Bagley	Geography
1911–1920	Janet Algar	Science
1912–1914	Evelyn L. Vernon	French, German, Latin

1913–1914	Mildred J. Benton	Elementary work – Lower School
1913–1915	Winifred C. Francis	Piano, Violin, Harmony & Theory
1913–1917	Evelyn Wilkins	English, Hygiene, Games, Swedish Drill
1913–1919	Gwynneth Lamb	Drill – visiting. Later school Accountant and Guides (pupil at Bancroft) 1914–1915
1914–1915	Elizabeth M. Eldridge	English and French
1914–1915	Kathleen White	History, Geography
1914–1919	Laura Lee	German, Singing, Piano
1915–1916	Margaret G. Saunders	Temp. Kindergarten Mistress
1915–1918	Lucy E. Palmer	English and French
1915–1920	Gladys E. F. Pennefather	History and Geography (pupil at Bancroft – Miss Gosnell's niece)
1915–1920	Edith H. Macintosh	Piano, Violin, Harmony
1916–1922	Kathleen F. Williams	Full charge of Kindergarten
1917–1919	Helena Newton (Mrs.)	Mathematics, Geography, English, Junior Needlework
1917–1920	Martha A. Button Second Mistress	Mathematics
1917–1950	Ruby C. Read	Handwork, Games, Kindergarten Mistress 1924
1918–1919	Marie E. Marien (Mlle)	Housemistress, French, Needlework
1918–1920	Constance Davies (Mrs.)	English Language and Literature
1918–1920	Isabel Mercer	French and German
1918–1920	Mary L. Powell	General Subjects – lower forms

Also mentioned are Miss Dobson and Miss Joseph, both of whom taught Art. No further details are available.

The Years in Bancroft Street, 1889–1908

Early Days

The Governors of the Grammar School (Foundation) bought the whole of the property known as 'The Woodlands', in Bancroft Street, Hitchin, in December 1889, eight months after the Hitchin Grammar School actually opened. Negotiations had, however, been going on for some years prior to this since the trusteeship had been in the hands of Alfred and William Ransom acting on behalf of the three Misses Peckover, who, from the death of their grandfather in 1871, were minors. The youngest came of age in 1882. In the intervening years this substantial gentleman's house had already been converted for use as a school and the outbuildings at the rear adapted for use as school rooms. There were also extensive gardens, shrubberies and a plantation at the rear for the development of outdoor pursuits. It seems possible that, from the start, the unique shape of the land made it ideal for the construction of two separate schools and was chosen with this in mind. In addition it occupied a central position in the town and had easy access to the railway station. It therefore offered an ideal location for the founding of the new Hitchin Grammar Schools.

Though the boys' and the girls' schools were to share the same site, they would be strictly segregated, with separate entrances, head teachers and other staff. The girls were in the original house and the boys in the converted stables and outbuildings at the rear.

Girls' Grammar School, Bancroft, Hitchin.

All candidates for admission to the Girls' Grammar School, 'must provide a certificate of good conduct and must pass an entrance examination consisting of, at least, Reading, Writing from dictation, Sums in the first four simple rules of Arithmetic with the Multiplication Table'. Having been accepted, the pupils must then pay £2. 10. 0 per term up to the age of 12 years and £3. 10. 0 thereafter. Stationery etc. to be 3/6d per term.

There were to be four scholarships in the first year – two to be partial and two total exemptions from the payment of fees. One of the latter would be for a student of three or more years from a Public Elementary School in Hitchin and the second for a pupil from Holwell, Pirton, Ickleford or Lower Stondon (preference being given to a pupil from Holwell under the terms of the Rand Charity). The number of scholarships was later increased to thirty-two; half of them free to Hitchin children and those from the villages associated with the Rand Charity and the remaining places half-free to all comers.

The prospectus shows that Miss J. E. Gosnell had been appointed the first Head Mistress and was 'Late Assistant Mistress of the Ladies' College in Jersey', though she had spent the past four years at Cheltenham High School. Her salary was £100 per year with a small capitation fee for pupil numbers.

On the 1st May 1889, Miss Gosnell, with her assistant Miss Arblaster, received her first seven pupils. The introductory syllabus lists seventeen subjects in addition to Religious Instruction and the 'Three Rs' – a daunting prospect for the two ladies.

There is some confusion as to which seven pupils took their places on that historic morning though the names Ethel M. Widdows and Eleanor Dawson were mentioned from two different sources. A special school magazine, published in 1939, added the names, Mary Carling, Emily Warren, Alice Warren, Mabel Roberts and Annie Hare to these two. Grace Plowman (Carling) gives the remaining five as herself, plus Margery Shepherd, Katie Andrews, Gertrude Seebohm and Mary Gibson. Sadly, no written records survive, but it seems clear that all these girls – plus Daisy Chalkley, another contender – were at the school by the start of the September 1889 school year, though not necessarily amongst the first seven.

On that May morning, Miss Gosnell and Miss Arblaster joined these few girls in the dining room, with the windows overlooking the garden, to hold the first school assembly and morning prayers.

By September, the numbers had grown to thirty-six and new teachers were appointed to cope with the increased school roll. Of these early pupils, Ethel Widdows went on to become a teacher herself, devoting thirty-five years to the profession; and Grace Plowman (Carling) gained a B.A. degree in 1902, the first pupil of the school to do so.

The Building and Grounds

The popularity of both Grammar Schools soon made clear the need for expansion and only two years later, in 1891, the boys moved to new premises built on land behind the original buildings and the girls were then free to take over the whole of the remaining site. This allowed more room in the house to accommodate the boarders who had been accepted, on a weekly basis, from the beginning of the school.

As the years went by, an assembly hall was built and part of the old garden had to be sacrificed in order that new classrooms might be added. A Cookery School – a simply equipped room across the yard – was considered a wonderful institution when it was added in 1892. A trained mistress, from South Kensington, arrived every week in the winter months and demonstrated in the morning before the girls spent the afternoon in practical work. Samples of their work were greatly appreciated by the parents who visited the school for the annual Prize Giving.

There were beautiful gardens, shrubberies and the old plantation at the rear of the school where there were tennis courts and a croquet lawn. There was also much room for other games and great opportunities for 'hide and seek' in the grounds. This also provided the setting for the annual Shakespeare productions, and 'A Midsummer Night's Dream', 'The Tempest', 'As You Like It', 'The Merchant of Venice' and 'King Lear' were all performed in the garden. When lessons were finished there was dancing in the hall and concerts were given by the staff and pupils.

The Kindergarten

Aillie Latchmore was one of the first three kindergarten pupils – the others being Muriel Gilbertson and Norah Shillitoe – when it started in 1896. She was the youngest member of the school, being taken there by perambulator at the early age of three and a half years. The Kindergarten commenced in Miss Gosnell's office, the room on the left inside the main entrance. As numbers grew, it moved into the dining room on the right of the front door and later into a still larger room up the school yard. Miss Finlayson was the first mistress – 'great fun and much loved by the children' – to be followed by Miss Bingham. Some of the children were also boarders and, in 1907, Doris Baron was one of the youngest, being only nine years old. The dormitories were shared bedrooms with about four girls in each, and she still remembers her first night in this strange new world. She arrived with a sniffly cold and one girl irritably complained. 'If you keep blowing your nose it will come off'. The poor child believed her and sobbed miserably. Next morning, seated beside Miss Gosnell, who always ate with the pupils, she was given hot bread-and-milk for breakfast. There were about ten boarders at that time. Miss Gosnell had a personal maid, Miss Frances Holloway, always called 'Leckie' by the

"Bancroft House School," Hitchin.

SPRING TERM COMMENCES JANUARY 20.

FOR PARTICULARS AND PROSPECTUS APPLY TO THE
Principal—GEO. HOULISTON, M.A.

Young Ladies' School.

MISS BARKER, BUCKLERSBURY, HITCHIN.

Next Term commences January 20th, 1890.
A LIMITED NUMBER OF BOARDERS TAKEN.

Young Ladies' Educational Establishment,

"LINDEN HOUSE," BANCROFT, HITCHIN.

THOROUGH ENGLISH, French, Music, Drawing, Singing, Calisthenics, Plain and Fancy Needlework. Large lofty Schoolrooms, well ventilated.

A Vacancy for Two Boarders. Fees very moderate.

Principal—E. M. PEIRSON, assisted by M. & A. PEIRSON.

NEXT TERM COMMENCES MONDAY, JANUARY 20th, 1890.

HITCHIN GRAMMAR SCHOOL.

HEAD MASTER—J. E. LITTLE, M.A., late Exhibitioner of Lincoln College, Oxford.
ASSISTANT MASTERS—R. LEWTHWAITE, B.A., Late Scholar of Magdalene College Cambridge; and W. H. ENGLISH, ESQ.
DRILLING—SERGT.-INSTRUCTOR C. SHORT.

NEXT TERM BEGINS TUESDAY. JANUARY 21st.

The Entrance Examination will be held on that day at 9 a.m.

There will be an Election to Scholarships later in the year, of which notice will be given.

The School has an excellent playing field close to the present premises, and almost adjoining the proposed site of the new buildings.

Forms of application may be obtained from Mr. C. HALES, the Market-place, or from the HEAD MASTER.

Girls Grammar School, Hitchin.

Head Mistress—MISS J. E. GOSNELL, B.A.

THE TERM BEGINS TUESDAY, JANUARY 21st.—The Entrance Examination will be held on MONDAY, January 20th, at 10 o'clock.

Term and Weekly Boarders are received by the Head Mistress.

Hertfordshire Express, January 1890   [British Newspaper Library, Colindale]

girls, who acted as matron to the boarders and was a very comforting and kind person, always ready for a cuddle and a 'goodnight' story. She also took her young charges out to visit, or for tea with friends in the town. She showed great affection to Doris, the 'baby' of the house. Watson, the gardener, was a figure much loved by the children and he was clearly devoted to them and the school. He kept the walled gardens beautifully. In the centre of the lawn was a large yew tree, the fruits of which the girls used to eat. They avoided the otherwise fatal consequences of this by spitting out the seeds! He caught Doris, and her friend Jeannie, in the act of taking a plum each from the garden wall and reported it to Miss Gosnell. They were both 'carpeted' and still, more than eighty years later, in recounting the story, Miss Baron became quite emotional. 'I can see and hear her still (Miss Gosnell). She raised a finger and said, "My dears, even if it is only a pin, if it is not yours, you must not take it". She was so kind, a wonderful woman and I have always remembered her words.' Mr. Seebohm visited the school, resplendent in grey top hat and long grey hair. 'Is that the king of Hitchin?' asked Doris, to everyone's amusement.

Pupils' Recollections

Tuesday, market day, was remembered by several pupils as a great trial of courage, in having to negotiate the cattle market taking place under the school's windows. One morning, Eva Switzer with her little brother, Christopher – children of the curate of St. Mary's – were bravely passing the cattle when one of the cows tossed Christopher. Pressure was then put on the Urban District Council to have the livestock market removed and it was eventually sited in Paynes Park.

Pupils arrived at the school by many means and Grace Plowman, who lived near Henlow, was one of those who travelled daily by train, walking each day to and from the station, whatever the weather. Since school did not finish for the day until quite late, this often entailed a walk home in the dark. Jessie Hall, later head girl,

1897–98. Kindergarten Class. *Back row L. to R.:* —, George Newton, —, Anthony Spurr, Walter Spurr, Raymond Halsey. *Middle row:* ? Kittle, Marion Gatward, — Kittle, Muriel Gilbertson, Miss Finlayson, Connie Fowler, Norah Shillitoe. *Front row:* May? Kittle, ? Farnham, Ida? Kittle, Aillie Latchmore, John Ransom, Lilian Gatward, Jack Goldsmith.   [Aillie Latchmore]

c.1899.   The Kindergarten. First left is Lillian Farnham and fourth is Waller Sworder.   [Anne Sworder]

lived on a farm at Offley and came to school in a pony and trap called 'The Tub'. Later, she had a fixed wheel bicycle and strict instructions to walk down Offley Hill, which were conveniently forgotten when she was late!

Several of the earliest pupils remembered learning to write on specially lined paper to ensure that the loops and hooks all had their allocated size; a system known as 'pot hooks and hangers'. Spelling was given great attention, even in the Kindergarten, and regular 'spelling bees' were a feature of school life. Aillie Latchmore recollected one School Prizegiving in the newly completed Town Hall, when several girls survived for an extraordinary length of time, correctly spelling words hurled at them from the audience. With only herself and Muriel Gilbertson remaining, Aillie failed to spell 'eschscholtzia', a word she ever after spelled correctly. Coincidentally, many years later, Marion Wood remembered difficulties with the same word, in class, when she was at school in the 1940s!

Miss Gosnell believed that the girls should work for love and not for the marks they gained. Originally there were no marks for the term's work, only for examinations, and there were no prizes. Marjorie Russell, a pupil from 1904–1908, remembers painting the form motto, 'Whatever your hand finds to do, do it with all your might', which seems to epitomise Miss Gosnell's approach to her school. By 1895, there was a change regarding the awarding of prizes, and Miss Phillipa Fawcett came to the school to present them to the pupils. She was an eminent educationalist of her day and a Senior Wrangler. This was the title, peculiar to Cambridge University, given to those who had attained the first class in examination for mathematical honours.

Several relations of the Head Mistress were connected with the school. There are

29

references to her sister being at Bancroft, one suggestion being that she was matron of boarders. There were also the five nieces, Pennefathers and Gosnells.

Other notable pupils were Lady May Lyon, who was at the school from 1897–1900 and Lady Rose Bowes Lyon who was a pupil there at the turn of the century. These were the elder sisters of Queen Elizabeth the Queen Mother. Though they stayed at school for lunch, they never ate with the other girls but had a private room with their governess and at 'play time' the three walked together and often conversed in French. Lady May Lyon later married Lord Elphinstone and was invited to open the new School Hall in 1939.

Times of Change

In 1902, the Balfour Education Act made the County Council responsible for the provision of adequate secondary education in the County. Happily, the wants of the Hitchin district were already partially supplied, but a thorough inspection of the Grammar Schools, made in 1904 by the Board of Education, resulted in the report that the schools were overcrowded. Looking to the future, any additions made to provide for both schools on the same site 'would be a make shift' and 'under the circumstances it became a matter for serious consideration whether, if the necessary funds could, from some source or other be obtained, the Girls' School should not be moved to an altogether new building on a more spacious site'. The Governors, having so far relied almost entirely upon the liberality of those interested in the school, were reluctant to have to resort to the help of public funds. It was, however, agreed with the County Council that the new building should be a

c.1902. Miss Gosnell and her staff in the garden at Bancroft. The Second Mistress, Miss Mabel Ward, who taught English, is seated on Miss Gosnell's left. One past pupil, on seeing this photograph, declared it a very poor likeness of Miss Gosnell which does not flatter her in the least. (Photograph by T. B. Latchmore.) [Sylvia Perkins]

joint venture and, after several generous donations, building was started in 1905. In 1906, two Catholic, private schools opened in the town: Sacred Heart School, founded by a group of nuns from France, started as a Convent School in Verulam Road, with three girl pupils, and St. Michael's, in Grove Road, a private school for boys, was completed and operational in the same year.

In 1906 the Girls' Grammar School had 121 pupils and ten teachers in addition to Miss Gosnell. A charming photograph was taken of them all, sitting under the yew tree, in the garden behind the school.

With the excitement of the new school in the offing, work still continued in Bancroft. External examination successes were high and a Sketch Club was started with a very enthusiastic membership. The Games Club had done very well, especially at hockey where they had success in seven matches of the ten played. Miss Gosnell bemoaned the unsuitability of the plantation for the playing of cricket, it being suitable only for tennis and croquet. The Public Swimming Baths, in Queen Street, were very popular with the girls but presented great difficulties since 'the times the baths are open to ladies does not fit in with the school time-table'. There were also 'slipper baths' on the same premises where the less wealthy could take a bath. One 'old girl' remembers the notice painted on the wall – 'Soap only on Saturdays'!

Miss Gosnell appreciated that some girls could not avail themselves of the opportunities to take part in the sporting activities because of the distances they had to travel home but regretted that more local girls did not play. 'They should join, not only for their own benefit, but to foster public spirit.'

As early as 1905, Mr. Seebohm had approached his old friend, Lord Lister, for a contribution towards the equipment required for the new school. In response, he was sent a microscope, a signed photograph and a letter which are still on display in the Biology Department.

Joseph Lister

12, PARK CRESCENT,
PORTLAND PLACE.

26 Oct 1905

Dear Mr Seebohm

In remembrance of old school days at Hitchin, I have pleasure in presenting this microscope to the Girls' School in which you take so deep an interest.

Very sincerely yours

Lister

In late 1907 the building was completed and the necessary equipment was slowly installed. Gwendoline Bryant later remembered 'The move up to the new building was grand fun; toiling up Windmill Hill carrying books and plaster casts for the Art Room and all kinds of impedimenta. How coldly clean the new building was – how bare – and how far away from the boys!' At last, in early May 1908, just nineteen years after its beginning with seven girls, the Hitchin Girls' Grammar School finally turned its back on its premises in Bancroft and marched into its future as 'The School on the Hill'.

Official Opening of the New School Building
25th July 1908

After completing the move into the new school building, Miss Gosnell, her staff and pupils had only a few weeks to ensure that they were fit and ready to receive their visitors, on Saturday 25th July 1908, when the school was formally opened by Dr. Butler, Master of Trinity College, Cambridge.

Mr. Aldis Wright, Chairman of the Governors, presided and the platform was filled with many of those responsible, both financially and practically, for the building of the new premises.

The Chairman started proceedings with a short history of both Grammar Schools, since the original John Mattock Foundation in 1639 until the present day.

Mr. Frederic Seebohm followed by thanking all those individuals who had made gifts towards equipment for the school, including the students and staff who had made all the curtains and blinds for the dormitory with material provided by the Governors.

Mr. Wright then made reference to the late Chairman, the Rev. Canon Hensley, who, he said, would have enjoyed seeing the new building completed and opened, as in the case of the boys' school seventeen years before, by the Master of Trinity – a college which had close links with both schools since their inception.

Dr. Butler then rose and noted that 'one of the most marked features of this assembly is that it represents a more than ordinary combination of private zeal and private munificence, with enlightened public aid'. After a speech of appreciation he concluded, 'The space reserved for the boys is no more than is necessary for their growing requirements and you have before you now this beautiful building, no more than is necessary for your need but still one feels . . . the building will be sufficient for your needs and those who follow you for some time to come'.

Mr. Millington thanked, on behalf of the Governors, the Head Mistress, Miss Gosnell. She now had 'greater facilities for carrying on her work, greater opportunity for exercising her influence and he had no doubt she felt they had also laid upon her greater responsibilities; that she would enjoy the facilities which had been given to her and that she would use her new opportunities to the utmost'.

Subsequently the visitors inspected the building and partook of tea.

Two days after the official opening, the girls celebrated their new school by staging a dramatic performance in the new hall. They gave 'The Dream Lady' – a little fantasy, and several scenes from Sheridan's 'The Rivals'. The whole performance was a credit to Miss Edith Johnson, the games and elocution mistress, who hoped that the performance would clear a £10 debt for the Games Club. The enthusiastic audience was pleased to subscribe twice this amount.

The newspaper advertisement for the new school year, in September 1908, reflects the great pride felt in the new school building and its facilities.

GIRLS' GRAMMAR SCHOOL, HITCHIN.

Head Mistress—MISS J. E. GOSNELL, B.A.

The New Buildings, opened in July, have been specially designed to meet the requirements of Modern Education, and contain Central Hall, Large Class Rooms, Art Studio, Laboratory, Music Rooms and Library.

The accommodation for Boarders is excellent.

The building is warmed throughout, and the ventilation is on the best modern principles.

There is a large and fully qualified Staff. The Education is thorough, and there is no over-pressure. Special attention is paid to Physical Culture. There is a

PREPARATORY DEPARTMENT

For Children (boys and girls) under eight years of age.

The Winter Term begins on Tuesday, September 15,

For Prospectus, &c., apply to the Head Mistress, or to the Clerk to the Governors, F. SHILLITOE, Esq., 2, Payne's Park, Hitchin.

Hertfordshire Express, 5th September 1908.　　　　　[British Newspaper Library, Colindale]

1909 & 1910–1911

After all the publicity given to the new Hitchin Girls' Grammar School in 1908, there are no records at all of events in 1909. Doris Baron recollects that Miss Gosnell decided that the girls and staff must all do 'fire drill' and climb down a rope ladder from an upstairs window. This caused great hilarity amongst the pupils when it was observed that one of the teachers, Miss Kelly, was not wearing knickers!

Reginald Hine, the historian, has written that the first school magazine appeared as early as 1906 but, sadly, the first copy known to survive is for Summer 1910. As if to mark the emergence of a new age, the first report is an eye witness account of the funeral procession of King Edward VII.

Elsie Warren gave a very evocative report of her work as a medical student in the Royal Free Hospital, working among the very poor of Islington and Holborn. She describes plans to work in a 'heathen' country, where women, no matter how ill, could only consult a woman doctor. Gladys Pennefather was nursing at Great Ormond Street.

The new school Debating Society considered 'The world is growing better' – a motion carried with a majority of twenty. A later debate decided that 'The franchise should be extended to women' but rejected the suggestion that 'A universal language is desirable'. They also voted against 'Homework should be abolished', probably influenced by the fact that the Head Mistress opposed the motion!

The Games Club lost two hockey matches at home during the winter and in an Oxford v. Cambridge match, the school provided three players for Cambridge and two for the Oxford team which won the match. This was followed by dancing and playing games in the hall. No fixtures were played outside the school in the autumn and the hockey field was taken up and relaid in December. The tennis club had twenty-six members and had two courts available for games at dinner time and until six o'clock on three nights a week. At the end of the summer term a tournament was held and was won by Miss Kelly and Kathleen Wilkinson who were presented with a cup given by the mistresses.

The Hertfordshire Art Society held its Annual Exhibition and M. Perkins won a 1st Prize in the Still Life, Amateur section; S. Chatron was Highly Commended for

c.1910. A sad tale is associated with this photograph of the boarders, taken about 1910. It depicts, amongst others, Muriel and Dot Wright and their friend Doris Baron. The latter formed an attachment to Don Wright, brother of her friends, and when he was killed in 1917, the original of this photograph was found amongst his effects. *Back row L. to R.:* Eileen Heale, Phyllis Gosnell, Barbara Field, Muriel Wright. *Front row:* Margaret Smyth, Doe Pennefather, Doris Baron, Ellen Chambers, Joan Gosnell, Dot Wright. [Doris Baron]

a study of Palm and J. Mitchell was Commended for a study of flowers.

The Dowager Countess of Lytton attended the Prize Distribution and Sports at the end of July. The most interesting item was a slow bicycle race in which the competitors wore fancy dress. A prize for the best costume 'to cost no more than one shilling' (5 new pence) was awarded to M. Dyer dressed as a teddy bear.

The list of prize winners was impressive, totalling thirty-eight for all areas of school work and almost as many prizes for the Sports Day. Acknowledgement was made to Frederic Seebohm, William Ransom, George Spurr and members of the staff for donating the prizes. After all the prizes had been distributed, there was an address by Canon Jones and a short musical programme followed by tea and an inspection of the school by the visitors.

In 1910 the boarders had a superb viewpoint from their dormitory window to see the passing of Halley's Comet with its long fiery tail, 'a lifelong thrill' for one pupil. The Dormitory, too, was the scene of a disgrace when one girl was expelled for climbing on to the high cross beams in the roof.

1911–1912

The most notable event of this school year was the death, on 6th February, of Mr. Frederic Seebohm who had been a Governor and Treasurer of the School from its opening in 1889. It is difficult to exaggerate his contribution to the development of the Hitchin Girls' Grammar School. He had been a founder, trustee and fund raiser for the original school and for the new building, as well as being a generous contributor himself. He had given the land on which the present school was built. A great educationalist, he was concerned that the school should have a worthy library and had presented many valuable books and the cupboards in which to keep them. With his death, the school had, indeed, lost a real and irreplaceable friend.

The Debating Society was still very active and, in December, held a 'Hat Night', to involve more members in actually speaking. Of the subjects taken from the hat, the discourse on 'Cats' by D. Russell was considered one of the best speeches. A debate, 'That Home Rule should be given to Ireland', was, at the February meeting, defeated by two votes.

The hockey players had a very mixed year in winning a match against Letchworth Ladies but losing against Royston and Luton and suffering two resounding defeats against Bedford. Honour was redeemed when they beat Caldicott boys by two goals!

There was a very full Christmas programme starting with a French Concert, in early December, to which visitors were invited. The familiar 'Sur le Pont d'Avignon' sung by the first form girls started the entertainment, which followed with other songs, sketches and a short interpretation of 'Sleeping Beauty'. A very pretty girl, Louella Whittles, was the princess and Doris Baron the prince. Due to an unfortunate lapse Doris cried, 'Lavez vous' (wash) instead of, 'Levez vous' (arise). 'It nearly brought the house down', she remembers. Red Riding Hood was also performed and appeared again, as part of the Boarders' Concert at the end of the term. The School was 'At Home' just before breaking up for the holiday and presented a varied programme of choral and solo singing before the Kindergarten 'stole the show' with their presentation of 'The Selfish Goblin'. This was enjoyed as much by the children as by the visitors and earned an encore. After the entertainment, tea was provided before the visitors were free to inspect the building and to see the Christmas decorations.

The School Sports Day, in June, started off well, and halfway through the programme, an exhibition of Swedish Drill was given by the Upper School. Fancy marching followed, but by this time rain was falling heavily and the rest of the sports were abandoned in favour of an impromptu concert in the hall. Prizes, for those events completed, were awarded by Mrs. Jones. The Sports were concluded the next afternoon and again included a fancy dress slow bicycle race. Phyllis Gosnell won a prize as a freak and Mary Browne for the prettiest costume.

Following the success of the Swedish Drill, Mr. Albon took a photograph and gave, to the school, eighty copies which were sold for 2d. each in aid of the magazine funds.

1912.   Swedish drill.   [School Magazine]

1912–1913   Head Girls: Gwendoline Bryant & Jessie Hall

Prefects, Autumn, 1912: *Library (before dinner):* L. Carlisle, M. Ellis, K. Warren; *(after dinner)* D. Donson, M. Hailey, D. Ellis. *Dinner Hour:* F. Meier, R. Parkinson, M. Smith, D. Williams. *Cloak Room:* 1.45 p.m.: K. Fitch, M. Walker. *Recreation:* D. Armstrong, B. Chalkley, D. Pennefather.
Heads of Forms, Spring, 1913: *Va:* K. Fitch; *Vb:* P. Hall; *IV:* M. Gardner; *IIIa:* D. Stout; *IIIb:* E. Chew; *II:* M. Bax.

During the autumn, Hitchin suffered a bad attack of measles but the school escaped with comparatively few cases.

The Rev. Mr. Shepheard-Walwyn addressed the girls on 'How to live healthy lives, both physically and morally'. He also left a list of 'improving' books to be read. There was also a talk on 'Temperance'.

A prize offered for the best essay went to Molly Gardner who wrote an account of the fatal aeroplane accident at Graveley, having been an eye witness to the tragedy. A memorial obelisk still stands on the Willian to Great Wymondley road, at the edge of the field from which the aviators flew. A further prize for the best sketch in any medium was won by Marjorie Hailey.

At the end of the autumn term, a large parcel was sent to the hospital containing gifts to be given to the children when they went home. The toys, dolls and useful articles were much appreciated.

Just before Christmas, the boarders gave an entertainment of songs, dances, sketches and two plays. Arrangements were upset a few days before the performance when Phyllis Gosnell fell ill. As she was a principal performer, her parts had to be undertaken by several different people at short notice. Despite this, the concert was a great success.

There was a Christmas Hockey Dance attended by members, visitors and some 'old girls'. Some of the mistresses provided the music and the refreshments which contributed towards a very happy evening. It did, in part, compensate for the disappointing playing year. The measles in the town and the bad weather both conspired to cause the cancellation of most of the games. Only two were played.

Jessie Hall left at the end of the school year. She had been a prefect and joint Head Girl with Gwendoline Bryant, as well as Games Captain. A talented pianist, she would be missed for her playing at morning assembly and at other school functions. She later studied under Dame Myra Hess.

The Debating Society agreed that 'The Balkan States were justified in making war on Turkey' and also that 'Mathematics is essential to a girl's education'. A resounding victory was won by the proposition, 'That England is shirking her responsibilities among the nations of the world', clearly demonstrating attitudes in the months before war was declared.

The Sketch Club decided that the girls would no longer vote for the drawings but that members of the staff, unfamiliar with the different styles of work, would do this instead.

There was a Concert just before Easter in which the pupils and staff combined to make an excellent programme of vocal and instrumental music in the first half of the evening, followed by 'The May Queen Cantata' after the interval.

It had been some years since the school produced a Shakespeare play so it staged 'The Taming of the Shrew'. Expenses were very heavy but even so, there was a surplus of £10 which bought an oak dresser for the studio and books for the library. The production required a great deal of work and dedication from the cast and those responsible for producing the costumes and scenery, but the resulting production was a credit to all involved in its creation. Such a great deal of time and effort had been expended in the staging of 'The Taming of the Shrew' that it was decided to hold no Sports Day in 1913.

1913   "THE TAMING OF THE SHREW."   [Anne Sworder]

DRAMATIS PERSONÆ

Baptista, a rich gentleman of Padua … … … …	M. WALKER
Vincentio, an old gentleman of Pisa … … …	K. LITTLE
Lucentio, son to Vincentio, in love with Bianca … … …	L. CARLISLE
Petruchio, a gentleman of Verona, suitor to Katharina…	H. FITCH
Gremio ⎱ servants to Bianca … … … … …	M. HAILEY
Hortensio ⎰	R. PARKINSON
Tranio ⎱ servants to Lucentio … … … …	M. ELLIS
Biondello ⎰	A. STEEDMAN
Grumio ⎱ … … … … … … …	F. MEIER
Curtis ⎰ servants to Petruchio … … … … …	A. HILLMAN
Peter ⎰ … … … … … … …	P. GOSNELL
A. Pedant, who poses as Vincentio … … … …	L. GOODLIFFE
Tailor … … … … … … … … …	B. CHALKLEY
Haberdasher … … … … … … … …	E. FOX
Katharina, the Shrew ⎱ daughters to Baptista … … …	K. FITCH
Bianca ⎰	M. MAYHEW
Widow … … … … … … … …	K. MEARS

1913–1914   Doris Armstrong

Prefects: *Responsibility for neatness of School:* M. Hall, P. Hall, K. Warren, W. Brooks, D. Pennefather, P. Gosnell, D. Donson, A. Hillman, E. Foster. *Library:* M. Hailey, M. Smith, E. Fox, D. Burrows. *Cloakroom:* D. Armstrong, B. Chalkley.
Heads of Forms, Spring Term, 1914: *Va:* D. Armstrong; *Vb:* M. Gardner; *IV:* D. Stout; *IIIa:* M. Ebbutt; *IIIb:* R. Mothersill; *II:* W. Jackson; *I:* R. Pirkis.

1914.   She Stoops to Conquer.   [Anne Sworder]

This was a happy school year since the gathering clouds of war did not break until the summer holidays.

The girls joined the boys, in the old Grammar School plantation, to hear a lecture on 'China', given by a missionary who had lived there for thirty years. This must have been of special interest to the girls from Lavender Croft, the Quaker Missionary home in Wymondley Road. Winefrede Jackson was just one of those whose parents were in China.

Miss Gosnell again held, just before Christmas, her 'At Home' for parents and friends. There was a varied musical programme and a report on the girls' successes in the preceding year. Following tea, the visitors inspected the work on display.

In February the school staged two plays, 'She Stoops to Conquer' and 'Fleur de Neige' – the first by the senior pupils and the second by the Kindergarten. There was both a matinee and an evening performance, enjoyed by everybody who attended.

The Hockey Club had a successful year, winning five out of the six matches played. A Basket Ball Club was formed by the newly arrived Miss Wilkins, which offered a popular alternative sport. No cricket matches were held in the summer other than those arranged within the school. Tennis became so popular that, despite a fourth court being made on part of the hockey pitch, a booking system had to be introduced. Varied successes attended the tennis matches, but by far the most popular fixture was that played against the boys of Caldicott School; won by the girls 87–48.

The first Inter-Form Gymnastics Competition took place in April, for the Gymnastics Challenge Shield. Each form, from the second up, took part and the competition was very keen. By a very small margin, the winners were Va. In June the staff and pupils were both surprised and honoured by the unannounced visit of Lady Salisbury, accompanied by the Misses Seebohm. En route to another

1914.   Fleur de Neige.   [Bernard Sanders]

PROGRAMME

"FLEUR DE NEIGE."

Reine	...	...	...	GWEN ELLIS.
Fleur de Neige	...	...	...	WINIFRED GOODLIFFE.
Miroir	...	...	...	RUTH MASON.
Prince	...	...	...	WILLIE ROPER.
Chasseur	...	...	...	OWEN GATWARD.

Gnomes ... ...
{
WINIFRIEDE JACKSON.
LILY KILBEY.
ALFRED DAVIDSON.
JOYCE ELLIS.
UNA BERRY.
NANCY CATFORD.
BERNARD SANDERS.

Scène 1.   Palais royal.   Scène 2.   La forêt.

Scène 3 et 4.   Chaumière des gnomes.   Dans des gnomes.

engagement, her ladyship wished to inspect the 'new' school and its buildings. Miss Gosnell, in a short speech of welcome, reminded Lady Salisbury that her last visit had been to award the prizes at a Prizegiving at the Old Town Hall. This practice had now been abandoned in favour of 'Virtue is its own reward', but the Head Mistress did encourage Form Competition and asked her Ladyship to present the Challenge Shield.

40

1914–1915

Prefects: P. Gosnell, D. Pennefather, M. Gardner, M. King, K. Mears, K. Warren, M. Hailey, D. Donson, D. Burrows, A. Hillman, M. Hall, P. Hall, M. Mitchell, M. Peck, E. Partridge.
Heads of Forms: *Va:* K. Warren; *Vb:* E. Haysom; *IV:* B. Agombar; *IIIa:* Madge Stallard; *IIIb:* M. Kidman; *II:* J. Ellis; *I:* G. Baron.
Hockey: *Captain:* P. Gosnell; *Vice-Captain:* A. Steedman; *Secretary:* K. Warren; *2nd XI Captain:* M. Smyth.
Net Ball: *Captain:* M. Hall; *Vice-Captain:* F. Day; *Secretary:* D. Donson; *2nd VII Captain:* M. Gardner.

Before the school reassembled, the Great War had begun, and life would never be the same again.

At a more personal level, the school lost a link with its history as well as a governor, in the death of Mr. William Ransom. He had been a driving force in the siting of the original Grammar School building in Bancroft, and, in the new school, had given generously towards the building and its equipment. Since its opening he had donated £10 each year towards building up the Library.

The school affiliated to the Girls' Secondary Schools Patriotic Union. As part of its contribution, the pupils spent the autumn term, at special working parties, making shirts, bedjackets, jumpers, gloves etc. and were able to send a large box to the St. John's Ambulance Association. In the latter part of the term, children's frocks and nightshirts were made so as to maintain the customary Christmas gift to Hitchin Hospital for distribution to the poor of Hitchin. Funding for all the materials was started by donations of money from all the girls and the staff. Thereafter, all paid 1d. per week. In addition, the Hockey Dance raised £2 and the Patriotic Concert £10 for the same purpose.

The concert was well supported; every girl wore a small Union Jack and the stage was decorated with flags. As might be expected, it had a very patriotic flavour with National dances and the singing of the National Anthems of all the Allies.

There were several other concerts throughout the year to raise funds for patriotic purposes; besides the usual full school entertainment at Christmas, both Va and the Prefects staged concerts of their own and gave as much pleasure to their audience as they took in performing.

The Hockey Club did not have a very full fixtures list but enjoyed the games that they did play. An innovation in the School Magazine was a full criticism of each girl's play – 'must work harder in the circle', 'not fast enough on the ball', etc. Net Ball reported much enthusiasm and mixed match results as did the tennis. Cricket suffered from the weather.

The Inter-Form Gymnastics Competition took place for the second time, and the quality of the work showed a great improvement over the year before. Form Va retained the Shield.

The school year ended in July with a dance, the proceeds of which went to buy comforts for five Belgian soldiers who had been in the trenches since the previous August.

1915–1916 Kathleen Warren

Prefects: *Cloak Room:* Monica King. *Preparation 12.30–1:* Agnes Hillman and Molly Gardner. *After Dinner, Monday:* M. Mitchell; *Tuesday:* Kathleen Mears; *Wednesday:* Dorothea Stout; *Thursday:* Lilian Goodliffe; *Friday:* Ida Taylor.
Heads of Forms: *VI:* K. Warren; *Va:* M. King; *Vb:* W. Taylor; *IV:* R. Reynolds; *IIIa:* D. Craft; *IIIb:* L. Symes; *II:* E. Davidson; *I:* G. Gibb.
Hockey Captain: Kathleen Warren.

An important development for the school was the founding of the Old Girls' Association, when sixteen old pupils attended an inaugural meeting in March 1916. It was decided there would be a Summer Gathering and a second meeting just before Christmas.

There were, in the autumn, two lectures illustrated with maps and pictures, to show the progress of the war, and the school continued its support of the war effort by making clothing. This went to the St. John Ambulance Brigade and the Red Cross Society. Letters of thanks also came from the Serbian Relief Fund and a hospital in Cambridge.

Near Christmas the School Concert offered a most varied programme, from recitations by the Kindergarten, through musical pieces and a 'Moth Dance', to drilling and marching. The latter was as much appreciated by the wounded soldiers in the audience, as by the parents and performers. The Prefects held their own concert about the same time and sent the proceeds to provide parcels for Belgian troops in the trenches.

The Fourth Form staged an 'Entertainment' at Easter which consisted of a fortune teller, 'catch penny' stalls and competitions. The entrance fee gave free seats to the two sketches which were performed. It was both a social and financial success, the proceeds from which went to the Needlework Fund.

Despite the published individual criticisms of their play, the Hockey Club claimed 'great joy when the hockey season came round'. They won all their matches in the autumn term and beat the 'old girls' 6–0.

Form Va won the Gymnastics Challenge Shield for the third year.

The first Old Girls' Summer Gathering took the form of a cricket match against the School. Despite their foreboding of advancing years and creaking joints, they soundly beat the school team by 95 runs to 46!

The school year ended with a Garden Fete in aid of the Star and Garter Home. There were the usual stalls and sideshows and, after tea, a concert in the hall. This had been a great effort on the part of all the school and its resounding success was reflected in the £50 raised. The needlework stall alone made £20, while the children's frocks and overalls left unsold went to support the Waifs' and Strays' Society.

1916–1917 Phyllis Hall

Prefects, Spring Term, 1917:
12.30 to 1 o'clock (Form IV) – *Monday:* W. Brewster; *Tuesday:* M. Ebbutt; *Wednesday:* B. Agombar; *Thursday:* E. Hillman; *Friday:* M. Thair. *1.30 to 2 o'clock* – *Monday:* J. Gosnell; *Tuesday:* D. Hawkins; *Wednesday:* W. Jardine; *Thursday:* M. Smyth; *Friday:* F. Graham. *Cloak Room:* I. Cook, W. Taylor.
Heads of Forms, Spring Term, 1917: *VI:* P. Hall; *Va:* J. Gosnell; *Vb:* M. Cooper; *IV:* M. Cole; *IIIa:* A. Mallows; *IIIb:* E. Druce; *II:* G. Gibb; *I:* E. Bell.

To increase still more the contribution of the school to the war effort, a War Savings Association was formed and in less than a year £110 was saved. This, however, was not judged to be good enough and the magazine exhorted each girl to 'help her country' in saving as much as possible. To encourage the idea of citizenship among the girls, a 'Corpus Comitum' was formed in June 1917 under the auspices of Miss Wilkins. The whole school was divided into six companies, each with members from all age groups, with a teacher as 'captain' and three 'lieutenants'. The activities seem to have had some affinity with the Girl Guides, with the signalling, camp fires and first aid. A strip of ground by the hockey pitch was used as a potato patch, with each company tending its own plot.

The Winter Gathering of the Old Girls' Association (O.G.A.) planned a hockey match but, on the day, the weather was bitterly cold and the pitch covered in snow, so the fixture was cancelled. This was just as well, since a train bringing some of the players from London was delayed, first by fog and then by an engine breakdown, and arrived in Hitchin 1½ hours late! The tea, dancing and games, did go ahead, so redeeming an otherwise disappointing day.

The hockey teams also suffered greatly from the weather, playing only three matches, all of which they won. By the summer, the weather was still causing problems for the tennis players, although the cricketers felt they had enjoyed an excellent season.

The previous year the Gymnastics Shield was retained by Va with a half mark lead over Form IV, who this year won by four marks over IIIa.

The school continued to support the war effort with its sewing and knitting, but a letter of thanks illustrates a new generosity, considering the wartime food shortages. It comes from 'The Maples' Hospital – later to be the nurses home for the North Herts. Hospital – thanking the staff and girls for a decorated fruit cake which had been sent for the soldiers in their care.

The staff staged a charade, 'The Three Gossips', at Easter, in aid of the Library fund, which made a novel departure from having the pupils on the stage and the staff in the audience!

The school year again ended with a Garden Fete, once more with tempting stalls and sideshows calculated to make visitors part with their money. Tea was served in the courtyard and, 'owing to war conditions, the Food Controller's restrictions were duly observed'. £40 proceeds were sent to the St. Dunstan's Hostel for Blind Soldiers.

1917–1918 Winifred Taylor

Prefects: E. Moore, M. Kidman, E. Cross, J. Holland, G. Gibb, J. Shillitoe, J. Smyth.
Heads of Forms: *Va:* W. Taylor; *Vb:* E. Cole; *IVa:* A. Mallows; *IVb:* M. Wade; *IIIa:* L. Dear; *IIIb:* G. Gibb; *II:* M. Ashby; *I:* E. Holland.
Games Captain: M. I. Barlow.
Hockey Captain: Maud Kidman.

In May the school welcomed special visitors when a surgeon, Sir Rickman Godlee, came to give a talk on the life and works of his uncle, Lord Lister. He also had other ties with the school in that his wife was Juliet, daughter of Frederic Seebohm. After the talk, Miss Lister gave a few personal reminiscences of her uncle, before presenting the school with his portrait.

Miss Wilkins left the school at the end of the summer term, and, in the following autumn, her place as organiser of the Corpus Comitum was taken by Miss Read. The corps had a very active year, and each company was detailed to give a short entertainment for the mistresses at Christmas. These varied from an excerpt from 'A Midsummer Night's Dream', tableaux of Nursery Rhymes, and several other plays. After Christmas, the structure of the corps was changed; the membership was put on a voluntary basis and the companies reduced from six to four. A badge and 'promise' were introduced; proficiency badges for needlework, first aid, signalling, music, etc. were suggested. The motto 'Play the Game' expressed the hope that the corps would be a great power for good.

The hockey club suffered from losing most of its best players in the summer of 1917 and was therefore playing below standard. A 'knockout' tennis tournament was organised – won by Maud Kidman – and an American tournament at the Summer Gathering was won by Miss Read and Winifred Barker. There were

1918. The Merchant of Venice.   [Edith Russell (Hawkins)]

enthusiastic inter-form cricket matches and those between the companies of the Corpus Comitum. The staff and prefects also played the school, the delighted school being the victors.

Empire Day was given over to a day of patriotism with saluting of the flag at assembly and a lantern lecture by Miss Gosnell on 'A Trip Round the Empire'. An evening of 'patriotic entertainment' included the speech of Henry V before Agincourt and plays entitled 'Children of the Empire' and 'Britannia's Hope'. It concluded with a tableau of 'Britannia and the Allies' as the girls sang 'Land of Hope and Glory'.

Form Va staged 'The Merchant of Venice' in April to raise money for the Red Cross funds and made £20. This was a good team effort by all the girls, whose form mistress, Miss Button, was stage manager, coach and general assistant. Other staff helped to make the costumes and made their contribution to the success of the venture.

The annual Sale of Work and Garden Fete was even more successful than in previous years, and £65 was sent to the Star and Garter Home to provide furniture for the invalids.

1918–1919   Ruth Mothersill

Prefects, Spring Term, 1919: *Va:* Muriel Barlow; *Vb:* Hilda Purrott; *IVa:* Enid Cross; *IVb:* Edith Bishop; *IIIa:* Joan Holland; *IIIb:* Gladys Course; *II:* Dorothy Bowden; *I:* Mary Chick.
Heads of Forms: *VI:* Ruth Mothersill; *Va:* Ella Thornley; *Vb:* Agnes Mallows; *IVa:* Ida Foster; *IVb:* Marion Dearman; *IIIa:* Dorothy Ames; *IIIb:* Marion Higgott; *II:* Margaret Belcher; *I:* Winifred Kilbey; *Prep.:* Francis Bell.

This time, the last event of the school year must be mentioned first because, in many ways, it was the greatest social change to overtake the school. After deferring her departure for five years, Miss Gosnell retired after thirty years' devoted service since the Grammar School first opened its doors in Bancroft.

It was a momentous year nationally too, with the ending of the war in November 1918, and a peacetime Britain looking forward to happier times ahead.

During November, a severe epidemic of influenza which was sweeping across Europe afflicted the town and made it advisable to close the school for a fortnight, giving the pupils an unexpected holiday.

A new development was the merging, in the spring, of the Corpus Comitum into the establishment of the 1st Hitchin Company of the Guide movement, with four patrols and Miss Read as Captain. A Brownie pack was also started with Miss Williams as Brown Owl, which attracted keen support among the younger pupils.

The staff entertainment at the end of the Spring Term included a repeat of 'The Three Gossips' which had been so popular two years before. Since the proceeds were to go to the 'Musicians' Gift' – a fund to provide good music for the army of occupation – it was appropriate also to stage a variety of musical items.

At the beginning of the Christmas term the pupils were asked to sacrifice some sugar in their tea in order to make a collection for The Maples Hospital. Nine pounds of sugar were thus given and used for the refreshments at a Hospital Fete in aid of the Red Cross.

The needleworkers were still busy and three cases of clothing were sent to assist the people returning to their wrecked homes in the devastated areas of France.

There were two lectures in the spring on widely differing topics. The first was on 'Tennyson and Byron Compared', by Dr. Lyttleton, and the second on 'The Development of the Aeroplane', organised by Miss Button in support of War Bonds Week.

The last event of the year, the Old Girls' Summer Gathering, was overshadowed by the retirement of Miss Gosnell. E. Tyler wrote, 'We were about to take leave of a FRIEND who had helped to mould whatever good there might have been in us'. Miss Gosnell, too, showed emotional tension as she bade farewell to all 'her' Old Girls and was presented with a silver tea service and tray, on their behalf, by Jessie Hall.

Miss Johnson, herself about to leave after thirteen years as a popular art mistress, represented the staff and gave Miss Gosnell a gold wrist watch and filigree brooch.

With the departure of Miss Gosnell, one phase of school life had ended and a new one was about to begin.

INNOVATIONS DURING MISS GOSNELL'S TIME. 1889–1919

Examinations, Prizes and Awards

1910   Oxford Local Examinations – Senior and Junior
      Associated Board – Royal Academy of Music and Royal College of Music.
       (Higher, Lower, Elementary, Primary)
      Royal Drawing Society Exhibition – Divisions – IV, III, II, I (Honours or Pass)
       (discontinued 1916)
      Annual Elocution Exhibition – Luton and South Beds.
1911   Meyer Memorial Prize – Best Bursar
1914   Hertfordshire Art Society – 1st, 2nd and 3rd Prizes (only in 1914)
      Dawson Memorial Botany Prizes – Senior and Junior Nature Diaries
1919   Cambridge Higher Local Examination

Games and Sports

1909   Hockey – versus other schools
1910   Tennis – Staff v. Girls Tournament
      Tea Dances & Games
      Sports – Sack race, slow bicycle etc.
1911   Hockey – Oxford v. Cambridge
            School v. Caldicott Boys' School
      Hockey Club
      Hockey Dance
1913   Sports – Swedish Drill Display and Races
      Cricket
      Basket Ball
1914   Games Club Dance
      Inter-Form Gym Competition for Challenge Shield
1915   Cricket XI
1917   Inter-Form Gym Competition Senior and Junior
       (Snr. Challenge Shield – Jnr. School Cup)
      Knock out Tennis Tournament

ANNIE MURIEL CHAMBERS
1882–1962
Head Mistress 1919–1945

Annie Muriel Chambers came to the Hitchin Girls' Grammar School, in 1919, with the difficult task of making her mark in a school which had been entirely moulded by her predecessor. She set to with a will.

Her scholastic record was impressive; she had been a pupil at Cheltenham Ladies' College before winning a scholarship to St. Hilda's College, Oxford. There she read Modern History for which she was awarded an Honours Degree in 1905 and in 1920 became a Fellow of the Royal Historical Society. The new Headmistress was, from the first, determined to keep a full record of the happenings within her school – the Red, the Yellow and the Green Record Books. The first contained the weekly record of general behaviour and performance in each Form; the second was more specific about individual pupils and the third contained the scholastic record of each pupil within the week. Besides this, there was the ceremonial marking of the register each morning after prayers. An 'absentee monitress' was appointed from each form and it was her duty to call, in her turn, the names of absentees for the day. Since some of these were late rather than absent, corrections were also necessary for the day before and all was marked by Miss Chambers in the Register. As the school became larger this daily ritual made greater and greater inroads on the time allocated to the first lesson.

Miss Chambers was a most able administrator, and all the girls seem to have had happy recollections of their time in the school when it was under her direction. Some pupils hero-worshipped her with a devotion which extended far beyond their school life whilst others were more aware of her human frailties. She quite clearly had her favourites who could do no wrong and conversely, other girls who could not put a foot right. On the less favoured, her sarcastic tongue and humiliations left a lasting mark. One ex-pupil, now a university professor, remembers that Miss Chambers had a very clear sense of one's station in life: daughters of professional men went to university, trade returned to trade, and the scholarship girls into nursing or shorthand typing. This rigidity was challenged when, during the war, an evacuee presented herself at the school, accompanied by mother, to claim the scholarship place won in the East End of London. Miss Chambers decreed that Hitchin Girls' Grammar School would be a most unsuitable establishment for the girl and only the intervention of County Hall dissuaded her.

With attitudes like these, it would seem that the nickname 'Charity' was rather inappropriate. It stemmed from Miss Chambers' fondness for quoting 'Faith, Hope and Charity, these three, but the greatest of these is Charity'. (Miss Squire and Miss Radway were 'Faith' and 'Hope' when in her company). It was commonly held that 'cold as Charity' was a better source!

Despite her short-comings, Miss Chambers could be charming and was adept at persuading others to undertake all manner of projects on behalf of the school. Though, like Miss Gosnell before her, she did not encourage reward for individual merit, she accumulated a vast array of trophies and prizes for distribution for collective effort and was always ready to provide some of the smaller prizes herself.

Several pupils remember one of her habits: Miss Chambers used regularly to

a. M. Chambers.

Miss Annie Muriel Chambers, Final Hons. Oxford, F.R.Hist.Soc. Headmistress 1919–1945.

1925. Miss Chambers in the Morris car she bought from Sanders Garage.   [Rosemary Russell (Cook)]

stand in front of the fire, skirt hitched up and directoire knickers displayed, warming the backs of her legs. Yet this strange stance never led to giggling fits. 'She was such a lady, that she couldn't be inelegant if she tried', said one ex-prefect.

Though primarily an academic, Miss Chambers had a wide range of other interests and talents. She was one of the first people in Hitchin to own a motor car and bought a beige, 'bull nose' Morris from Sanders Garage. Bernard Sanders, former 'Prep' school pupil and 'still only a lad' himself, taught Miss Chambers, Miss Squire and Miss Read to drive in the days before a driving test was necessary. 'Not always easy to teach a school marm to drive', is his laconic comment now.

Miss Chambers was an accomplished needlewoman and a keen gardener. She was particularly interested in alpines, and her blue and white garden is still remembered. When she was worried about the roses, Isobel Harkness was instructed to ask the advice of her father. His reply, 'Tell her to put on her "wellies" and stamp them in' was never relayed!

Another story related to the garden shows the kinder side of Miss Chambers' nature:– Two of the Kindergarten boys had been very naughty – they had thrown all the muddy wellingtons over the toilet door and buried the boy inside – and Miss Read sent them quaking to be punished. Both were given a good 'ticking off'. A few days later, Robert Stutley decided to 'get back into Miss Chambers' good books' and at break, sneaked into her private garden and picked a bunch of her prized flowers. He then presented himself to the Head Mistress who thanked him and instructed her maid to bring him milk and biscuits. He felt this was a very good idea, but when he tried the same trick a few days later he was told that Miss Chambers was busy!

Throughout her years at the school Miss Chambers always had a dog and brought with her 'Scott', described as a red coated Chow, which always led the boarders' 'crocodile' as it took off down the drive. Next came 'Jimmie', a black labrador with the gentle nature of his breed. He could be seen, sunning himself, sitting upright on the garden seat beside his mistress and surveying his domain. Next came 'Pi', a brown spotted dalmatian with a great love of tennis balls who came to an untimely end through chewing wood and swallowing the splinters. Lastly came a small Sealyham pup – 'Timothy', who liked nothing better than to dash onto the hockey pitch and steal the ball.

When Miss Chambers came to the school, her friend Miss Squire came too and took up an appointment to teach games and gymnastics. In 1945 Miss Chambers retired and within three years, Miss Squire retired also. They lived together until Miss Chambers' death and in the late 1950s they were seen by an old pupil, happily holidaying by Lake Lugano.

| Surname *Chambers.* | | Christian Names | *Annie Muriel* | | Style { Mr.? / Mrs.! / Miss! } | 67 |

1. Date of Birth.	2. Date of appointment on probation.	3. Date of definitive appointment.	4. Date of leaving.
5 May 1882.	9 April 1919.	Sept 1919	

5. Schools and Colleges at which educated, with dates. State names and types of institutions.	6. Particulars of Public and University Examinations taken, and certificates and degrees obtained, with dates.
Private Schools 1892 – 1899. Cheltenham L. College 1899 - 1902 St. Hilda's Hall. Oxford. 1902 - 5	Ox. Senior Local. 1899. Camb. Higher Local. Full Hons C. 1901. Scholar. St Hilda's H. Oxford 1902 Final Honours School of Modern His. Cl. I 1905 1920 F. R. His. S.

7. List of teaching posts held, with dates.	8. Particulars of training in teaching, if any, and certificates or diplomas obtained, with dates.
York High School Sept 1905 – Dec 1907 Literary Work - Jan 1908 - May 1909 Bedford H.S. May 1909 - July 1917 Berkhamsted Schools for Girls Sept 1917 – Aug 1919	
	9. State external teaching or official work undertaken, if any, in addition to duties in the School.

10. Special subject or subjects.	11. State principal duties assigned, and subjects taken. (Any subsequent changes and their dates to be indicated in red ink.)	
History	Some History & Scripture throughout school. Duties of Head mistress. Charge of Boarding H.	

12. Total annual emoluments.		13. Particulars of retiring allowance, if any.
Salary, with scale, if any. £ 500. Capitation Fees, if any. April 1924 £550 Estimated value of board and lodging if given as part of emoluments.		14. Post, if any, taken up after leaving the School.

From Staff Register, Book I.

50

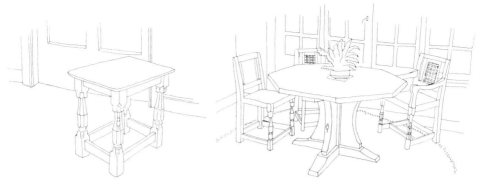

Drawings by Amanda Birkinshaw 1980–87.

The O.G.A. planned celebrations for Miss Chambers' eightieth birthday but it was not to be: two months before her birthday she had a stroke and died.

A collection was made to provide a memorial to her, and an oak table, chairs and a stool were purchased from 'Thompsons', the master craftsmen in Yorkshire, whose trade mark is a small carved mouse. A carving of St. Francis of Assisi was also bought and all are now in the entrance hall of the school.

Miss Chambers spent twenty-six years at Hitchin, in which time the school held an excellent reputation for the standards of teaching, discipline and loyalty found there. This was her true epitaph.

MISTRESSES APPOINTED DURING MISS CHAMBERS' TIME 1919–1945

1919–1945	Muriel A. Chambers, Head Mistress	History, Scripture
1919–1943	Margaret H. Forbes	Needlework, Cooking, Laundry, Hygiene
1919–1921	Phyllis E. Hayes	Geography, Latin, English
1919–1920	Margaret L. Missen	Mathematics, Science
1919–1928	Lydia K. Pearce	Art
1919–?	E. Vera Rimmington	Piano, Singing, Ear Training
1919–1948	Ruth Squire	Games, Gymnastics
1919–1926	Eveline G. Thomas	French, English
1920–1947	May A. Flinn, Second Mistress	Science
1920	N. Mabel Holt	History, English
1920–1948	Violet H. Hughes	English
1920–1921	Sarah A. Hunt	Mathematics
1920–1923	Dilys A. Jones	French
1920–1926	Elizabeth V. Lloyd-Williams	History
1920–1923	Alice L. Mather	Scripture, Secretarial
1920–1949	Marjorie Mortimer	French
1920–1937	Anna W. Osborne	Dancing (Visiting Mistress)
1920–1922	Alice L. Raby	Piano, Violin
1920–1958	Dorothy M. Radway	Mathematics
1920–1923	Kathleen M. Weatherley	Class Singing, Piano, Ear Training
1920–1927	Mabel C. Williams	Botany, General Subjects
1921–1922	Millicent S. Campbell	Geography, Latin
1921–193?	Evelyn G. Clark	Mathematics
1921–1924	Helen Murray	English, Games, Shorthand

1922	Mabel E. Haworth	Geography, Latin
1922–1927	Elizabeth E. Sandercock	Geography, Latin
1922–1948	Ruth Saunders	Music, Choir
1923–1924	Patience N. W. Collet	French
1923–1924	Gertrude E. Mockridge	Charge of Kindergarten, All Subjects, Drawing, Painting
1923–1926	Doreen O'Brien	Music, Singing, Ear Training
1923–1924	Phyllis M. Spenser	General Subjects in Middle School
1924–1927	Elsa M. Bavin	Junior Games, Secretarial
1924–1928	Eleanor C. M. Rountree	French
1925–1935	Alfreda C. Bullmore	Violin, Orchestra, Piano
1926–1931	Evelyn Cryer	English
1926–1929	Irene M. Gay-Price	Music
1926–1931	Cicely Tower	History, English
1927	Cecile A. Essex	French, Mathematics
1927–1928	Lois M. France	English
1927–1933	Gwendolyn B. Howells	Geography
1927–?	Dorothy H. Street	Games (Visiting Mistress)
1927–1932	Menevia S. Young-Evans	Classics
1928–1965	Elizabeth D. Allright, Acting Headmistress '62 Deputy Headmistress '63–'65	Head of Science, Biology
1928–?	? Arthur	?
1928	Nancy Bilney	Games (Temporary)
1928–1931	Katherine G. Harvie	Mathematics
1928–1930	Mary G. Knight	Gymnastics, Games
1928–1930	Shirley M. Smith	Art
1928–1931	Una D. Strognell	Languages
1929–1935	Margaret Beckwith	Music, Class Singing, Piano
1929–1930	Hilda Hooker	Kindergarten, Junior Subjects
1929–1930	Georgina L. MacKinlay	French, Junior English
1930–1948	Julia Cartwright	Head of Art, English, School Magazine
1930–1931	Margaret Hooley	Gymnastics, Games
1931–1934	Phoebe G. A. Ashburner	English
1931–1945	Ada Console	French, German
1931–1933	Cecilia M. Grant	Gymnastics, Games
1931–1935	Elizabeth J. Rees	History
1931–1935	Mary J. Wolverson	English, Scripture
1932–1936	Marjorie J. Burnand	Classics
1932–1946	Daisy E. Wright, Senior Mistress '45–'46	Geography, Librarian
1933–1937	Dorothy J. Harris	English
1933–1936	Joyce M. Pearse	Gymnastics, Games
1935–1943	Joyce Abraham (Mrs. Cannon)	Mathematics, Junior Subjects
1935–1938	Mary E. Barnes	Piano
1935–1937	Mary A. Cavenagh	English
1935–1938	Barbara E. Coyle	Violin, Orchestra, Piano (Part-time)
1935–1948	Janet W. Wells, Senior Mistress '46–'48	Head of History
1936–1941	Ursula Gibbon-Davies	Classics
1936–1938	Nancy W. Shaw	Physical Education

1937–1941	Sylvia C. Topsfield	English
1937–1941	Florence J. Baldwin (Mrs. Huggins)	Mathematics
1937–?	Nancy W. Harding	Dancing
1938–1939	Audrey Baker	Games
1938–1945	M. Frances Nicholls	Piano, Singing
1939–1943	Margaret Boulton	Games
1939–1942	Stephanie Hess	Violin
1940–1943	? Rooth	?
1941–1962	Mary Chrystal Senior Mistress '54–'56	Head of English, Librarian
1941–1947	Phyllis B. Dunning	Mathematics, Physics
1941–1944	Freda B. Hewitt (Mrs. Dennis)	Classics
1941–?	Elizabeth B. House	Modern Languages
1942–1945	Joan M. Eyre	Junior Subjects
1943–1944	Una P. Charlick (Pupil '35–'38)	Music (Visiting Mistress)
1943–1949	Christine S. Griffiths	Domestic Science
1943–1955	Vivien Litchfield	Languages, Careers Officer (later)
1943–1944	Eileen J. Pierotti	English, French
1943–1946	Margaret R. Steel	Physical Education
1943–1945	Betty M. Williams	History, English
1944–1946	Elizabeth L. Bygrave (Pupil '16–'21)	Piano (Visiting Mistress)
1944–1945	Judith D. Roddick	Junior and General Subjects
1945–1970	Ann K. Stanier Senior Mistress '50–'52	Head of Classics, Librarian, School Magazine
1945–1953	Moira J. Monk, Mrs.	General Subjects

Aso mentioned in the 1940s: Miss Burton, Physical Education.

1919–1920   Eileen Moore

Form Prefects, Summer, 1920: *I:* E. Curry; *II:* W. Kilby; *IIIb:* H. Morris; *IIIa lower:* F. Bullmore; *IIIa upper:* A. Logsden; *IVc:* —; *IVb:* M. Prater; *IVa lower and upper:* N. Logsden, S. Stuart; *Remove:* —; *Vb:* E. Cross; *Va:* A. Glew; *VI:* E. Moore, E. Cole, M. Cooper, V. Snare.
Games Club Captain: M. Barlow.

A new milestone in the history of Hitchin Girls' Grammar School was reached in September 1919, with the arrival of its new Head Mistress, Miss Chambers, who in her first year made many minor changes, while the peacetime expansion allowed for some major changes as well.

Three large classrooms and a cloakroom were built on the site of the kitchen garden and connected to the school by a covered way; one classroom was converted for Domestic Science use and great additions were made to the gymnastic apparatus. These reflected the growing number of pupils in the school.

Amongst the minor innovations was the awarding of yellow deportment girdles and a 'Deportment Picture' for the Form which attained the highest number of them. Another picture, 'The Tidy Picture', was awarded to the Form with the tidiest classroom.

The system of marking was changed from numerical to alphabetical and would now range from A–E.

A School Choir was organised to consist of twelve members, one from each form, and it was soon noted that the singing at Prayers had greatly improved.

The Hockey, Net Ball, Tennis and Cricket Clubs were now to be 'The Games Club', with a Games Captain. The first was M. I. Barlow. Unfortunately, games, in all fields, had a disappointing and undistinguished year.

A short but pleasant concert was performed at Christmas when the Kindergarten sang carols and there were other musical items. Before it, Miss Seebohm gave to the school, on behalf of Mr. Hugh Seebohm, a beautiful, framed photograph of Miss Gosnell, to be hung in the Hall.

The Girl Guides celebrated their first anniversary and were congratulated on their progress in working for proficiency badges and their Second Class awards. Only five girls had 'found it too great a strain to even try to keep the Guide Law and Promise. These have retired', wrote the Captain, Miss Read. A senior patrol for girls over sixteen was formed. Ivy Pettengell wrote in 1939 'Miss Read was awe inspiring, especially in her Guide uniform'; a view recently confirmed by Bernard Sanders – then in the Kindergarten – who said, 'I think I was rather overawed by her, because she was such a big woman'.

Miss Chambers addressed the Winter Gathering of the O.G.A. and suggested that they might benefit from putting the constitution on a more practical basis and by doing some useful work for other organisations in the town.

Dr. Murray visited the school, in February, to give a lantern lecture on the work of women doctors and ended by telling of the wonderful work being done by the Children's Hospital which was in urgent need of funds. More than £10 was subsequently sent.

This was the first recorded instance of a 'lantern lecture' in the school, in which a light source and transparent glass slides were used in much the same way as by a modern slide projector.

At the end of the summer term, the girls gave a display of country dancing for their parents and friends, each form dancing its own special contribution. This was followed by folk songs and an action song performed by the Kindergarten.

1920–1921   Mary (Esther) Cole

Form Prefects, Autumn, 1920: *I:* M. Lovelace; *II:* J. Newberry; *IIIb:* R. Morris; *IIIa lower:* H. Morris; *IIIa upper:* D. Farrin; *IVc:* F. Bullmore; *IVb:* G. Pearcy; *IVa lower and upper:* M. Prater; *Remove:* M. Baker; *Vb:* V. Parrish; *Va:* E. Cross; *VI:* M. Cole, M. Cooper, I. Goldsmith, C. Halstead, C. Haworth, A. Mallows, H. Purrott, D. Saunderson, A. Whiteman.
Form Prefects, Spring, 1921: *I:* C. Cannon; *II:* M. Baron; *IIIb:* J. Thomas; *IIIa lower:* W. Prater; *IIIa upper:* C. Evans; *IVc:* M. Western; *IVb:* A. Logsden; *IVa lower and upper:* D. Tyler; *Remove:* N. Logsden; *Vb:* A. Lewis; *Va:* E. Cross; *VI:* M. Cole, M. Cooper, I. Goldsmith, C. Halstead, C. Haworth, A. Mallows, H. Purrott, D. Saunderson, A. Whiteman.

This year again saw several innovations introduced by Miss Chambers. Form Councils were established and reported to be doing 'good work'. A School Orchestra was formed and a Form Running Competition was reported for the first time. For this, teams of twelve girls from each form competed for the 'Running Clock', which was held by the winners for one term. A pleasing development was the time allowed to the Upper School for private reading in the Library. Of this facility, Grace King wrote:– 'The liberty one found in those final school years, to browse at will, was to be one of the happiest experiences of school life'.

The mistresses performed 'Scenes from Cranford', in early December, and the £20 profit was divided between several charities. They themselves were later entertained by the prefects who invited the mistresses to a Social Evening.

Just before school broke up for the Christmas holidays, the Rev. A. R. Runnel Moss came to give a recital of 'A Christmas Carol'. (Almost sixty years later, one ex-pupil remembered this.)

In the spring there was a production of 'A Midsummer Night's Dream', which included in its cast these four attentive, if solemn, fairies.

1921. *L. to R.:* E. Terry, Z. Maw, M. Lewindon, L. Grishwood. [Barbara Wheldon]

There were two theatre trips to Luton, first to see an old morality play, 'Everyman' and in the summer to see 'Twelfth Night'.

Autumn and winter lectures varied, from the Bible Society speaker telling of the difficulties of translating the Bible into Chinese to a lantern lecture on 'Bees' and a talk on 'Careers for Educated Girls'. In February, a talk on 'Beethoven' was musically illustrated.

The Guides attended their first summer camp during the 1920 holidays. This was reported by Miss Read to be '. . . such a jolly, healthy time'. Held at Welwyn, it was a divisional camp with seventy girls from the area.

'Ruby' Read was also a Kindergarten teacher and, as such, is associated with a recollection of Bertha Jackson, a seven-year-old in 1920. 'Miss Read asked for a 'stationery monitress', and I put up my hand thinking it was something to do with travelling from Hitchin to Letchworth station by train!'

Both hockey and netball teams reported great improvements over the previous year. The hockey players still faced published, individual criticisms but the whole netball team was told – 'It is a pity that netball people can never be left to take their own game occasionally and take it decently. Put this right next year!' Tennis players, too, had a better season and rounders seemed to have displaced cricket.

1921–1922   Ida Goldsmith

Hockey Captain: Hilda Purrott
Netball Captain: Ida Goldsmith.

In February of this school year, Princess Mary was married and a cheque was sent from the 'Marys' of Hitchin Girls' Grammar School, which was duly acknowledged.

Miss Seebohm gave a Literature Prize to the school and this was offered, by Miss Chambers, for good essay work done by the girls during the Christmas holiday. She also appealed for donors of other prizes and awards for the school.

A further development in 'self-government', after the successful setting up of the Form Councils last year, was the establishment in the winter term of a School Council.

Lectures this year included a speaker from the Bible Association, Reginald Hine giving an imaginary 'Walk down Bancroft', and Mrs. Adams, a governor of the school, enlightening the girls on 'Old Ideas of Education'. A further talk on 'Greig and his Works' was musically illustrated at the piano and by pupil participation in songs. There was, later, a similar talk on 'Chopin'.

The Choir now numbered twenty members and the School Orchestra, though few in numbers, had great enthusiasm. There was a Summer Concert at which parents and friends were invited to hear their efforts, augmented by class choral singing and recitations.

Before Christmas, the school went to the Playhouse, in Market Place, to see 'Twelfth Night' and in June, a party went to see the same play in Luton.

A small exhibition of Drawing and Design was staged in the Art Room (Room 1), just before Christmas. In the adjoining Science Room (Room 2) was a display of the toys and 'woollies', mostly hand made, which had been collected by the pupils and would be sent as Christmas gifts to various hospitals.

'Toll for the Guides. The Guides that are no more!', thundered Miss Read, whose own enthusiasm was not shared by enough pupils to keep the Company going. A few remaining enthusiasts would remain, a Lone Patrol 'Heather', and would meet in one another's homes. The Brownies survived but pleaded that 'recruits would be gladly welcome'.

The O.G.A. had enjoyed an encouraging year and had established a Fellowship Fund with the object of 'assisting old girls in distress and present girls in difficulty in regard to completing their education'. In future the Winter Gathering would be in January rather than just before Christmas. This was a popular move to the majority of members.

A good hockey season and a 'tremendous improvement all round' for the netball players, though there were still some sharp remarks about their play. Tennis at the top of the school was good but the Middle School was criticised; the rounders team had also improved.

At the Sports Day, the cup was won by Vb which gained the largest number of points. In presenting it, Miss Chambers declared that the school was in sore need of trophies and cups and asked for subscriptions towards this end. Mr. Course responded promptly and gave a cup to be devoted to the Lower School Form matches and there were three generous donations towards providing another.

1922–1923 Gwendoline Dear

Hockey Captain: Doris Tyler

A far reaching development in the school's social awareness came in October 1922 when Miss Douglas came to tell the girls about the United Girls' Schools' Mission. Her talk about the work done, and still left to do, so inspired the girls that at the end of the morning the pupils decided to join the Mission and help in its work. Within a year the school magazine reports, '. . . from time to time we see, in the News Sheet, little things which we can send. . . .'. This was in addition to the weekly collections for this cause. In response to a request for flowers to brighten the Settlement, the school decided to send them regularly. Each form agreed that in its turn, it would deliver the weekly flowers, on Friday, to Hitchin Station, from which they would then travel by train to London. This practice survived for many years.

Miss Chambers continued to ask for trophies for sport and academic prowess and reported that Miss Seebohm had given a second Literature Prize, to be given for the best year's work in English. There would also be prizes for the best entries submitted to the Magazine.

In November the school had a Sale of Work to raise money for a new hard tennis court. Parents, friends, pupils and staff all worked hard to pile the stalls with tempting goods to buy for Christmas presents; sideshows too showed imagination and Miss Murray, dressed as the Town crier, was positioned by the weighing machine! Teas were also on sale at one shilling each. The result of all this hard work was a very creditable £173. 11s. 3d.

Mrs. Hine, had, with her husband, visited the League of Nations Conference in Geneva and came to the school to talk about it. This preceded a lecture in the Town Hall to all the children of the town on the same subject. The Hitchin branch of the League offered junior and senior prizes for essays on 'The League of Nations'. Phyllis Longley won the over-14 years, and Ruth Norcott the under-14 years awards.

Empire Day was still celebrated in the customary fashion and this year, as a special treat, Miss Seebohm lent a record of the King's speech which was reproduced on the gramophone.

Mr. Sorabji visited the school twice – once to talk about 'India' and the second time 'Kashmir'. There was an unusual lantern lecture on 'Flowers in Shakespeare' and Miss Lister made a return visit to talk about 'Palms', wonderfully illustrated by slides and her own sketches. There were two musical lectures, the first on 'Grieg' and the second on 'Schumann', both incorporating appropriate songs and music.

A Choir from the Senior Singing Class went to compete in the Hertfordshire Music Festival in Hertford. The first choir they heard was Ware, which they feared was performing better than they were able to. In this judgement they were right, since Ware went on to win the first prize, but the Hitchin girls were placed second and resolved revenge next year. Within the school, the choir took part in the School Concert in July when the small orchestra performed well but sorely needed more string players.

All the games teams reported improved performance throughout the year. The cup presented last year and to be known as the Course Cup was awarded for inter-form netball matches.

Seventeen senior hockey players made a collection and were pleased to give Miss Chambers a clock, to be used as a trophy. This would now allow the award of a senior and a junior 'Running Clock' for form running. The O.G.A. decided, this year, to print a Rule Card to be sold for 2d. each, and chose a design to provide an O.G.A. blazer badge.

1923–1924   Ivy Pettengell

Back Row: Lottie Bird, Winnie Rayment, Margaret Bell (H.G. 1924/25), Edith Newling, Marjorie Goodgame, May Bell. *Front Row:* Florence Lewis, Esther Brooke, Ivy Pettengell (H.G. 1923/24), Miss Chambers, Barbara Morris, Doris Tyler, Marjorie Swannell.   [Mrs. Jill Grey]

This year was outstanding for the number of lectures which were fitted into the school timetable. Mr. Hine spoke of 'The Art of Reading'; Mr. Mockridge on 'Greek Mythology'; Miss Currey on 'The League of Nations' (again); Sir William

Vincent on 'Thackeray' and Miss Knight-Bruce on 'Call of the Empire'. Mr. Edmunds, who spoke of 'Burmah. Its People and Customs', illustrated his talk with lightning sketches and Mr. Sorabji again paid a visit. Lantern lectures were given by Mr. Turtle, from the department of the Sergeant-at-Arms of the House of Commons, who spoke of 'The Houses of Parliament'; Mrs. Shore on 'Famous Artists in the National Gallery' and Mr. Maxwell on 'A Trip to Australia to Study the Eclipse of the Sun'. He had many slides of both Australia and New Zealand. A third lantern lecture, 'Childhood in Animals', was also seen by the Kindergarten which was allowed to join the 'big school' for the first time. This year they also had a report in the magazine stating that they were very pleased to be able to play on the new hard tennis court on the days when the grass was too wet. Formerly, play had been on the gravel drive which led to many grazed knees and, as one pupil remembers, liberal applications of 'Zambuck'!

The musical lectures remained popular, and this year Mr. Robson gave a lecture-recital on the instruments that combine to make an orchestra.

The Choir again went to the Hertfordshire Music Festival, this time held in Hitchin. They were disappointed to be awarded only third place in their class but obviously forgave the Ware Choir for the defeat last year and entertained them to tea at the school.

The School Concert was now an annual fixture in July and had expanded to include the Kindergarten Band and action songs; the school orchestra played and duets and solos were performed by vocalists, pianists and violinists. Recitations and choral singing were also in the programme.

'The First School Debate' was heralded at the end of the Easter term and was so successful that it was decided to form a Debating Society. The school had, for many years, of course, a flourishing Debating Society, under Miss Gosnell, until the outbreak of the Great War when talking had given way to more practical help for the war effort.

A collection was made for the Hertfordshire Nursing Association and the £8 collected was presented, by Ivy Pettengell, to the Duchess of York at a Hatfield Fete in May.

At the end of May, the Vth Form girls went to Wymondley, where they were taken to visit the site of the ancient Roman villa – 'Many of the girls obtained pieces of Roman tiling'. Afterwards they were shown traces of the old open field system before going on to Great Wymondley to visit the church. Mr. and Mrs. Hailey then provided tea on the lawn at their beautiful home, 'Delamere House', before taking the girls on a conducted tour.

Two very successful performances of 'Alice in Wonderland' were staged in the spring term – a very ambitious project requiring many players and elaborate costumes. Parents and friends were specially thanked for the work they had put into making these, at little cost to the school. The only criticism of the youthful players was that, for the Croquet Match, they kept falling over one another in the confined space 'rather spoiling the effect of the game'! Despite this, all involved had a thoroughly good time and were able to donate nearly £45 to the Old Girls' Fellowship Fund. From this gift the O.G.A. bought a picture by Perugino to hang in the Hall, and provided the oak table for the Hall platform which is still in use.

The winter team games suffered from the weather and the netball captain complained, 'We shall never beat Luton until we strengthen our defence'. Tennis had a good season and reported 'marked improvement'. The tennis captain reported, 'a good many people have really mastered the over-arm service now', reminding us that in the recent past ladies served under-arm. In June a junior tennis couple – M. Mackintosh and V. Bedwell – took part for the first time in the Inter-Schools Tennis Tournament. They succeeded in winning the cup though their

criticism, in school games, as printed in the magazine, say that one shows 'much improvement' but the other '. . . needs to use her head . . . placing weak'.

At the Sports Day, a special mention was made of F. Lewis, who jumped 4ft. 9ins. in the Senior High Jump, breaking the school record. This year, hurdles were borrowed from the boys' school and, for the first time, the girls had a Hurdle Race. A new Junior Cup was presented to IIIb. This had been a leaving gift by Miss H. Murray who had taught games at the school for the past three years. Junior Deportment Girdles were awarded for the first time. These would be similar to the Senior ones, but a little narrower. As with the Seniors, there would be a Deportment Picture for the form with the most girdles in the term.

1924–1925   Margaret Bell

Form Prefects: *VI:* M. Bell, L. Bird, E. Brookes, F. Lewis, E. Newling, W. Rayment; *Va:* M. Course; *Vb:* A. Sainsbury; *Special V:* G. Lewindon; *IVa¹:* J. Newberry; *IVa²:* K. Norris; *IVb:* S. Lawmon; *IVc:* M. Lewis; *IIIa¹:* J. Wallace; *IIIa²:* M. Titford; *IIIb:* D. Foxlee; *II:* J. Taylor; *I:* M. Purdy.
Games Club & Hockey Captain: W. Raiment.
Netball Captain: J. Thomas.

During the Summer Term, the Governors decided to award a School Leaving Scholarship, to the value of £40 a year, for three years, to be competed for by those girls going to university. At the same time, Miss Chambers decided that the summer holidays would be more enjoyable if the pupils had something to occupy their spare time. She therefore set up the Holiday Competition and offered prizes in each of fourteen classes. These ranged from handicrafts and keeping diaries to a 'pot pourri' class designed to cater for anything not covered by the others.

Canon Veazey visited the school and told the girls something of the work of the United Girls' Schools' Mission which they had supported for two years. This was a prelude to the visit, by a party of girls headed by Miss Chambers, to attend the annual service in Southwark Cathedral. After the service, the party went to the Settlement in Camberwell, the Mission hall and then on to the two houses where the Mission started. Representatives of the school would attend the service each year and visit the area.

Sir William Vincent came to the school twice, each time speaking about Dickens. The first time, he also presented prizes for the 'Henry Esmond' paper and promised to give similar prizes for 'Barnaby Rudge' when he returned later in the year. Another speaker chose 'The Catacombs'. Lantern lectures included 'Protective Colouring in the World of Nature', by Mr. Rowntree, and two visits by Canon Perkins. His first talk on 'William the Conqueror and the Bayeux Tapestry' was later followed by 'Westminster Abbey'. The latter complemented another lecture, by Miss Chambers, on 'The Architecture of English Cathedrals'.

The Kindergarten now had Miss Read in charge, following the departure of Miss Mockridge at the end of the summer term. The children held their own Harvest Festival, after which the fruit was sent to the Hitchin Hospital. In May, there was 'The Understanding and Appreciation of Music' by Major Bavin, who illustrated

1925. Music Festival. *Back row:* Doris Franklin, Kathleen Thomas, Jenny Purdy, Joan Flex, Phyllis Taudevin. *2nd row:* Dorothy Cobbett, Grace King, Vanna Cuenis, Phyllis Tyler, ? ? , Irene Skoiles. *3rd row:* Agnes Sainsbury, April Hoffman, Ena Hanscombe, Miss Saunders, Barbara Higgins, Grace Garrett, Mary McMath. *Front row:* Marjorie Lewindon, Kathleen Baumber, Jean Jackson, Phyllis Marriott, Catherine Harrison, Margaret (Peggy) Mackintosh, Connie Macdonald, Kathleen Hillman, Dorothy Bland, Connie Thomas, ? ? , Phillis Winter.   [Phyllis Marriott (Turner)]

his talk on the gramophone. The Music Festival was held at Hatfield and once again the coveted Challenge Shield was just out of grasp. Hitchin was again in third place with 83 marks while the winners had only two marks more.

The Debating Society held its first debate of the year, 'Newspapers are of use to the Community'. The affirmative vote was important since it decided the fate of the recently introduced 'Newspaper Lesson' in the lower forms. Other debates followed throughout the year and the Society prospered.

The boarders went to visit the Priory at Little Wymondley, an ancient house, formerly a Canonbury. Here monks had studied and used herbs for healing purposes, using the main building as a hospital. Nearby, a barn, thought to predate William the Conquerer, still shows interior signs of being a baronial hall. After visiting the church, Mrs. Foster at Wymondley Bury gave the girls tea.

The Gymnastics competition was judged by Miss Disney who told of her work at the Princess Mary Village Homes. In response, the school donated a silver cup for competition in their netball matches and the letters of thanks fully show how it was appreciated.

'Considering the weather, we did not have a bad season', claimed the Hockey captain, and the improvement in the Netball team meant '. . . we beat Luton!' In contrast to the winter weather, summer was kind to the tennis and rounders teams.

The highlight of the summer term was a display of country dancing on the lawn and an Art Exhibition in the school building. All the girls were in appropriate dress, as 'lads and lasses', and the sun shone on a happy crowd of school girls, parents and visitors. This event was recalled by Zoe Maw as a very pleasant memory, though she remembered that there was no shade from the newly planted trees!

61

1925. Country dancing.   [Jean Jackson (Butlin)]

Sports Day finished the school year on a lovely day but attendance was disappointing, owing, it was thought, to the country dancing three weeks earlier.

The O.G.A. held their usual winter and summer gatherings. In summer, in contrast with former years, no organised tennis tournament was arranged, though some 'past' played some of the 'present' girls, while others just wandered and gossiped. Miss Gosnell and Miss K. Johnson had both attended regularly but this year were unable to come. In the afternoon, Aillee Latchmore told of her work in the Girls' Club, in Queen Street and asked for help – especially with hockey. Tea in the courtyard was followed by the A.G.M. after which the chairs were taken to the Garden where the members of staff performed A. A. Milne's play 'The Princess and the Woodcutter'.

1925–1926 Joan Taudevin

School Prefects: *VI:* J. Taudevin, M. Ashby, J. Fauvel, G. King; *Va:* M. Lewindon; *Vb:* J. Newberry; *Special V:* M. Baron; *IVa¹:* K. Hollis; *IVa²:* M. Lewis; *IVb:* E. Tickle; *IVc:* J. Wallace; *IIIa¹:* M. McCarraher; *IIIa²:* M. Powell; *IIIb:* D. Farris; *II:* M. Purdy; *I:* M. Shillitoe.
Hockey Captain: P. Mackintosh.

Sir William Vincent again gave prizes for literature – this year his author was Sir Walter Scott, and the book 'Redgauntlet'. Other speakers were M. Nabokoff talking about 'Russia'; Major Cartwright on 'Movement in Dancing and Sports' and Mr. J. E. Little, past Headmaster of the Boys' Grammar School, on 'Trees' with allusions to their influence on place names such as Ashwell and Aspenden. Mr. Hine spoke, in July, of 'Poets I have known'. Amongst these illustrious people were Walt Whitman, Rupert Brooke, W. B. Yeats and Walter de la Mare, examples of whose poems he also read. Miss Green came to keep the school up to date on the Settlement and told of the different clubs and social evenings enjoyed there. Miss Brook-Smith came from a Mission school in Travancore, and told of her life in India. There were also three lantern lectures, two geographical about 'North Wales' and 'Morocco and Algeria' and a third about 'Michelangelo'.

It is notable that the pupils were ever ready to help those less fortunate than themselves. Miss Brook-Smith requested books, and two large boxes were collected and sent to India; the Children's Country Holidays Fund was sent enough money to send four poor East End children to the country for a holiday; the Mission had regular cash donations and five cases of goods had been made or bought and sent to the Settlement. A large hamper was sent to Hitchin Hospital and toys to an Orphanage.

At the end of the Christmas term, the girls of the Vth and VIth forms were invited, by the staff, to a fancy dress party – reported as 'very grown up' – because it did not start till 6 p.m. All the staff, including Miss Chambers, were in fancy dress, mostly demure and very ladylike, though Miss Forbes as a Naval Officer, 'seemed quite accustomed to wearing trousers'. Prizes were given to staff and pupils before the boarders' play 'Japhet in Eskimoland' – Joan Proctor as the snowman was specially mentioned for standing still!

Also in December the Grammar School Players from the boys' school staged 'She Stoops to Conquer', at Hitchin Town Hall and in the spring, the staff of the girls' school gave a fine performance of 'Captain Brassbound's Conversion'. Half the fun of this was to see which member of staff took which part since the whole production had been shrouded in secrecy. Not to be outdone the Sixth Form performed scenes from 'Hamlet' in the summer. Rather strangely, 'The school's appreciation of the Tragedy was strangely mirthful' – perhaps because it was the end of the school year.

A form Choir Competition was successfully held, for the first time, and Miss O'Brien gave a statuette of Peter Pan to be awarded to the successful Junior Form. Miss Weatherley gave a picture to be awarded for Sight-Singing. Once again the Choir entered the Hertfordshire Music Festival and were at last rewarded by winning the Shield. Sadly, their victory was rather hollow since the effects of the General Strike meant that only one other choir could get to the venue in Letchworth.

After its first rush of enthusiasm, the Debating Society complained of poor attendance and falling membership saying that the subscription of 3d. a term only paid for the buns served before each meeting.

'The worst season we have ever had as regards weather and illness' reported the hockey players, who congratulated Miss Bavin on her selection as Reserve for the England Hockey team. The Senior High Jump was especially exciting at the Sports Day, when P. Tyler beat last year's record by one inch and cleared 4ft. 10ins., whilst B. James jumped the same height and beat her own former record of 4ft. 7ins. D. Aldridge set another new record with 75yds. 1ft. for 'Throwing the Cricket Ball'.

1926–1927   Grace King

School Prefects: *VI:* G. King, I. Smith; *Va:* M. Lewindon; *Vb:* E. Curry; *Vc:* K. Hollis; *IVa¹:* E. Eddy; *IVa²:* W. Swain; *IVb:* J. Wallace; *IVc:* M. Feesy; *IIIa¹:* B. Pott; *IIIa²:* J. Taylor; *IIIb:* M. Purdy; *Preparatory:* N. Bloom.
Hockey Captain: P. Mackintosh.

The outstanding thing about this school year was that, for the first time, the school uniform was modified in the summer and the girls wore blue cotton slips – a popular choice after formerly sweltering in blue serge and black woollen stockings!

Several old friends, and some new, visited the school to give talks and lantern lectures. Sir William Vincent updated the work of the 'League of Nations'; Mr. Squires came to expand his colleagues' talk, last year, about their mission work in Travangore; in similar vein, Archdeacon Mather spoke of his work in South Africa and asked for financial contributions towards providing a nurse for his area. A collection was made and sent to him. Captains Pike and Barlow both gave lantern lectures; the first on 'Dramas in the Wild' and the second on 'America'. Miss Proctor came to tell about, and show, 'Eclipses', and Miss Lister followed her slides of 'Switzerland' with showing her watercolours of Swiss flowers.

Major Bavin made his annual visit, this time choosing 'Music and Literature', while Miss Gay Price spoke of 'Beethoven' with musical examples using some musicians and a gramophone. The Choir travelled to St. Albans for the Music Festival but in the face of increased competition came third, no mean achievement since they had been in the first three every year since the festival began.

School Singing and Sight Reading Pictures were presented for the first time during this school year.

A Sale of Work was held in December, to raise funds in order to make a contribution for the Shakespeare Memorial Theatre. Once again, the school rose to the occasion with great enthusiasm and generosity. All sections took part; from the

1927.   VI Form stall on Sports Day.   [Jean Jackson (Butlin)]

Kindergarten with its Hoop-la to 'Squire's Super Scrumptious Toffee' and 'Forbes' Famous Fruit Cake' provided by members of staff. They were able to add £100 to the fund as a result – the largest contribution sent by any school up to that time.

Sports Day was the usual success and, fired with the success of the sales stalls at the Christmas Sale of Work, the girls of the Sixth form had a produce stall in the courtyard which did good business amongst the visiting parents and friends.

After the reverses of the previous year, the Debating Society reported improved fortunes though there was some complaint that the lower forms never had anything to say!

The magazines are invaluable in discovering the minutiae of school life so long ago, and it is a source of regret that little attention can be given to the fiction and poems contributed. Since all sport and games were, this year, undistinguished we give you instead:–

HOCKEY FEVER

Parody on 'Sea Fever'

I must go down to the field again,
    To the wintry field and the sky,
And all I ask is a white ball,
    And a stick to steer it by,
And an eye quick and an arm strong,
    And a grip firm and ready,
And a frightened look on the foe's face,
    And our own team steady.

I must go down to the field again,
    For the call of the open air
Is a clear call and a stern call,
    Which means I must be there;
And all I ask is a referee
    With an eye on 'sticking',
And for 'foul throws' and for 'off-side',
    And the art of kicking.

I must go down to the field again,
    To the scene of battle and strife,
For the games' way is the only way
    To secure a healthy life;
And all I ask is the luck to score,
    Whilst our goal's well defended,
And the sweet sound of the whistle's blast
    When the hard fight's ended.

Nancy Peel, IVa[1]

1927–1928 Jean Jackson

The great generosity shown by the Seebohm family to the school continued down the years. Every year there was reference to the gift of prizes, pictures and books. Now the Misses Seebohm gave to the school a gift of adjacent land which, when some of the trees had been cleared and the ground levelled, could be used as a field for games and the wood for botanical study and recreation.

The New John Rand Leaving Exhibitions and two Junior Bursaries were, at the end of the school year, awarded to girls on the results of the Midsummer examinations.

The school had so grown in numbers that two new forms were created and IIIb temporarily 'found a home in Mrs. Gould's house over the road'. The Preparatory school and Kindergarten were this year referred to as separate entities.

Mr. Coleman visited the school to talk about St. Andrew's parish and showed some photographs of the area. Miss Tseng told of the rise of Communism in China.

A lantern lecture in French was given by Comtesse de la Croze, 'La Bretagne', and Mr. Linlott Taylor showed slides of Rhodesia.

Great excitement was generated by the cinematograph showing of 'Up in the Far North' by Mr. Dadley. The Junior School and 'as many seniors as could fit into the Hall' were enthralled. . . . 'We all gazed with delight at the natural colour photographs . . . icebergs . . . harpooning whales . . . swimming of the polar bears and their struggles for freedom. There was a great outburst of applause when the baby bear was released.'

In the Easter term a party of the seniors went to Bruges, when they had a day trip to Ghent and another to visit the battlefields of Ypres. Nearer home were a trip to the Welgar Shredded Wheat factory at Welwyn Garden City and another to 'King Lear' at the Old Vic.

Small changes in the year included the introduction of a competition for the writing of a One Act Play and the setting up of a National Savings Association branch following the visit of Major Firth who explained the scheme to the pupils. The Debating Society had now changed its name to The Literary and Debating Society. Play readings would alternate with the debates.

Staff v. School hockey matches had been played for several years, but this time the weather caused the fixture to be postponed for a week. Since the refreshments had already been prepared by the girls, with country dancing to follow, that went ahead as planned. For the first time, the staff also played the school at netball after the Inter-Form Running but lost both this fixture and the hockey match several days later.

1928–1929 Helen Gray

Form Prefects, Autumn, 1928: *VI:* H. Gray, E. Curry; *Va:* E. Eddy; *Vb¹:* V. Bennett; *Vʀ:* M. Sainsbury; *Vb²:* B. Jackson; *IVa¹:* M. Colson; *IVa²:* P. Scoot; *IVb:* N. Long; *IVc:* J. Bennett; *IIIaᴘ:* B. Bayes; *IIIa¹:* P. Richford; *IIIa²:* J. Lee; *IIIb:* F. Flex; *Prep:* R. Williams.
Form Prefects, Spring, 1929: *VI:* H. Gray, M. Lewis; *Va:* B. Hennell; *Vb¹:* M. McCarraher; *Vʀ:* D. Hertz; *Vb²:* M. Flex; *IVa¹:* M. Hawkes; *IVa²:* M. Morris; *IVb:* G. Major; *IVc:* J. Bishop; *IIIaᴘ:* J. Bush; *IIIa¹:* G. Tanner; *IIIa²:* J. Parrott; *IIIb:* A. Bush; *Prep:* R. Gray.
Form Prefects, Summer, 1929: *VI:* H. Gray, M. Lewis, M. McCarraher; *Va:* L. Kelly; *Vb¹:* V. Bennett; *Vʀ:* R. Barker; *Vb²:* B. Cobbett; *IVa¹:* V. Williams; *IVa²:* J. Inman; *IVb:* M. Watson; *IVc:* G. Harradine; *IIIaᴘ:* O. Folds; *IIIa¹:* M. Ellsmore; *IIIa²:* M. Strong; *IIIb:* J. Shepherd; *Prep:* M. Cooper.
Hockey Captain: Helen Gray.

At the start of the school year the foundations were laid for a new building – the West Wing – and by the beginning of the summer term it was complete and in use.

It would now relieve the pressure for form rooms and all the girls could be accommodated on the main site. One of Miss Chambers' academic incentives was that a day's holiday would be declared for the whole school, if any girl had an 'A Week'. This entailed being classified 'A' in every subject – the chances of which must have been so remote that the resultant endeavour well outweighed the chances of success! In October, Marion Lake, in IVb, achieved this apparently impossible feat and the school took its holiday in November.

After months of impatient waiting, the new field was at last levelled and brought into use for games whilst the lovely wood could be used for nature studies.

Miss Seebohm, generous as ever, gave the school an epidiascope. It was then reported that the school had 'never had pictures projected with such definition before . . . not only can slides be reflected but postcards, pictures from books and botanical specimens'.

Miss Hansell visited the school and reported on happenings at the Mission and Dr. Joy lectured on 'Birds'. Lantern lectures remained popular; Miss Richardson showed 'Historic Costume'; Mr. Murray Urquhart, 'Rembrandt' and Miss Hancock slides of 'Canada'. When Mr. Burt came, with 'Beasts of African Jungle and Plain', the whole school from the Kindergarten to the Vth forms were fascinated, especially by those photographs taken by the animals themselves by activating the camera with trip-wires.

Miss Saunders played the piano and spoke of 'Schubert', using gramophone records to illustrate orchestral works. This year, in celebration of the school's twenty-first birthday on the present site, there were two concerts instead of the usual one. It seemed fitting that, at the Music Festival, held in Hitchin, the girls should win the Challenge Shield. They also tied for first place in the Sight Reading with Hitchin Boys' Grammar School, and were presented with an appropriate certificate.

Miss Chambers offered a prize for 'The Best Buttonhole'; by the next year it would be for 'The Best Darn' and seemed destined to become the Needlework Prize.

The Debating Society, which only a year ago added 'Literary' to its title, had now been swallowed by the newcomer and only The Literary Society remained.

The staff put on two performances of 'The Admirable Crichton' and kept secret the cast list until the characters appeared on stage, adding to the enjoyment of the play. On Saturday, soon after the stage direction 'night falls with tropical swiftness', right on cue, it fell rather more than was intended when the lights fused. The admirable Watson soon saved the day.

A party of two hundred girls was taken to see 'Twelfth Night' at The Play House and a trip was made to the Central Hall, Westminster, to see 'The Hockey Film'. This proved very helpful and interesting to all who went.

Other 'games news' this year was the success of the 'Junior A' couple, Marguerite Colson and N. Long, who were successful in winning the Junior Shield at the Inter-Schools Tennis Tournament. It was also a source of pride that the H.G.G.S. was the only one there whose girls offered to umpire.

Generosity to those in need was a regular feature of school life at this time and a fully detailed list would be tedious. One gift, this year, of historic interest was the donation to the Mansion House Fund for Miners suffering acute hardship after their long strike. Two sacks of boots, shoes and warm clothing were also sent to the miners' families in Lancashire.

1929–1930 Margaret McCarraher

Form Prefects, Autumn Term, 1929: *VI:* M. McCarraher, J. Mantle, F. Hart, F. Weeden; *Va¹:* P. Keller; *Va²:* B. Jackson; *Vb¹:* M. Hawkes; *Vr:* V. Jones; *Vb²:* P. Scoot; *IVa¹:* G. Major; *IVr:* B. Washington; *IVa²:* M. Colson; *IVb:* G. Middleton; *IVc:* J. Middleton; *IIIa¹:* M. Bennett; *IIIa²:* S. Richford; *IIIb:* R. Gray; *Prep:* D. Flawn.

Form Prefects, Summer Term, 1930: *VI:* M. McCarraher, J. Mantle, F. Hart, F. Weeden, M. Brookes, E. Eddy, O. Gobby, L. Kelly, M. Ward, E. Wood; *Va¹:* P. Keller; *Va²:* l. George; *Vb¹:* J. Crump; *Vr:* J. Cox; *Vb²:* P. Scoot; *IVa¹:* G. Major; *IVr:* I. Walker; *IVa²:* M. Crooks; *IVb:* J. Eddy; *IVc:* M. Brooker; *IIIa¹:* F. Crabb; *IIIa²:* S. Richford; *IIIb:* B. Hall; *Upper Prep:* B. Bishop; *Lower Prep:* D. Sullivan.

The trial flight of the ill-fated R101 took place in the autumn of 1929, when it flew to London from its construction hangar at Cardington. This caused great excitement in the school, which was assembled on the hockey pitch to see 'a beautiful silver-grey fish . . . we all marvelled at the ingenuity of her structure'.

Miss Seebohm gave to the school a wireless set which caused great excitement when it was fixed up in the Big Room – now Rooms 11 & 12. There was great anticipation at the prospect of 'listening in' next term.

The Preparatory had now grown to such proportions that there would be an Upper and a Lower class for the first time, each with its own mistress.

There was a lecture, in French, about Paris and, later in the year, a visit to the French Society in Cambridge for some of the senior girls to see a play by Molière. In contrast, there was a lecture on 'Coal Mining' and another about the Empire Marketing Board. Miss Chambers gave a lantern lecture on 'Church Architecture' and Miss Radway, another member of staff, spoke about 'Birds' and offered a prize for the best 'Diary of Bird News', recorded from December to July. Mr. Klostergaard talked about 'Hans Christian Andersen' and showed slides of places associated with him, and Mr. Rowntree, following his success some years ago, returned with 'The Childhood of Animals'. Mr. Urquhart, another old friend, gave a series of lectures on 'Italian Art', which culminated in a visit to Burlington House to see some of the paintings.

The musical highlight of the year was the retention of the Challenge Shield at the Music Festival. The choir scored 187 out of a possible 200 marks so the standard set was very high indeed.

The Literary Society moved from strength to strength and now had nearly 150 members. This threw great strain on the catering arrangements so, though the buns would still be available, tea would not longer be served.

There was an overseas trip, when twelve girls and four staff went to Geneva. Apart from the visits to the Castle of Chillon and a watch factory, the party visited the headquarters of the League of Nations. As a result of this, and a subsequent lecture, it was decided to have a School branch of the League. This entailed having each country represented by a senior and two or three other delegates who met in the Big Room and hoped 'To carry out some good work in aiding the League'.

1930–1931   Janet Mantle

Form Prefects, Autumn Term, 1930: *VI:* Janet Mantle, Freda Weeden, Esmé Wood; *Va¹:* Mary Titford; *Va²:* Margaret Flex; *Vb¹:* Gwen Major; *Dom. V:* Melody Colson; *Vb²:* Gwen Cooper; *IVa¹:* Marjorie Baumber; *IVa²:* Pamela Richford; *IVb:* Ivy Andrews; *IVc:* Betty Stratford; *IIIa¹:* Betty Hall; *IIIa²:* Thelma Bowskill; *IIIb:* Sybil Russell; *II:* Jean McCarraher; *I:* Pat Woolard.
Form Prefects, Summer Term, 1931: *VI:* Janet Mantle, Freda Weeden (Second Head), Betty Adams, Esmé Wood, Doris Baker, Evelyn Ellsmore, Bertha Jackson, Pegeen Keller, Mary McCarraher, Marjorie Street, May Wilson; *Va¹:* Mollie Hawkes; *Va²:* Dorothy Legg; *Vb¹:* Vera Woolard; *Dom. V:* Melody Colson; *Vb²:* Barbara Bayes; *IVa¹:* Joan Eddy; *IVa²:* Vivian Trimming; *IVb:* Phyllis Matthews; *IVc:* Audrey Owen; *IIIa¹:* Helen Smith; *IIIa²:* Enid Burgess; *IIIb:* Isabel Theobald; *II:* Pat Gardner; *I:* Lucinda Angwin.
Hockey Captain: Pegeen Keller.

'The History of the Hitchin Grammar School', written by Reginald Hine and published by Paternoster and Hales, was on sale for 2/6d. per copy. Mr. Hine had a family interest in the Girls' School because his daughter, Felicity, was a pupil there at the time.

A generous friend was lost when Miss Hilda Seebohm died during the year. She had, along with her sister, been a regular and welcome visitor to the school and had been one of its governors.

A school inspection was held in the summer term. Though these occasions put the pupils and staff on their mettle, there was no need to fear.

The girls who left the school between Easter 1930 and Easter 1931 presented an Honours Board and two pictures with the proceeds of their collection.

There were very few lectures this year. Mr. Spikesman gave a lecture on National Savings and returned later in the year with lantern slides of the Empire and stressed the help that could be given to the Empire by supporting the National Savings scheme. Mr. Weber gave an illustrated talk on the magazine 'Punch'; Miss Cherry Garrard had slides of 'Palestine, Egypt and Syria' and Mr. Garrard brought his of 'Wild Flowers'.

There were only two choirs competing at the Hertfordshire Music Festival, held at Hatfield. The choir again won the shield and came first in the sight reading test.

The school remained very keen in its support of the League of Nations. Its Junior Branch had a speaker, attended a meeting at Welwyn Garden City to see a film 'The World War and After' and had debates. There were also plans to correspond with children in the majority of the League member countries. Mr. Hine asked the school to provide a poster for display in the station booking hall. A prize would be given for any poster used and the words 'Join the League of Nations Union' had to appear on all entries.

There was a performance of 'The Dragon' at some time during the year. The report is so sketchy that it would not warrant recording were it not for the photograph, given by Amy Purdy, showing the players and the orchestra, which had been re-formed a year earlier. Amy, the violinist next to the piano, left school in this school year. She subsequently taught the violin in most of the local schools until her retirement in the early 1980s.

The Literary Society had many playreadings throughout the year and Miss Harvie told of her visit to see the Oberammergau Passion Play the previous summer. She spoke of the origins as well as the play itself and had many photographs which she had taken.

1930.   The Dragon   [Bertha Jackson (Leech)]

A party of girls travelled up to London to see an exhibition of Persian art at Burlington House, and a second group went to the National Gallery and British Museum. Nearer home was a visit to see 'Macbeth' at Hitchin Town Hall.

Down the years, the school's financial and practical support for the U.G.S. had continued unabated. They still helped the less fortunate, and some visited and even did holiday work at the Settlement. Now a new Settlement building was about to be opened and Janet Mantle, the Head Girl, was chosen to represent the school. Queen Mary was to accept, from each girl, a white silk purse, embroidered with the school crest and holding a note of the donation made. Janet wrote, 'Those who were to present the purses were to wear long-sleeved white frocks, black shoes and stockings, no hats and white gloves. . . . As her Majesty entered the door, we all craned our necks to see her. She was exactly as she appears in photographs – very dignified and regal. She was dressed in silver-grey, a toque hat, a coat trimmed with chinchilla fur, a bunch of violets and grey shoes and stockings.'

1931–1932 Pegeen Keller

Form Prefects, Autumn Term, 1931: *I:* Morwenna Shearne; *II:* Pat Woolard; *IIIb:* Joan Gladwin; *IIIa²:* Doreen Norman; *IIIa¹:* Miriam Fleming; *IVc:* Ruth Dawson; *IVb:* Marion Bennett; *IVa²:* Betty Stratford; *IVa¹:* Ava Bush; *Vb²:* Ruth Bishop; *Vb¹:* Kathleen Gray; *Va²:* Jean Russell; *Va¹:* Gwen Major; *VI:* Pegeen Keller, Mary McCarraher, Doris Baker, Marjorie Street, May Wilson.
Form Prefects, Spring & Summer Terms, 1932: *I:* Morwenna Shearne, Daphne Russell; *II:* Jill Gardner, Vivien Kipling; *IIIb:* Mary Weeber, Pat Kipling; *IIIa²:* Pat Gardner, Margaret Alexander; *IIIa¹:* Vera Arnold, Lois Thrussell; *IVc:* Betty Austin, Joan Kortright; *IVb:* Helen Smith, Mary Whitby; *IVa²:* Julie Shepherd, Gwen Barker; *IVa¹:* Joan Fay, Anthea Hughes; *Vb²:* Deirdre Gray, Marjorie Purdy; *Vb¹:* Barbara Bayes, Kathleen Gray; *Va²:* Melody Colson, Dorothy Haywood; *Va¹:* Jessie Clay, Florence Roberts; *VI:* Doris Baker, Mary McCarraher, Marjorie Street, May Wilson, Pegeen Keller.

The school, in conjunction with the Boys' Grammar School, held its first Founder's Day. This was to take the form of a memorial service in St. Mary's Church, Hitchin, at the end of the summer term and would honour the memory of some of those who had, by their service and generosity, helped to build and maintain the two schools.

Mrs. Margaret Tuke, a Governor of Hitchin Girls' Grammar School, became a Dame Commander of the British Empire in the New Year's Honours List.

The new Letchworth Grammar School was opened as a co-educational establishment. A friendly relationship was formed from the first when Mr. Wilkinson, the headmaster, came to Hitchin to address the Junior branch of the League of Nations on the subject of Japan and its problems. (Japan successfully defied the League, over Manchuria, for eighteen months before leaving the League in May 1933.) Miss Seebohm gave to the school, this year, a micro-projector which would be most useful in Botany and Biology, with its ability to magnify and project the image on to a screen.

The school had its 'first' fire drill but, as with the 'first' debating society, this precaution had been taken when Miss Gosnell was at the school.

Talks for the year were again few; Miss Cherry Garrard returned with a lantern lecture and chose 'Climbing and Winter Sports' as her subject; Miss Seebohm showed her slides of Egypt and Miss Turner chose 'Inland Birds'. The musicians were very well served: Mr. Bavin gave a series of talks on 'The Art of Listening to Music', using the gramophone to demonstrate his points; Miss Cropper gave a song recital tracing the history of English songs and Miss Beckwith gave an interesting account of the life of Haydn, and both staff and pupils took part in the concert which followed. Since the Orchestra had regrouped and there was a rising interest in the subject, it was fitting that the school decided to form a Music Society.

In February the staff staged the play 'Prunella', which was commended for its charm and the delightful scheme of colouring and lighting. The play was enjoyed by every one and the proceeds made a generous donation to the Old Girls' Fellowship Fund. This money was to help form the Music Society and to buy a music stool and music dictionary.

There was one trip, to see 'Julius Caesar', at His Majesty's Theatre.

Mr. Hine judged a Verse Speaking Competition organised in mid-June. He commented on the high standard of performance and prizes were awarded to the Seniors, the Middle School and the Juniors.

Miss Chambers organised a History cross-word puzzle which taxed the knowledge of the seniors throughout the autumn term. Two prizes were given. During the year, it was decided to raise funds in order to build an outdoor swimming bath. To this end, a display of country dancing took place at the end of June. All was ideal; the sun came out and promised a lovely day; the dresses and bright smocks were colourful and appropriate; the dancing was pleasing and the folk songs provided contrast, while the Orchestra played valiantly. The display concluded with the whole school dancing before breaking into a march which ended with all the girls in one huge hollow square. Even the Kindergarten joined in and enjoyed the day with the rest of the school. With the proceeds of the stall and of a 'Mile of Pennies' laid on the hard tennis court, £26 went into the Swimming Bath Fund.

1932–1933   Doris Baker

Games Captain: Marguerite Colson

The highlight of the year was the building of the new swimming bath, which was opened in early July. It was in a beautiful setting, among the trees, just below the school main buildings and would be a great asset for the foreseeable future. Now, most of the girls would have the opportunity of learning to swim and benefiting from this healthy outdoor pursuit. This was of course at the end of the school year.

Much fund raising had taken place and in autumn 1932 the school held a special Sale of Work to raise funds for the proposed swimming bath since some money would be needed before work could even begin. In order to raise the maximum sum it was planned to open on Friday afternoon and again on Saturday, so a lot of work was needed to stock the stalls and tempt the visitors. It was a grand team effort; the Kindergarten had a bran tub in their room; the Hall and the Big Room were crammed with goods; a pierrot clanged a bell to summon the audience to the boarders' entertainment in the Art Room. Cruel fate took a hand in affairs when a thick fog enveloped Hitchin on Saturday making firesides more tempting, to many, than visiting the school. Despite the set-back, the sale raised more than £200 and the Swimming Bath fund was under way.

Mr. Spurr, long time governor and draper in the town, died in June – 'our very sincere friend for many years, who always had time to give to our affairs', was how Miss Chambers spoke of him.

Mr. Heald-Jenkins came to lecture about 'Sir Walter Scott' and described the centenary celebrations which he had visited in Edinburgh. Miss Ashmore was very helpful with 'Careers for Girls' whilst Miss Sterling spoke of 'Indian Children' and showed examples of their handiwork. Two lantern lectures were of 'English Cathedrals' by Mr. Jarrett and 'Wings of Empire' by Mr. Simmons. He described the difference that aeroplanes had made to the communications between parts of the Empire.

Musical interests were well served by a recital of 'Songs of Shakespeare' by Miss Cropper and a concert, given by members of the staff, of the works of Mozart. Some girls were also able to hear, on the new wireless, a concert, conducted by Sir Walford Davies, which was a special Schools Broadcast. The school orchestra was appealing for more members, especially to play the viola since the musical balance was at present poor. The Choir went to the Hertfordshire Music Festival, in Ware, and once again provided formidable opposition to all comers by retaining the Challenge Shield for the third consecutive year and also came first in the Sight Reading.

Just before Christmas, Form Va^2 gave a performance of a 'Yorkshire Symphony', to support the fund. 'The efficacy of their instruments, amongst which were combs, cymbals and medicine bottles, was much admired', stated the magazine's critic.

The Literary Society had a full programme and reported several debates. Other activities were mainly play readings. A new club was formed, the Science Club, which illustrates the growing influence and interest in science as part of girls' education.

There was a handwriting competition, with prizes, showing that old values still prevailed alongside the new.

A School journey to Axbridge took place in May. The girls travelled by train to Bristol and from there completed the journey by open bus, being able to see the Clifton Suspension Bridge and Bristol far below. The rest of the holiday was varied and there were outings to Cheddar, Glastonbury and Wells.

Nearer home, Mr. Bloom took a party of girls to Hitch Wood to search for fossils. The outing to this lovely wood was enhanced by the discovery of several fossils which were collected and taken back to school.

The previous year's sixth form leavers presented an electric clock which was put in place over the entrance to the Hall.

1933–1934   Gwen Major

Second Head: Grace Mayles.
Head Boarder: Jean Ingram.
Prefects: Grace Mayles, Jean Ingram, Lorna Newton, Joyce Thomas, Gladys Harradine.
Form Prefects, Autumn Term, 1933: *Va^1:* B. Castle; *Va^2:* G. Barker; *Vb^1:* E. Burgess; *Vb^2:* B. Dent; *IVa^1:* P. Gardner; *IVa^2:* D. Norman; *IVb:* M. Weeber; *IVr:* B. Bishop; *IVc:* M. Willmott; *IIIa^1:* M. Lobban; *IIIa^2:* V. Kipling; *IIIb:* S. Crabb.
Form Prefects, Summer Term, 1934: *Va^1:* J. Eddy; *Va^2:* N. Kelly; *Vb^1:* J. Sheppard; *Vb^2:* B. Rayment; *IVa^1:* V. Arnold; *IVa^2:* M. Alexander; *IVb:* D. Lawson; *IVr:* M. Powers; *IVc:* P. Hodges; *IIIa^1:* J. Soden; *IIIa^2:* M. Wilkinson; *IIIb:* D. Russell.
Games Captain: Gladys Harradine.

Two milestones in the history of Hitchin were celebrated on consecutive days in November and parties of girls attended each.

The first was the centenary of the birth of Frederic Seebohm, when a blue plaque was unveiled on the wall of the furniture shop at the junction of Hermitage Road and Bancroft. This now stands on the site of the former Seebohm home. In honour of his memory, the school was granted a day's holiday the next week. The second event was the opening of the new X-Ray Department of the Hitchin Hospital, strangely held in the Playhouse where a film was shown.

Staying with the hospital theme, Dr. Winifred Symmonds, the school doctor and first woman doctor in Hitchin, came to talk about 'Old Hospitals' and a sister from the London Hospital spoke of nursing as a career. Mr. Lugg lectured on 'Julius Caesar' and Professor Hall chose 'Burma' for his talk. Mr. Nott-Bower gave a lecture about 'Policemen' and, after taking fingerprints from some of his audience, projected them on the screen to show 'criminal types'. Another fascinating lantern lecture was by Mr. James M. Scott, who had been part of the Arctic expedition to plot a British air route over the Pole.

The involvement with the U.G.S. and the work of the Settlement was brought nearer to home when Margaret Flex, an old girl, now working at the Mission, came to tell of her work. Canon Veasey also returned with more slides to show the progress which had been made in helping all ages, from the very young to the old, in these poor areas. The weekly flowers were still being sent as well as money and gifts of clothing. Two huge hampers of garments were sent before Christmas, as were other gifts throughout the year. At this time, flowers were also being delivered regularly to the Hitchin Hospital and gratefully acknowledged by the matron.

A new innovation, on Friday morning after prayers, was that members of the sixth form took it in turns to read, for a few minutes, on any subject of topical interest. Ominously with the 'Icknield Way' and 'Madame Curie' were 'Hitler's Germany' and 'German Labour Camps'.

The League of Nations group still had regular meetings, but the first rush of enthusiasm seems to have waned. The Literary Club, renamed the 'Arts Club' so as to widen its scope, got off to a flying start with a series of lectures, debates and play readings. They read, for the whole school, Sheridan's 'The Rivals'. (It is amazing how often this play, above all others, was chosen for performance.) The Science Club also had a full programme and was able to make two visits in the locality. They went to the Rubber Works at Letchworth and were able to see the raw material converted into 'familiar things such as rubber buttons'. They also went out to the hills at Pegsdon to see the dew pond and the chalkland flowers.

The games have had 'little to report' for several years, but this time an English International Hockey player showed a film and advised the senior girls on their play. Both first and second eleven teams were taken to Cambridge to see the American Women's Hockey Team play the East of England. Old Girl Margaret Mackintosh played for the home team which won by six goals to one. The tennis enthusiasts also had an outing when they went to Wimbledon and saw Dorothy Round beaten by the American Sara Palfrey.

1934–1935   Grace Mayles

Second Head: J. Thomas.
Head Boarder: M. Clarke.
VI Form Prefects: N. Balls, B. Hancock, P. Beddoe, M. Cahill, M. Clarke, B. Corble, F. Crabb, J. Eddy, J. Ferrier, Mgt. Hicks, Mj. Hicks, J. Lake, D. Peake, M. Routh.
Form Prefects: Va^1: E. Burgess; Va^2: B. Farwell; Vb^1: B. Robarts; Vb^2: A. Doble; IVa^1: M. Street; IVa^2: J. Taylor; IVa^p: M. Harland; IVb: M. Wilkinson; IVc: D. Reed; $IIIa^1$: O. Holmes; $IIIa^2$: S. Crabb.
Games Captain: B. Hancock (Spring), R. Gray (Summer).

The event which dominated both the national and the school life in 1935 was the Silver Jubilee of the accession of King George V. The King sent a message to all children:–

> 'You are the heirs to a great past; but the future is yours, and it is your high responsibility. Each of you must try to be a good citizen. To this end you must make the best use of all your powers. Strive to grow in strength, in knowledge, and in grace. If you persist bravely in this endeavour, you will work worthily for your family, your country, and for mankind. So to live, in whatever sphere, must be noble and be great.
> My confident trust is in you. *George R.I.'*

The school enjoyed two days' holiday in celebration of the King's Jubilee and on their return, the staff organised an afternoon of fun and games. The school was divided into two groups. Half the pupils were involved in sports where the races relied not so much on skill as on ingenuity. The other group went to the lower field which was set out in fair-ground fashion, with coconut shies and other sideshows. When everything was over, each child was given a box of Jubilee Chocolate, provided by the Urban District Council. To round off a happy day, no girl had prep. in the evening.

Further celebration took the form of a dramatic entertainment, where five plays were performed by different factions in the school and the sum of £24 raised was divided amongst three charities, including the Jubilee Fund. In acknowledgement of this came a receipt bearing the signature of the Prince of Wales. There was also, strangely, a French and German party where various forms contributed and games were played but no one was allowed to speak English!

Back with the normal routine, Mr. Lugg lectured the seniors on 'Macbeth'; Mr. Nott-Bowers told of 'Roads' – their development and the traffic on them; Mr. Balls showed slides and told of his six months' trip to Turkey, in order to collect specimens of plants and seeds for Kew Gardens.

Miss Chambers announced the intention of starting a second, junior, Orchestra and a Music Club was formed. The Arts Club devoted its whole efforts to drama, with play readings and full performances. The League of Nations Union had, in common with the other societies, a rather curtailed programme because of the Jubilee celebrations, but reported an increased interest amongst the younger pupils.

An unusual event on the sports field was the holding of a hockey tournament where each player paid a small fee, the proceeds of which went to support the National Playing Fields Association.

1935–1936   Joan Eddy

Second Head: Freda Crabb.
School Captain: Ruth Flex.
Prefects: Pat Beddoe, Betty Corble, Janet Ferrier, Margaret Hicks, Enid Burgess, Doreen Eddy, Betty Stratford, Joan Weaver.
Form Prefects: *Va¹:* Sylvia Bone; *Va²:* Betty Reynolds; *Vb¹:* Pat Gardner; *Vb²:* Sybil Russell; *Remove:* Nina Baxter; *IVa¹:* Joyce Lowrie; *IVa²:* Sylvia Locke; *IVb:* Barbara Clarkson; *IVc:* Molly Hewitt; *IIIa¹:* Joyce Jenkins; *IIIa²:* Audrey Ewing.
Tennis Captain: Freda Crabb.

After the celebrations last year, the school shared the sorrow of the whole nation in January, when the king died at his country home in Sandringham. The pupils were taken down to the railway station where they stood in silent respect as the funeral train with its black coach passed slowly by on the way to London. A Memorial service was later held in St. Mary's and attended by representatives from the school. Three months earlier, the pupils had been granted a day's holiday, to celebrate the marriage of the Duke of Gloucester to Lady Alice Scott. Her first public engagement was the opening of a new ward at the Hitchin Hospital, performed at the Town Hall, where some girls were given seats. The rest lined Hollow Lane, standing in the snow, to cheer as she passed by.

Miss Seebohm ceremonially planted a small Atlantic Cedar in the grounds. This seedling was from trees in her own garden, and it seemed fitting that it should find a place in the woods which she had given to the school.

The Magazine format changed radically, for the first time in twenty-five years; the page size increased greatly and the cover changed from blue to cream. The editor still made the regular plea for more items of greater interest, especially from the middle school. To promote this there would be a competition, with prizes for work from pupils under fourteen and another for those older. In the magazine this year were a couple of reports which, unwittingly, raise a smile. First in respect of the school trip at Easter, to Normandy:– 'We left Newhaven in great spirits, but the weather was unkind and our numbers were soon sadly depleted'. The second, reporting the speech at the prizegiving for the Swimming Sports:– 'Mr. Widdows thanked all concerned and commented on the extraordinarily fine summers we had had since the bath was opened. This put an end to an extremely enjoyable day.'!

Miss Gilbert again came to advise the girls on career prospects and Mr. Lowe returned with more, ever popular slides of animals. This year he chose 'Animals of the Forest', Miss Croker came to talk about 'Chinese Art' as a prelude to a visit, by girls in the upper school, to an exhibition in London. Current affairs were not neglected and Mr. Grant came to tell of 'The European Situation', where Hitler was causing anxiety to Mr. Baldwin. In contrast with the programme of play reading, The Arts Club were taken, by Mr. Hine, to visit Hitchin Priory. The Science Club, in addition to a programme of talks, went to the Rothschilds' museum at Tring.

Those tennis players who went to Wimbledon were fortunate to see both Kay Stammers and Dorothy Round win their singles matches. The hockey players were proud to know that Margaret Mackintosh, an old girl, had been chosen to play for the England Ladies' Hockey Team on their tour of America.

The O.G.A. had continued for years with their regular summer and winter Gatherings. Now they intended to be more ambitious with a weekend of activities, the members from Hitchin offering accommodation to those coming from a distance. The next time, there was a highly successful meeting in London which they intended to repeat.

1936–1937 Margaret Hicks

Second Head: Janet Ferrier.
Head Boarder: Sheila Lock.
Prefects: Enid Burgess, Doris Perry, Gweneth Powles, Doreen Eddy, Wendy Shollick, Lois Thrussell.
Form Prefects: Va^1: M. Crooks; Va^2: P. Padley; Vb^1: M. Lobban; Vb^2: R. West; IVa^1: M. Sayer; IVa^2: B. Purdom; IVb: A. Ewing; IVc: S. Lambert; IVc^p: J. Cholmeley; $IIIa^1$: D. Fooster; $IIIa^2$: M. Allingham.
Games Captain: Diana Keller.
Tennis Captain: Pauline Mallett.

For the third successive year, events beyond the school boundary had a greater influence than those within. The coronation of King George VI led to rejoicing, unusual school activities and extra holidays, Miss Chambers gave to the school two magnolia trees which were planted in the grounds to commemorate the coronation, and each pupil received a spoon and a book, given by Hitchin Urban District Council. There was a Youth Rally at the Albert Hall, when representatives came from every part of the Empire and Hitchin Girls' Grammar School was represented in the audience. The first part of the programme consisted of speeches from Rt. Hon. L. S. Amery, Lord Snell, the High Commissioner for India and the Prime Minister of Australia. After a break in the programme, the words of the next speaker, Mr. Baldwin, were broadcast to the Empire. The Empire Service of Youth was held, next day, in Westminster Abbey and relayed to Westminster Hall.

1936.　The Tempest.　　　　　　　　　　　　　　　[Sheila Ridgon (Wintle)]

Two weeks later the King visited a huge Youth Rally held at the Empire Stadium, Wembley, where young people demonstrated all the gymnastics, folk dancing, games etc. associated with youth the world over. Seven Canadian girls stayed in Hitchin and came to learn how an English school compared with theirs at home. Miss Chambers organised 'tea and games' at a party to bid 'farewell' to the visitors.

Within the school day, it was decided to have two forty minutes' lessons and then twenty minutes' preparation period each afternoon. This would make the school day ten minutes longer but should result in more free time in the evenings. It was decided to have a school bookplate, and the design submitted by Barbara Brown and Joyce Perrin was chosen for its clarity and simplicity. There would be a 'Hobbies Trophy', a modern carving of a girl's head bowed over her work with a needle in her hand. This would be given to the form exhibiting the best collection of work, and stars were given to individual entries which showed ingenuity or excellence of execution.

The school staged two performances of 'The Tempest', at the end of November. The quality of the production was confirmed by the Hitchin Pictorial, which wrote, '. . . diction and sincerity determine the success . . . In both directions the girls excelled. . . . The performances were almost above criticism and the players merited the highest praise.'

The girls leaving the previous year, gave money with which to buy two chairs, which matched in design the arm-chair already on the platform.

IVb[1], the winners of the Junior Gymnastic Cup. *Back row:* J. Downing, J. Watts, C. Galbraith, K. Knowles, D. Flint, A. Ewing, D. Prentice, B. Rudkin. *Middle row:* D. Robinson, G. Lewis, J. Watkins, J. Castle, A. Cresswell, I. Stutier, R. Hand, G. Jones, M. Mostyn. *Front row:* J. Nicholson, B. ? , J. Jenkins, Miss U. Gibbon-Davies, K. Bellew, B. Barker, M. Saunders, M. Clarke.

[Kathleen Bellew (Davies)]

78

Two unusual successes: Zoe Maw, an old girl, had, with her architect partner, won third prize in a design competition held by the Royal Institute of British Architects (R.I.B.A.). The Head Girl, Margaret Hicks, had a story accepted by the Young Artists' Programme of Children's Hour and read the story herself for the broadcast.

The writer S. P. B. Mais came to tell of his 'Delight in Books', and Mr. R. Hine told of Hertfordshire's place in English History.

Mrs. Elliott came to the school to give a violin recital, and burgeoning interest in music led to the creation of a Music Club wherein each form would contribute a few items to the programme. They also visited the Westminster Hall for a special 'Concert for Children'. The Science Club went to Hitchin Gas Works and the Arts Club broke with their traditional play readings. In the autumn they had two mock trials and after Christmas, following an inspiring talk on 'Puppet Shows', they made puppets; with the help of Miss Abraham, a theatre was built and their own plays were performed.

1937–1938   Enid Burgess

Second Head: Doreen Eddy.
Head Boarder: Gilian Dalgliesh.
Prefects: Silvia Bone, Gwen Dolling, Diana Keller, Brenda Burbidge, Kathleen Grant, Catherine Matthew, Adeline Doble, Winifred Illingworth, Lois Thrussell, Lottie Fraser, Pat Hawkins, Joan Oakley, Hope Whincup.
Games Captain: Diana Keller.

The school was greatly saddened by the death of Dr. J. H. Gilbertson. As a governor he had been a familiar sight at school functions and festivities and had given the Hockey Cup in the season 1921–1922.

A Home Science Course was started for those girls in the Vth Form who would not be taking School Certificate. They would sometimes spend a whole day in the Domestic Science room, learning dressmaking and other needlework skills, cookery and the theory of domestic science. As one girl commented: 'we should be transformed into model housekeepers'.

The first meeting of the School Council was reported. There had been a school council started in 1922 but no more had been heard of it since. It is reasonable to assume that it just faded out.

Geography and current affairs dominated the lectures. Mr. Lowe came with slides of 'St. Kilda's'; Mrs. Goudie spoke to the Senior School about 'South Africa' and the Kindergarten and the Lower School heard about life in Ceylon from Mrs. Jessop. With the deepening international crisis, Mr. Grant came three times to clarify the confusing details. First he spoke of 'Japan' and its expansionist policies. The next visit, to speak of 'Central Europe', was just one week after Hitler marched into Austria (i.e. mid-March 1938) and the pupils were warned that Czechoslovakia was in danger of being the next victim. His third visit told of German influence in Brazil; the importance of Palestine on Germany's air route to the east and the recent Czech border incident.

The school was now so active in charititable works that for the past three years they had been drawn together under the umbrella title of 'Social Services'. Support for the U.G.S. had regularly grown, with the school being involved in several different Settlements with their nursery schools, clubs for the elderly and practical help for the poor. Some girls had worked at the Settlements during the long holidays. Through the same associations there was aid to the Children's Country Holidays Fund. Save the Children Fund received a donation, as did the King George Memorial Playing Fields Fund. Gifts were also sent to hospitals and orphanages.

The Hertfordshire Inter-school Hockey tournament took place on the school grounds. The home players did extremely well, for not only did the 1st XI win the tournament but the 2nd XI was second! The County Hockey Match between Hertfordshire and Bedfordshire was also played on the school pitch and Hertfordshire beat Bedfordshire 11–0. Diana Keller would be leaving at the end of the school year. She had been Games Captain for two years; had played in the hockey 1st XI for four years and the 1st netball team for five years. This constituted a record in the school. A party of girls went to Wimbledon to see the first day's play in the Wightman Cup and were fortunate to see Kay Stammers play Alice Marble as well as the following match between Helen Wills Moody and Peggy Scriven.

1938–1939   Adeline Doble

Head Boarder: Margaret Saunders.
Games Captain: Enid Bryant.

School Prefects: Back row L. to R.: Mary Halliwell, Anne Graham, Pat Hawkins, Lottie Fraser, Margaret Saunders. *Front row:* Enid Bryant, Maisie Street, Adeline Doble, Hope Whincup, Mary Lobban.   [Enid Bryant (Foster)]

This year, the school celebrated the tercentenary, and the Golden Jubilee, of its foundation; for it was in 1639 that John Mattock founded the Hitchin Grammar School, 'in order that the children . . . of Hitchin should be taught and instructed. . . .' It was also the Golden Jubilee of the Girls' school, which had started in Bancroft with seven pupils, and now it had more than 400. Once again expansion was needed and building undertaken. A temporary wing was demolished and in its place would be a new Hall, Art Room and Laboratories. In the meantime, four of the forms found accommodation in the Hermitage Halls, each pair spending half a day there. In the middle of the morning, the younger girls were taken up to play on Windmill Hill before 'getting into line' and crossing the Belisha crossing to resume their lessons until dinner time.

The Opening Day, on 28th June 1939, was a milestone in the history of the school. Lady Elphinstone – sister of the Queen and an old pupil in the time of Miss Gosnell – came to perform the official opening. Miss Gosnell and Miss Chambers were both on the platform, and all three ladies were presented with bouquets by children from the Kindergarten. Mr. Hugh Seebohm, Chairman of the Governors, presided at the ceremony supported by the governors and members of the Education Committee and of the Hertfordshire County Council. Miss Seebohm, dear and faithful supporter of the school, was also a guest.

Due to gifts from a staff concert, from Miss Seebohm and last year's school leavers, it had been possible to purchase a grand piano for the new hall, in place of an upright, and an H.M.V. Radiogram. The O.G.A. had given a 'solid and dignified' arm-chair for the platform.

After the official opening the assembled company inspected the new building and watched a country dancing display before being entertained to tea.

In honour of this occasion, a special souvenir edition of the School Magazine was produced bearing an appropriate golden cover and containing recollections of the school since its early days in Bancroft. Miss Gosnell contributed, as did Mr. Hine and a host of old girls and staff. (From this have come many of the anecdotes in this book.)

Despite the international unrest, a party of girls went, in the summer holidays of

1939.   Miss A. Chambers, Lady Elphinstone and Hugh Exton Seebohm   [Lorna Glenwright]

1938, to a League of Nations Summer School in Geneva. In ten days there were fifteen lectures, three receptions and five excursions. The lecturers came from places as diverse as China, America, India and Spain.

Back to school came Miss Wright who had spent a year teaching in the U.S.A. whilst her counterpart, Miss Flemington, had spent a year in Hitchin. The VIth form gave a party for sixty of the children who were connected with the Mission at Peckham.

The Chair, presented by the Old Girls for the platform of the New Hall.

1939. H.B.G.S. and H.G.G.S. hockey teams. *Back row:* Cliff Darlow, Pete Folland, Joe Barrett, John Foster, Philip Spikesman, ? Nicholls, E. Leete. *Middle row:* Pete Shadbolt, Don Shaw, Bunty Kartwright, Mary Lobban, Diana Loughlin, Phyllis Tosband, T. Waters, J. Wittenbury. *Front row:* Lorna Smith, Mildred Roe, Barbara Clarkson, Winifred Illingworth, Rosemary Dorman, Pauline Cooper, Enid Bryant. [Enid Bryant (Foster)]

Nona Martin achieved an 'A' week in November. She was the second girl in ten years to achieve what was thought to be impossible. Perhaps this was reflected in the reward being a half day's holiday in place of the former whole day!

The proud history of hockey in Hitchin was exemplified in 1938 when there were four girls in the 1st, two in the 2nd and 2 reserves in the county hockey teams. The Boys' Grammar School was, of course, also celebrating its tercentenary, so it was decided to have a Boys v. Girls Hockey Match – appropriately on April Fools' Day! This was the first time that the two schools met on the hockey field. The girls put up a good fight, but the boys were faster on the ball and won by 5 goals to nil. In the teams' photograph, two of the players, John Foster and Enid Bryant, were later Head Boy and Head Girl of their respective schools. When nineteen and still in school, they became engaged, and married in 1943.

1939–1940 Lottie Fraser

Second Head Girl: Pat Hawkins.
Head Boarder: Barbara Clarkson.
Prefects: Lottie Fraser, Pat Hawkins, Enid Bryant, Mary Lobban, Phyllis McCombie, Margaret Privett, Mary Rose Watt, Barbara Clarkson, Sylvia Crabb, Margaret Lloyd, Margaret Low, Dorothy Reed, Mildred Roe, Daphne Russell, Mary Russell.
Games Captain: Enid Bryant.

The school was affected by the war from the very beginning of the autumn term. The Government decreed that no schools should reassemble before some air raid precautions were taken. Kathleen Bellew (Davies), '35–'43, remembers:– 'The trenches, dug round the sacred hockey pitch and designed for our safety in air raids, were never used as such and were anything but safe. Wings leapt over the top to avoid falling in and halves floundered in mud to retrieve lost balls.' These were later filled in when the lower corridors and basement were reinforced with timber props, and when the siren sounded, each form would go to allocated places.

Miss Chambers reported that school was only two days late in starting with adequate precaution for A.R.P. and the great 'blackout' well in train. She also writes of 'visitors' in the school but it is unclear whether these, at that time, were official or private evacuees. The school now had blackened window frames and netted glass with sand buckets in every room and spare corner. Miss Wells soon had a highly efficient Fire Squad, and the new court-yard was the scene of much furious 'stirrup pumping' during the dinner-hour. Rosalie Picton was a member of this squad and remembers that the fire fighters had a blue ribbon on the gas mask box which every person had to carry at all times.

Since economy would now be essential, Misses Squires and Wright started a 'second hand shoe shop', where outgrown shoes could be bought and sold. Knitting was very popular and most forms were given one period, in school time, when they could knit. Miss Saunders secured some inexpensive, good wool, which the girls could buy in the dinner-hours.

The Games Captain reported how lucky the school was to retain its games pitches intact, reflecting the plight of those less fortunate who had to surrender their grounds to support the war effort.

There had always been an annual service in Southwark Cathedral, which representative staff and pupils had attended. This had been a time when all those who supported the Settlements and Mission work in London could come together and renew their resolve before visiting some of the places which benefited from their efforts. Now it was deemed unsafe, and the service was cancelled.

The School Council decided to add the Red Cross to the list of charities supported by the school and were determined to raise as much money as possible. By Christmas they were able to send £11 for Polish Relief and sums to three other charities. Staff and girls descended on Dr. Gilbertson's barn, in Bancroft, where they sorted old clothes, bottles, silver paper and 'all kind of rubbish' which was sold, on behalf of the Red Cross, for £200. The knitters excelled themselves and, in addition to the usual recipients, were able to send some clothes and woollies for the children evacuated to Hitchin.

The Chancellor of the Exchequer made a special appeal to 'Save our Way to Victory'. The school had introduced National Savings many years before but resolved to renew their efforts. A cinema van came and showed a programme outlining how vital this money would be. The pupils were reminded that: '£4 buys a pistol, £700 a barrage balloon, £5,000 a fighter plane and £20,000 a bomber'.

After the de luxe edition of the Magazine, published the previous year, the Autumn 1939 edition was confined to ten pages and the type-face considerably reduced. Because of the increasing paper shortage, the magazine had, by the following summer, shrunk still further to one quartered broad-sheet, printed both sides.

In many small ways, the war had already left its mark on the school.

1940–1941   Enid Bryant

In a world where death had become almost commonplace, the school was still able to grieve for the passing of Watson, an old man, fortunate to die at home. He had served the school faithfully and well for fifty-two years, first in the gardens at the school in Bancroft and later as the official Caretaker and Groundsman at the School on the Hill. School days would never be the same without him.

Eastbourne High School had now been evacuated to Hitchin and used the school every afternoon whilst the Hitchin girls were there in the morning. Every spare corner was brought into use for teaching space but even so, many pupils had several afternoons 'off' each week, while others went down to Walsworth Road Baptist Church Hall to continue their studies. Due to all this, there was a holiday term of one month in August when school reassembled for a timetable of first aid, toy making, play reading and other less academic pastimes. Girls of the Upper School went to St. Mary's once a week for sketching and brass rubbing.

The School Council declared that a Good Causes Fund be set up and discussed plans for money raising. The success of their efforts must have exceeded even their own expectations because six months later more than £150 had been distributed to twelve charities. In addition, War Weapons Week had raised over £30 and some of the girls had helped with the demonstrations associated with it. The staff performed two plays and the silver collection of £11 was sent to the Spitfire Fund.

During the holidays, some of the senior girls returned to school to help with the fire-watching; Form IIIb and IIIr 'adopted' the minesweeper 'Grampian' and sent parcels of small gifts, letters and Christmas cards.

Some things never change, and the Annual Verse Speaking Competition, which had taken place for the past ten years, carried on as always. Marion Sayer, at school '34–'39, remembers: 'Everyone had to do it. We sat there and felt quite sick on the last day of term. Reginald Hine always came to adjudicate it'. Constant too was the Singing Competition, still with the faithful Miss Mary Ibberson (founder of the Rural Music School) judging it, and the Singing Picture went to the VIth form and the Sight Reading Picture to Va[1]. Sports Day and Form Running competitions helped maintain some of the old 'safe' pattern of school life. Other things were slightly modified to embrace the new situation; the annual gym competition was judged by Miss Knight of the Eastbourne High School and the Carol concert was a joint occasion. The magazine, restored to a slimmer version of its former self, would appear only once instead of twice a year.

A source of sadness and pride was the death, in the London Blitz, of an old girl Amy Noel (Steedman). As Commandant of the London Women's Legion, she, with two others, was killed when they took a mobile canteen to the relief of distressed families, the A.R.P. and the fire services in a badly bombed area. A message of sympathy was sent by the Queen to Amy's parents.

A mark of hope for the future was symbolised by the opening, in the autumn term, of the new Old Hale Way School. In 1956, this was to become the Bessemer School for Boys, when the Girls' High School opened in Bedford Road.

1941–1942 Diana Clarke

Captain: K. Bellew.
Prefects: Daphne Flint, K. Bellew, E. Bœson, C. Brockis, J. Downing, K. Ephgrave, B. Lewellen, E. McRitchie, D. Morriss, A. Morrison, M. Mostyn, D. Prentice, M. Saunders, P. Whitby.

Even in the midst of the war some humour always prevailed and so this year's calendar starts, rather than ends, with the Games report. A fixture to play the Boys' Grammar School had been arranged each year since the tercentenary; this year was no exception though the game was played with more enthusiasm than hope – the previous year the girls were trounced 11–0! The report of the game reads: 'We managed to get our annual match with the Boys and received the usual 'licking' – the worst we've had, but also the first time we've ever scored a goal against them – I think the goal-keeper must have become numb with the cold!'. Thus the national spirit was exemplified on the playing field of Hitchin.

This 'Are we down-hearted?' spirit was mirrored in the Mission parishes of the Settlement. Though the district had suffered badly in the blitz, it was being tidied up, clubs were in full swing and communal dinners provided. Even though clothing was short, the school still sent off two large sacks full of garments to be distributed to the children, most of whom were evacuated.

Shortages were beginning to be felt at school and an appeal went out for old paint boxes, in any condition. Though paints were still available, the boxes were unobtainable. (In these pre-plastic days, the boxes were made of metal – much too precious for such a use.)

For some obscure reason, the Government required nettles, and so, at Whitsun, the Upper School sallied forth with gloves and scissors to collect the required crop. This was crammed into sacks, slung one each side of a pony, and an afternoon's picking resulted in four large sacks and two dust sheets full. This harvest was then laid out to dry on various garage floors and the dried weight of one hundred-weight made the nettle rash seem worth while.

The Good Causes Fund still flourished with contributions from all kinds of fund raising schemes; socials, competitions, tournaments, concerts and sales of work, all helped swell the growing fund.

The VIth form were most enterprising by staging a pantomime, 'Cinderella'. As late as the dress rehearsal, it was found that the 'quick change' from rags to ball gown was not slick enough to avoid an awkward pause and the Ugly sisters – Tapioca, with her badges, and Semolina, in her bib – went about singing 'Pick yourself up, dust yourself down, and start all over again'. The demon king was plastered with green greasepaint, left this vital 'prop' at home one performance and had to improvise with cold cream and green chalk! Even then she was only just dissuaded from going on stage in her glasses. The cow was firmly pinned together because at one rehearsal the front half of the beast had walked and the rear had not! Tight pyjamas made excellent breeches, while in the ball scene the anxious

1942. Cinderella.   [Diana Morriss (Foster)]

86

producer dropped the gong with a tremendous clatter and then struck only nine strokes for midnight! The final loving kiss of Cinderella and Prince Charming was the result of much giggling rehearsal. We are indebted to M. Mostyn who reported all this at the time and made the production sound such fun, as well as most profitable for the war effort. The staff wondered if the VIth form would ever settle down to work again!

In the previous year the boarders had asked to rejoin the Guides and the 1st Hitchin Company was reformed. Now, a year later, it had become an open school company and there were thirty-three guides working in five patrols. The original company colours were proudly paraded on Empire Day. The Guides were busy raising money for the Baden Powell Memorial Fund and their Sale with Sideshows brought in £20 for this cause. Now the Brownie pack was about to restart too.

A poem was sent to Miss Seebohm, at Christmas time, telling of the school's great affection for and indebtedness to her. With it went a cheque, to which every member of the school contributed, for her to send to a charity of her choice. In her long affectionate letter of acknowledgement, she told of her intention of donating it to the 'Fairbridge Farm Schools' and so further demonstrated her commitment to children and their education.

1942–1943   Kathleen Bellew

Captain: Ann Morrison.
Prefects: Pat Arnold, Christine Brockis, Dorothea Edwards, Peggy Garnham, Kathleen Hill, Audrey Mole, Doreen Robinson, Joan Slow, Pauline Whitby, Rhona Garratt, Pat McCombie, Hilary Roe.

In the middle years of the war the country settled down to a regular pattern of living, and one effect of this was the return of many evacuees to their homes. Eastbourne High School went back at Easter 1943, after two and a half years in Hitchin. Both schools had made the best of their joint arrangement but were now glad to be going their separate ways. The Hitchin girls soon 'flowed into the empty spaces and now it seems impossible to believe that we ever housed some two hundred extra people and their belongings'.

Miss Forbes, 'The Gentle Dragon', left the school, after twenty-eight years. She had helped to train many generations of efficient little housewives in her den in the Domestic Science Room, and the school would never be the same without her.

Many of the girls went potato picking in October and November, in common with their contemporaries throughout the country. Some of the girls enjoyed 'life on the land' so well that they returned to help plant the new crop during the Easter holiday.

Kathleen Bellew (Davies), head girl at this time, has interesting recollections. She was responsible for the fire-watching rota and found fire watching one of the more frightening experiences:

'We chatted on equal terms with members of staff until bed-time, the moment of truth for two of us. By the dim light of a shaded torch, we crept into the old gym – no lights allowed, of course, because of the blackout. Old stories of the school being haunted returned to haunt us and we never slept. It was quite a relief when the siren wailed and we rushed to join the staff to anxiously watch the skies and stare in disbelief at the glow from burning London. The school was never hit but we did have our scares. One night there was damage to the railway lines and an unexploded bomb fell near Miss Seebohm's house. One day, soon after school finished, a Junkers 88 flew low over the school being pursued by a Spitfire. Photos of fighter pilots were pin-ups inside every desk lid along with film stars in uniform and family and friends away from home. Our number one tune was "Warsaw Concerto" from the film "Dangerous Moonlight". They were stirring times indeed but Miss Chambers insisted that school work and routine should go on.'

There were the usual lectures on a variety of subjects and musical evenings and concerts, many of the competitions and most school activities. Only the school societies seem to have fallen victim to the war as all disappeared to be replaced by the World Affairs Group.

Several innovations appeared in the school; a Visitors' Gallery was introduced at the School Council; the school play was revived; the first VI form party since the war took place at Christmas – and the First XI scored another goal against the boys in the annual Hockey Match! No away matches were played because of the national emergency. Some girls hoped to revive the playing of cricket but this was impossible because the necessary equipment was unobtainable.

A Greek tragedy was chosen for the play – 'The Alcestis of Euripides' – and for six months staff, principals and chorus worked to make this the best production ever. The costumes presented a problem since clothing was rationed: cheese-cloth was not, and a large bale was bought and dyed different colours, to provide every garment for the show. This rather messy undertaking took place in the Domestic Science Room. There were, at the first performance, a few mistakes, mostly attributable to nervousness. The worst of these was when two bearers managed to drop the body of Alcestis as they bore it off stage! Despite this break in the tense atmosphere, on only the one occasion, this was a production of which all concerned could be proud.

1943.   The Alcestis of Euripides.   [Anne Willmott (Dr. Millar)]

1943–1944   Pat McCombie

Captain: Hilary Roe.
Prefects: Anne Willmott, Jean Davey, Claude Fandre, Dorothy Crosoer, Rhona Garratt, Shelagh Brennan, Hilary Roe, Nona Martin, Rachel Squire, Pat Phillips, Anne Barker, Trixie Primmer, Jean Laney, Joyce Ramsey.

With the invasion of Europe, the country looked forward to the ending of the war. This, in some ways, made everybody try still harder to support the war effort; in others there were already signs of 'returning to normal'.

School numbers had risen to 510 and a number of applicants were, regretfully, turned away.

The School Savings Association joined the 'Help the Soldier' campaign and raised £336 saved by 82% of the school's number. Some forms achieved a 100% support and planned savings weeks of their own. By the end of the year, a further £500 had gone into savings.

Mrs. Nicholls allowed the school the use of the Red Cross Shop premises where toys, made by the staff and pupils, were sold for almost £100 to support the fund. There was a 'Book Salvage Drive' and nearly 3,000 volumes were sent off to be recycled.

The 580 Company of the Girls' Training Corps had been in operation at the Grammar School for two years, where some instruction, prior to joining the Forces, was given. In June, the Cadet Day celebrations for the North Hertfordshire

1943.   Kindergarten race. Barbara Whaley, first to the tape; Michael Hill on the left.   [Michael Hill]

Companies were held in Hitchin when Major Oldham took the salute while the band of the Hitchin Army Cadets led the march past.

The new Education Act came into force this year, and the Oxford School Certificate would be taken for the first time. The Preparatory Department would gradually disappear, along with the Kindergarten.

Lectures and films reflected the mood of the times. Italy, Russia and America were all covered as was 'The War' and 'The Navy'. An awareness of the future was displayed in 'Post-War problems in Housing and Education'.

The Music Club was revived and a pianoforte recital was given by Mrs. Branson. Dr. Redlich came to judge the singing competition, and afterwards gave a talk about 'Schubert', and played some of his piano works.

The Rev. Brown, vicar of Peckham, came to tell of prevailing conditions in London and answered the many interested questions from the girls. Cash donations and clothes had been sent every year and now, as a measure of faith in the future, the regular, weekly boxes of flowers were again sent to London. Even in winter, when fresh flowers were impossible, decorative twigs and berries were despatched.

Under the new Education Act, the provision of a hot mid-day meal became mandatory in all schools. Mr. Newsom, the Divisional Education Officer, came to explain the act to the girls. Since meals for all would cause complications on the school premises, a daily 'crocodile' of girls wound its way down the hill to the British Restaurant and Communal Feeding centre. Some also went to a 'well known' cafe in Hermitage Rd. called the Stay A While.

The united school effort for the Good Causes Fund was this year combined into a country dancing display, well rewarded by a collection of £37. For the whole of the summer term all the gym and some of the games lessons were devoted to learning the old, traditional dances. Suitable boys' smocks were not easy to find, but a round up of some of the participants in the last display, in 1939, produced a few – the rest of the 'Boys' wore domestic science overalls. On the great day the Orchestra took their places, and the colourful dancers took to the field to provide a performance which, for a while, made the war seem far away.

1944–1945 Anne Willmott

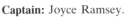

Captain: Joyce Ramsey.
Prefects: Rhona Garratt, Jennifer Chear, Dorothy Crosoer, Dorothy Clements, Constance Flemons, Jean Laney, Jean Morrison, Trixie Primmer, Joyce Ramsey, Gwen Roberts, Penelope Shepherd, Janette Kerr, Eileen Dawson, Mary Plummer, Jean Wren.

Within a year of the Great War ending, Miss Chambers had come to the Hitchin Girls' Grammar School. Now, just after the victory in Europe and with the ending of World War II in sight, she too handed over the reins to a younger woman and took a well earned retirement. In her years as headmistress, society had undergone an upheaval, not least in its attitude to female education but, under her guidance, the girls were well fitted to play their role in the wider world.

The new Education Act of 1944 raised the school leaving age from 14 to 15 years.

This affected the school very little since the girls rarely left before their School Certificate Examinations at sixteen.

Two days' holiday were declared to signal the end of the war in Europe and on 8 May, V.E. Day, a light shone from the turret, now called the bell tower, for the first time. The school was crowned with a small 'lighthouse', shining hope for the future.

The School Council discussed discipline marks, order marks and the forfeit system and decided to keep all three. Behaviour on the trains was causing concern and it was decided to review the list of train prefects and appoint extra girls where needed.

The major beneficiary from the Good Causes Fund was, this year, the Red Cross. Once again a concerted effort went into making goods for a Sale of Work at Christmas time and £127 was raised. Since the G.C.F. was formed in May 1940, the school, by its varied efforts, had collected £882 for the war charities.

The Fellowship Fund, started by the O.G.A. in 1921, had been maintained throughout the war and continued its charitable work of gifts and loans. In the past it had often been used to help fee-paying girls who, through unforeseen circumstances, would not otherwise be able to stay at the school. Since fees had now been nationally abolished this would no longer apply, but the Fund would still be used for helping pay for training of deserving cases which came outside the regulations.

Miss Chambers, in a letter to the Old Girls, remarked that she too would now join their ranks and that she would always be 'at home', in her new cottage at Todds Green, to any of them who wished to call on Wednesday afternoon.

The regular current affairs lectures by Mr. Grant now ranged further afield. His first talk was on 'The Future of Europe' but the second crossed the Atlantic to 'The Tennessee Valley Authority'. Mr. Hardy spoke of 'Birds' and Miss Lowenthal came twice: to talk of Flemish and of Eighteenth Century Art.

There was a concert by the Riddick String Orchestra, a second concert by three instrumentalists of the works of Beethoven and Locatelli. In addition there was a recital of piano and cello music by the Misses Stansfield and Barlow.

This year there was a Junior Carol Concert and a Senior Carol Service for the first time.

All the other school activities went on as they had always done; the Form Running; The Junior and Senior Gym Competitions; Games Tournaments, Sports Day and the Swimming Sports; School Concert and the Founder's Day Service. The school had well survived the problems of wartime.

INNOVATIONS 1919–1945

Year	Event	Reward	Given by
1919–1920	Tidy Form Rooms	The 'Tidy Picture'	
	Guide Company formed		
	School Choir		
1920–1921	Form Councils		
	School Orchestra		
1921–1922	School Council		
	Form Libraries		
	Holiday Essays	2 Prizes	
	Literature Comp.	3 Prizes	Miss Seebohm

1922–1923	Joined United Girls' Schools' Mission		
	Choir to Hertfordshire Music Festival		
	Magazine Comp.	3 Prizes	
	English – best yr's. work	Prize	Miss Seebohm
	Singing Comp.	Singing Picture	Mrs. Pryor
1924–1925	Form Choir Competition		
	Junior Singing Comp.	Peter Pan Statuette	Miss O'Brien
	Sight Singing	Picture	Miss Weatherley
	Holiday Comp.	Prizes – various	
1927–1928	Write One Act Play	Prize	
	Sewing Comp.	Prize	
1929	Diary, Bird News Comp.	Prize	Miss Radway
1931–1932	History Cross Word	Prize	Miss Chambers
	Verse Speaking Comp.	Prize	(Judged – Hine)
1932–1933	Handwriting Comp.	Fountain pens	
1934–1935	Best Form Marks Record	Flex Trophy	Mr. & Mrs. Flex
	Junior Orchestra formed		
1936	Hobbies Comp.	Carved Wooden Trophy	
	Magazine Comp. (new)	Prizes	
1938	Book prize – sen. & jun.		
1940–1941	Wartime Recipes	Prize	Miss Chambers
1944	Needlework Comp.	Picture – 'The Sampler'	

INTRODUCTION OF NEW EVENTS AND THEIR TROPHIES

Year	*Event*	*Reward*	*Given by*
1919–1920	Deportment Awards	Yellow Girdles	
	Highest Form Number	'Deportment' Picture	
	Net Ball		
	Form Running	Running Clock	
	Country Dancing		
1921–1922	Form Tennis Tournament	Prizes	
	Form Hockey Match	Cup	Dr. Gilbertson
	Sports Day		
	Form with most sports points	Sports Cup	
1922–1923	Inter-Form matches	'Course' Cup	Mr. Course
	Snr. Tennis	Cup	
	Jnr. Tennis	Cup	
	Snr. Rounders	Cup	
	Jnr. Rounders	Cup	
	Tennis Tournaments	Prizes	
1923–1924	Snr. Sports	Cup	
	Jnr. Sports	Cup	Miss Murray
	Jnr. Form Running	Jnr. Running Clock	Pupils
	Snr. Form Running	Cup (snr. clock now for 2nd)	Mr. Thomas
	Jnr. Deportment Award	Narrower Yellow Girdles	
	Highest Form Number	'Deportment' Picture	Miss Chambers
	Tennis Singles Champ.	Cup	Mrs. A. Lindsell
	(runner up)	Small Cup	Dr. Parry
1925–1926	Snr. Netball	Cup	
	Netball – Boarders v. Daygirls		

1927–1928	Junior Netball	Cup	
1932–1933	Snr. Swimming	Shield	Mr. Brown (WGC)
	Jnr. Swimming	Shield	Mr. Brown (WGC)
1934	Swimming Style	Cup	Mrs. Sainsbury (Old Girl)
	Diving	Cup	Mr. Shillitoe (clerk to the Governors)
	Royal Life Saving Soc. Examination	Bronze Medallion	
1934–1935	Jnr. Diving	Picture	Joyce Thomas (Old Girl)
1935–1936	Royal LIfe Saving Soc. Examination	Silver Medallion	
1937–1938	Inter-Form Swimming Comp.		
1942–1943	Jnr. Tennis Tournament	Bronze Figure	Mrs. Cannon

EXAMINATIONS, PRIZES AND AWARDS

1919	Cambridge Higher Local Examination
	Oxford Local – Senior and Junior
	Music – Assoc. Board R.A.M. & R.C.M. – Higher, Lower, Elementary
1920	London Matriculation – Div. II
1921	Royal Drawing Society (previously discontinued in 1916)
	London Matriculation
	Oxford Senior
	Governors' Bursary
1923	County Senior Scholarship
	Oxford and Cambridge School Examination Joint Board
	University of London
	London Institute for the Advancement of Plain Needlework
1925	Governors' School Leaving Scholarship (value £40 per year for three years' University study)
	Second Annual Governors' Bursary
	Oxford Local Exam – School Certificate
	Oxford and Cambridge – Higher Certificate
1926	'School' and Elocution Qualifying Examination
	Music – Piano and Violin
1928	John Rand Leaving Exhibitions
	Two Junior Bursaries – awarded on results of midsummer exams
	Responsions, Oxford
1934–1935	Headmistress' Annual Report & Exams
1935–1936	Civil Service Clerical Exams
1942–1943	Royal Academy of Dancing – Grades I, II, III, IV

M. A. Badland

Miss Mary Alice Badland, B.A.(Manchester), Head Mistress 1945–1962.

MARY ALICE BADLAND
1909–1971
Headmistress 1945–1962

Prior to her appointment to Hitchin Girls' Grammar School, Miss Badland had taken a Classics degree at Manchester where she was awarded a First Class Honours Degree in Latin and a Class I Teacher's Diploma. She then spent seven years teaching at the Bridlington and Rochdale High Schools and a further seven at Bury Grammar School for Girls.

Life could not have been easy for her when she first took up her new appointment. One pupil remembers:

'When Miss Chambers left, we looked forward to giving her successor a hard time. Miss Badland started at a distinct disadvantage; she was younger but not glamorous; quiet and with not so strong a personality as her predecessor. It was not really until the older staff had left, and none of the girls remembered Miss Chambers, that she ever really stood any chance of making her impression on the school.'

Even then her shyness meant that she remained a remote aloof figure to many of the girls. She hated having her photograph taken and would avoid the camera if at all possible. The 'old girls' remember best her appearance; tall and slim with a very upright carriage; always beautifully dressed in classical styles and with good colour sense.

A constant visitor to the Social Staff Room, Miss Badland would talk to anyone who sat near her, gave small informal coffee parties and joined staff theatre trips. To those who breached her reserve, she was charming and lively.

Miss Badland came to the school at an educationally difficult time, for her arrival coincided with a new Education Act and the re-organisation this always entails. She appreciated the advantage of education having a wide range of subjects and discouraged specialisation. A great deal of the former bookkeeping was dispensed with, and Parents' Evenings were started for each form group. In this, she was a pioneer in what has now become common-place. There was also a good deal more contact established with the Boys' School with lectures and concerts, games and dances. School trips were also organised on a joint basis. Another innovation was the greater involvement of the pupils in arranging the morning assembly.

Miss Badland visited every class each week and gave praise where it was due and slated those at the bottom of the form if it was thought they had not tried hard enough.

In 1949 she was awarded a travelling scholarship, which allowed her to spend five weeks in America in the autumn of that year.

Miss Badland, like Miss Chambers before her, arrived with her dog, a black labrador puppy called Coffee, which was boisterous and uncontrollable, jumping up on to everybody. He had an enclosure near the bike sheds and it was strictly forbidden to feed him. Of course the girls did and he was soon very fat. Following him came Romulus and Remus, two spaniels. Remus died early, but Miss Badland was devoted to the other dog which went with her when she left.

The headmistress, like both her predecessors, 'lived in'. At first she was in the school but later moved over to a flat at Highbury House. She was provided with personal maids, one of which was Polish and unable to speak a word of English. For

Surname **BADLAND** Christian Names } **MARY ALICE** Style { Mr / Mrs / **Miss** }

1. Date of Birth.	2. Date when service commenced in this school.	3. Date of definitive appointment, if later.	4. Date of leaving. (See also Head 14.)
22·6·1909	12·9·1945	Sept. 1946.	

5. Schools and Colleges at which educated, with dates. State names and types of institutions.			6. Particulars of Public and University Examinations taken, and certificates and degrees obtained, with dates.	
	From	To		Date.
Kidderminster High School for Girls	1920	1927	Cambridge School Certificate (Exemption of Matriculation)	1924
Manchester University	1927	1931	N.U.J.M.B. Higher School Certificate	1926
			,, ,, ,, ,,	1927
			B.A. Hons. Latin - Class I	1930
			Teacher's Diploma - Class I	1931

7. List of teaching posts held, with dates (month and year).			8. Particulars of training in teaching, if any, and certificates or diplomas obtained, with dates.
	From	To	Teacher's Diploma - Class I - 1931 (Manchester)
Bridlington High School for Girls	Sept. 1931	July 1934	
Rochdale High School	Sept. 1934	July 1938	9. Particulars of part-time employment and of any external teaching or official work undertaken in addition to duties in the School.
Bury Grammar School for Girls	Sept. 1938	July 1945	
			10. Subject or subjects for which specially qualified.
			Classics
			11. Principal duties assigned, and subjects taken. (Indicate if appointment is temporary.)
12. Total annual emoluments.			
SALARY SCALE, IF ANY.			Duties of Head Mistress

Commencing Salary.	Annual Increment.	Maximum Salary.

13. Particulars of retiring allowance, if any.

Capitation Fees (rate) and Special Allowances, if any. Burnham Scale

Estimated value of board and lodging or of house, and whether given in addition to cash salary or otherwise. £60 p.a. deducted by H.C.C. for unfurnished rooms, service etc. in Boarding House

14. Post, if any, taken up after leaving the School. (See also Head 4.)

From Staff Register, Book III.

hours on end Miss Badland patiently taught the girl to communicate until, by the time she left, the maid had a good grasp of the language.

Miss Badland was the first person to admit her shortcomings in practical matters and freely told and laughed about them. Whilst Miss Chambers was still in the school, the centre light bulb 'went'. The older woman asked if she would stand on the table to change it. This Miss Badland was quite incapable of achieving and Miss Chambers did it herself! Later, when an H.M Inspector, she visited a sewing class and found a girl in trouble. Miss Badland gave 'advice', only to overhear the teacher's scandalised tones as she asked, 'Whoever told you to do it like that?' The child, in a broad Yorkshire accent, replied 'That woman told me'!

At the Townswomen's Guild, she made contact with other women on an equal footing, enjoying their activities and serving as Chairman of the Hitchin Evening Branch.

Miss Badland left the Hitchin Girls' Grammar School in 1962 to become a Government Inspector of Schools in the Sheffield area, a position she held until a year before her death in 1971.

As a memorial to her years at the school, a service was held in St. Mary's Church and an inscribed oak seat bought for the grounds.

Miss Badland was an outstanding administrator and is remembered as always strict and fair by her pupils. She seemed remote to them but remembered every pupil by name and cared deeply about the development of her school. She, in her turn, contributed to the history of Hitchin Girls' Grammar School.

Drawing by Amanda Birkinshaw 1980–87.

STAFF APPOINTMENTS DURING MISS BADLAND'S TIME 1945–1962

1945–1962	Mary A. Badland, Headmistress	Classics, Timetable, Examinations Results
1945–1946	Barbara M. Bell, Mrs.	Music
1945–1947	Enid Roberts	French
1945–1946	Nora M. Thomas	French
1946–1949	Jean N. Butlin, Mrs. (Pupil '19–'28)	French
1946–1947	Doreen V. Hirst	Physical Training, Games
1946–1947	Jean M. Irwin	Class Singing, Piano
1946–1967	Abigail Lamb, Senior Mistress '52–'54	Head of Geography, Careers for 1 year VI
1946	Constance M. Leigh, Mrs.	Music

1947–1949	Doris M. Baxter	French
1947–1951	Audrey Errock (Mrs. Townsend)	French, German, Guides
1947–1948	Ada G. Freeman	Mathematics
1947–1948	Joyce M. Lazenby	General Science
1947–1955	Vivien A. Lewis	Physical Training, Games
1947–1972	Ruth B. Stovin	Head of Music, Choir, Orchestra
1948–1950	Honor E. Chamberlain	Mathematics, French
1948–1952	Audry C. Howard (Mrs. Milner)	English
1948–1963	Joan Williams Senior Mistress '56–'58	Head of History, Careers
1948–1950	Margaret Wood	Physical Training, Games
1949–1971	Kathleen Britton, Senior Mistress '58–'60 Deputy Headmistress '65–'71	Head of Modern Languages, Save the Children Fund '66
1949–1950	Cicely M. Fillmore	Botany, Zoology, General Science
1949–1954	Margaret H. Morrow (Mrs. Nicholls)	Head of Domestic Science
1949–1953	Janet Mothersill (Pupil '20–'25)	Head of Art and Crafts
1949–1952	Brenda M. Pettit	Physics, Chemistry
1950–1958	Gladys Anderton, Mrs.	Mathematics
1950–1967	Marjorie W. Covington, Mrs.	French, Latin
1950–1953	Kathleen M. Farmer	Geography
1950–1951	Mlle. Letoudal	French Assistante
1950–1953	Shelagh M. Morley	Physical Training, Games
1950–?	? Wilkins	?
1950–1955	I. June Williams	Chemistry, Biology
1951–1955	Josephine M. Daintree	English, Latin, Drama
1951–1954	G. Betty Hilsum, Mrs.	French, German
1951–1969	Edith M. Middlemast	Music, Piano
1952–1957 (+'72–'84)	Barbara Barker (Mrs. Graebe)	English, Drama
1952–1960	Eileen M. Corrigan	Head of Scripture, Latin
1952–1953	Marion Cox	Physics, General Science
1953–1957	Joan R. Hasler	History, Junior Latin
1953–1954 (+'58–'60)	Nicole A. Marzac	French Assistante
1953–1954	? Pull	Art
1953–1954	? Roberts	?
1953–1954	Heather M. Williamson	Geography, English
1953–1954	Jean M. Woodward	Physical Education
1954–1965	Claudia O. Critchley, Mrs.	Physics
1954–1957	Mary S. Eva	Physical Education
1954–1955	Janette Lees (Mrs. Lamont)	French
1954–1973	Margaret E. Naylor	Head of Art
1954–1958	Patricia Richardson (Mrs. Willmott)	French
1955–1957	Jean A. Baldock (Mrs. Mobbs)	Art, Craft
1955–1971	Elaine M. Bolton, Second Mistress '60–'62	Head of Mathematics, Head Year I & II
1955–1967	Marion E. Clarke	Latin
1955–1984	Patricia E. Fletcher, Deputy Head '73–'84	Head of Domestic Science and Needlework
1955–1957	Audrey A. Heap	English, Latin
1955–1959	Patricia Hughes	Head of Physical Education
1955–1959	Olive I. Othen	Geography
1955–1962	Ronald P. Weatherhead	Chemistry, Mathematics

1955–1956	Kathleen M. Wilden	French, German
1956–1957	Mlle. de Chanroud	French Assistante
1956–1964	Amelia R. Kaye	French
1956–1979	Maureen E. O'Connell	English, Latin, Drama, Classical Studies, Librarian '71–'79
1956–1959	Mary Smith, Mrs.	Physics, Chemistry, Mathematics, Magazine Treasurer
1957–1962	Rosamund Andrew	Art, Illustration, Lithography, Crafts
1957–1960	Olive F. Bentley	History
1957–1964	Margot D. Jefferis (Mrs. Sampson)	English, Drama
1957–1967	Nancy J. Waddilove	Physical Education, Head of Physical Education '59–'67
1958–1981	Isabel M. Blackman, Deputy Head '71–'81	Head of English '61–'79, Drama, School Magazine, Save the Children Fund
1958–1960 (+'53–'54)	Nicole A. Marzac, Mlle.	French, German
1958–1961	Sheila D. Penfold (Mrs. Maynard)	Mathematics
1959–1962	Frances B. Jenkins	Physical Education
1959–1962	Joyce A. Ransley, Mrs.	Geography
1959–1968	Margaret J. Stunden, Mrs.	Head of Biology, Mathematics, Careers, Timetable '62, Religious Education
1959–1969	Joan M. Wills, Mrs.	Mathematics, Magazine Treasurer, Savings
1960–1964	Sheila M. King	History
1960–1962	Mary B. Luker, Mrs.	Science, Mathematics
1960–1980	Enid F. Rock	French, German, Assistant Examinations Officer
1960–1971	Ada L. Shepherd, Mrs.	Economics, Geography, Scripture, English, Arithmetic
1961–1962	Rita M. Killick, Mrs.	Junior Mathematics
1961–1965	Gay M. Pierpoint	English

1945–1946 Gwen Roberts

Prefects: Joyce Burgess, Jennifer Chear, April Davis, Eileen Dawson, Constance Flemons, Mary Garnham, Janette Kerr, Renée King, Sheila Marshall, Eileen Northover, Mary Plummer, Margaret Potts, Josephine Thurlow, Jean Wren, Muriel Batt, Margaret Day, Pat Davies, Marguerite Delavenay, June Fuller, Betty Godfrey, Brenda Philpott, Molly Turner.
Games Captain: Joyce Burgess.

This was a year which produced great and far-reaching changes in the school. Not only was it the first year of peace time but there was a new headmistress, Miss Badland, and many changes in the staff, who struggled with the implications of the new Education Act. Three of the school governors died, including Mr. Hugh Exton Seebohm who had been Chairman of the Governors since 1931.

Some things remained constant in the continuation of regular school lectures and, in November, Mr. Grant spoke of the 'Aftermath of War in the Orient'; in December the senior School was addressed by Miss Ellis, the Warden of the

Settlement, and in June a lecturer from Cambridge spoke on 'Economics'. During the Easter term, in lighter vein, there was a marionette display and in June a swimming demonstration by Mrs. Badcock who had represented Great Britain in the 1928 and 1932 Olympic teams.

'What awful songs!' was the initial reaction to the selection of pieces for the singing competition but after some weeks' practice 'the songs were not so bad after all, in fact we enjoyed singing them!' Forms IVb and IVc took part for the first time and IVb were rewarded by winning the new Junior trophy. The Junior Sixth won both the Senior Trophy and the sight reading test. Further music was provided by a quartet and the usual carol concert in December whilst drama was represented by Laurence Housman's 'Bethlehem' at Christmas and 'Tobias and the Angel' performed by the Sixth form drama group in May.

A party of girls was taken to Southwark Cathedral for the first post-war Annual Mission Service and afterwards went to a church in Camberwell for 'a very good tea'. There they heard of the vicar's work over the past fifty years' ministry, and the recent sufferings of his parish during the blitz. One Sunday the Communion Service was abandoned in order to prepare breakfast for two hundred and sixty people who had lost their homes the previous night. Visits were also made to a Greek Art Exhibition and to the Science Museum before the end of the school year.

The Arts Club was restarted during the year and covered a wide spectrum of activities whilst the World Affairs Group maintained a varied programme, with a Cambridge town councillor talking about local government and an ex-administrative officer from West Africa telling how the Nigerian people were being educated for future self government. Perhaps most interesting of all were Mr. and Mrs. Chalkley telling of their experiences as internees of the Japanese along with pupils of the girls' school in the Chinese settlement where they had all lived.

The new Education Act brought change and reorganisation of the Library when more money was made available to replace and buy new stock. Various sections were moved to new positions and the boarders were thanked for their help with the manual work. The working of the new Education Act made possible the abolition of the library subscriptions, and the County Council now provided a grant for fiction as well as non-fiction books.

Va asked to be allowed to use fountain pens. Miss Badland agreed 'so long as pens were not lost and ink was not spilt'.

The magazine notes two effects of the recent war: Diana Cooper died as the result of an accident while serving in the V.A.D. (Voluntary Aid Detachment) in Singapore, and M. Putley returned to Va[3] after being evacuated to America where she spent five years in the appropriately named Bancroft School in Worcester, Mass.

1946–1947   Marguerite Delavenay

Prefects: April Davis, Betty Warren, Muriel Batt, Pamela Beckham, Evelyn Boesen, Monica Bransom, Claire Cole, Betty Coleman, Pat Davies, Margaret Day, Joyce Finlay, June Fuller, Betty Godfrey, Lalia Graydon, Isobel Harkness, Philippa Hesketh, Brenda Philpott, Rita Plumb, Nancy Sampson, Molly Turner, Sheila Brown, Mary Elizabeth Fyfe, Joan Wade.
Games Captain: Margaret Day.

The school magazine reflected the general easing of supplies after the war with its better quality paper and the appearance of several school photographs, including that of Miss Flinn who retired at the end of the summer term after twenty-seven years at the school – twenty-five of them as Second Mistress. A school group photograph is also recorded as having been taken in the early summer.

Lectures recorded during the year included one about 'The United States of America', 'Behind the Scenes in Broadcasting House', and 'Parliamentary Procedure'. There was a Nativity play and one actor took all the parts in a performance of 'Twelfth Night'. For the last week of term films were shown every day on the 'gebescope' – a piece of equipment which is now obscured by the mists of time and recollection! There was also a 'Macbeth' recital.

School life was slowly changing after the coming of peace with greater emphasis on widening horizons restricted for so long by the war. More visits were made: to see French Tapestries and the King's Pictures; to the Mission Jubilee Service; to 'L'Avare' at L'Institut Français; and to 'The Frogs', a play performed entirely in Greek at Cambridge. Less academic was the coach trip to Wimbledon where the girls saw Budge Patty, Bob Falkenburg, Jack Kramer and Yvon Petra, Louise Brough and Doris Hart either playing or being mobbed by the crowd. A group of Dutch children visited Hitchin and seven of the girls found hostesses at the school. All had a thoroughly good time and the English girls looked forward to visiting Holland during the summer holidays. The school had proposed a joint Dramatic Society of the Grammar Schools but the headmaster of the boys' school could 'see no means of making these arrangements possible at the moment'. He did, however, allow a joint Social near Christmas.

The games report states, 'The less said the better about our last hockey and netball season. All we can say is we were lucky to get a match the first and last Saturdays of the Spring Term!' Thus is the memorable winter of 1946 – faithfully recorded, most matches having been scratched owing to snow. It was nevertheless a good year for the games teams: only three matches were lost, all of them rounders fixtures, in the whole year.

A country dancing display in June caused some problems of dress for those girls dancing as boys. A few had pre-war 'hand-me-down' smocks, some made ingenious use of sacking and others performed miracles with old army shirts. While being eminently suitable, these were, in some cases, extremely short! The 'girls' fared better, needing only 'bright cotton frocks, gay hair ribbons and coloured ankle socks'. Visitors entered into the spirit of the afternoon and arrived in 'gay summer frocks and hats reminiscent of a pre-war Royal Garden Party'. Music was provided by two pianos, three violins and a drummer – all members of staff and pupils. All concerned had dreaded poor weather but the day 'began well and ended even better'. A collection was made at the end of the display, when more than £30 was collected and divided between the Association for providing Playing Fields and the Nursery Department of the Union of Girls' Schools in London.

With widening interests in other directions, both the Arts Club and the World Affairs Group complained of lack of members and interest.

It was generally agreed by the School Council that a biennial Sports Day should be held in future, but a proposal for extra games teams for younger members of the Senior School was quashed on the grounds of lack of time for practice and matches. The Senior VIth had complained at the general untidiness in the school. Some 'steps had been taken' and now 'the impression one gets is of more tidy lockers, corridors and grounds. May this continue until the "bad mark" book becomes unnecessary!'

Hitchin held a Safety Week in June with several competitions yielding prizes to our girls. In the Junior Section of the Poster Competition the first prize of £3 went

1947. A general view of the finale, in which all the dancers took part.
[Herts and Beds Express at Hitchin Museum, Miss M. Crystal]

to B. Vizard, second prize of £2 to A. Richards and the fourth prize to P. Pope. P. Tompkins was 3rd in the Fancy Dress competition, but the most notable success was that of P. Towlson who won a Raleigh cycle after correctly identifying its parts.

1947–1948   Margaret Day

Prefects: J. Finlay, B. Philpott, N. Sampson, R. Hesketh, M. Delavenay, S. Brown, W. Clements, M. Cooper, E. Coxall, E. McWhirter, M. Palmer, J. Sanders, N. Shepherd, M. Taylor, J. Wade, W. Cole, P. Fyfe, O. Hunt, D. Jeffs, G. Poulton, M. Stobart.
Games Captain: N. Shepherd.
Tennis Captain: F. Davies.
Swimming Captain: S. Brown.

A highlight of this school year was the celebration in April of the Silver Wedding of King George VI and Queen Elizabeth, which was declared a school holiday. Miss Squire and Miss Hughes both retired after teaching at the school for twenty-eight years, and the former presented the School with the Hymn board 'which now seems so much a part of the Hall that we wonder how we could ever have been without it!' Miss Saunders' service with the School was only a little less when she left after twenty-six years on the staff. The school magazine published, this year, a photograph taken at the summer gathering the previous year showing all three headmistresses, past and present, who had served Hitchin Girls' Grammar School. A unique record! In the Easter holidays the two games fields were completely reconditioned and sown with new grass seed, so marking still further the move to peace time. This proved to be so fascinating a sight to some of the girls that the windows were white-washed to help concentrate their minds on their school work!

Unusually, there were no lectures in the Autumn term but this was rectified after the Christmas holiday. Commandant Vivier spoke about France, and the pupils from the Boys' Grammar School joined us in hearing a fascinating lecture about Penicillin. In the summer term the Bishop of Armidale from New South Wales talked of his life in Australia and said that more immigrants were needed in that country, and that the girls would be sure of a warm welcome should they choose to make a new life 'down under'. This term there was a second talk about France, a lecture about Charles Lamb, and Mrs. Gavin Jones giving the girls some helpful advice about Flower Arranging. The Hogarth Puppets visited the school in the autumn and there was a film about Atomic Physics.

Music was well represented during the year, notably when the H.G.G.S. School Choir won the Challenge Shield at the North London Music Festival and received their prize from Princess Marie Louise. The choir was also invited, on four

1948.   Tennis coaching on the lower field courts.   [Pictorial at Hitchin Museum]

occasions, to sing at evensong in St. Mary's Church. There were two piano recitals, Intimate Opera, and a rendering of French songs. There was a visit by the Jacques String Orchestra in the spring; Miss Badland took a party of girls to the Central Hall, Westminster, for a special children's concert and there was a Chamber Opera by St. Christopher's Players.

The VI form gave a performance of 'The Housemaster', a comedy which seems to have produced a great deal of laughter, both intentionally and by accident. 'The cast was not ready in time and a flustered producer went in search of a "Pianist" to play SOMETHING' – the choice of music seems to have been rather inappropriate; then an ash-tray rolling under the sofa seems to have caused some problems which were compounded by finding a lighted cigarette smouldering on the upholstery. Smoking on stage also provided a vain attempt to light a cigar and as the final curtain fell, one performer fell backwards through it!

The first outing of the year was to the Children's Theatre in Letchworth to see 'The Immortal Lady', while a visit to the Royal Academy for an exhibition of Indian Art gave illustration to a lecture on the same subject the previous week. A party of girls went to the usual service at Southwark Cathedral and some went to the St. Albans Pageant. A hundred girls went to Wimbledon and were fortunate to see Drobny play Cucelli in a game which lasted for more than two hours. This was not the famous Drobny marathon since on this occasion he lost the match.

This year saw the revival of the first Flower Show since the beginning of the war. 'The number of entries was amazing' and all exhibits were on show in the Geography room where Miss Flinn came to judge them. Also in the school calendar were 'Dance' and 'Flannel Dance' for the first time. Alas, the school clubs were still in decline and it was proposed that they be either 'revived or abolished'. A small museum was set up this year and there was a request for 'the loan of things of interest, for one week'. It was proposed that the V and IV forms should hear the schools' broadcasts, but it was pointed out by members of the staff that the school had very few wireless sets and the broadcasts seldom fitted in with the syllabus. This revolutionary proposal was not pursued.

The school was fortunate, in May, to secure the services of two Lawn Tennis Association coaches. They guided a huge group of the IV forms in court craft and in improving their strokes before helping the School Tennis teams and giving an exhibition match.

1948–1949 Joan Wade

Prefects: B. Fuller, W. Cole, F. Davies, A. Fitch, V. Fox, P. Fyfe, D. Highton, O. Hunt, O. Knight, G. Poulton, E. Wood, V. Bidwell, M. Deacon, M. Lander, J. Luther, P. Monk, L. Morriss, P. Pope, M. Streeter, M. Whitby.
Games Captain: F. Davies.
Swimming Captain: J. Sanders.

The year started with some difficulty; work in the kitchens, which should have been completed during the summer, had not started when the pupils returned in the autumn, and for some weeks nearly 400 dinners had to be served daily with workmen in the premises where the food was prepared and cooked.

By the death, in April, of Reginald Hine, the school lost a historian and its friend. Mr. Hinks and Mr. Saunders, both governors of the school since 1940, also died, as did Mr. Shillitoe, who was Clerk of Governors before the school was taken over by the Hertfordshire County Council.

On a happier note, Miss Badland was awarded a travelling scholarship which she planned to use in the autumn of 1949.

Three new hard tennis courts were officially opened by the Headmistress with Mr. Widdows, Chairman of the Governors, 'cutting the tape', and three additional grass courts on the top field produced a new burst of enthusiasm for the game. The V and VI forms were allowed to use the hard courts after school 'if they provide their own equipment'.

A minor change in school dress rules allowed the wearing of summer frocks before the half term.

The library was completely re-classified during the year and changed to the 'Dewey System' commonly used in public and college libraries. This was a great undertaking and advice was needed: Mr. Jones at the Boys' Grammar School allowed inspection of the Mattocke Library; Mr. Ashby from Hitchin Public Library and Mr. Miles gave unstintingly of their help. The boarders were again pressed into service for moving books.

Only three lectures were given at the school; Mr. Speakman spoke about 'Local Government', Miss Waite about the 'Mission' and Miss Charlesworth spoke of the work of U.N.E.S.C.O. Pupils from five other schools were invited to attend the latter.

Visits were made to Letchworth for two 'Book' lectures and to hear Peter Scott talking about 'Wild Fowl' and the work of the Severn Trust. The girls also went to the Boys' Grammar School to see Hogarth's Puppets and to Berkhamsted Boys' School for a performance of Aristophanes' 'Birds'.

The National Youth Orchestra visited Hitchin during the Easter holidays and used the school for both rehearsals and accommodation. The girls had the

Down in the form gardens in the lower field. This photograph, taken five years later, shows that the hobby remained popular.   [Sandra Pickard, Ic]

boarders' dormitory and the boys slept in the gym with some classrooms also being used. Musical events in term time included a piano recital by Mrs. Peckett, visits to concerts in London and choral singing in St. Mary's.

The most ambitious undertaking by the girls was a production of 'Papageno' – an adaptation of 'The Magic Flute'. Provision of suitable costumes caused some concern since clothing was still rationed, but the girls were generous in providing clothing coupons with which to buy material. The 'queen's ladies' were strictly segregated from the 'slaves' in the dressing room – a 'colour bar' made necessary by the need to keep the slaves' 'blacking' off all the other costumes! Moving behind the backcloth was tricky since it was made of stiff paper and made a deafening rattle if brushed against.

Visits during the year included those to the British Museum to see the Elgin Marbles, the Tower of London, St. Albans and Wimbledon. A group of girls again spent an autumn week in the potato fields helping with the harvest.

A growing national interest in gardening was reflected in the school when plans were agreed to allow the Junior girls to have gardens in the lower field.

After a break of four years a Sports Day was organised in early June. Unfortunately the event was rained off after only three races so competitors and visitors retreated to the Art Room where the Flower Show was staged.

The H.G.G.S. first swimming match took place in June against a team from Christ's Hospital but sadly no record survives of the outcome.

1949–1950 Madge Streeter

Deputy Head Girl: M. Deacon.
School Captain: D. Drake.
Prefects: C. Baldwin, E. Wood, J. Bayley, V. Bidwell, C. Delavenay, J. Hales, M. Hardwicke, P. Monk, B. Preston, A. Taylor, B. Young, M. Whitby, J. Deards, P. Hesketh, K. Howard, A. Kirby, A. Newman, S. Overton, A. Patrick, M. Timms, J. Walsby.
Swimming Captain: M. Lander.

Miss Gosnell's death in October severed a long, affectionate tie with the first Headmistress of Hitchin Girls' Grammar School. Miss Mortimer retired after twenty-nine years' service, and Miss Read had seen all her pupils go into the 'big school' before taking a well earned rest. With her retirement went the tradition of a Kindergarten class at the School.

H.M. Inspectors visited for four days in the summer term and seemed satisfied with the standards of both staff and pupils.

A full calendar of extra-curricular activities included a lantern lecture on 'Camouflage in Nature' and a talk about Paris. Miss Badland returned from America and fascinated the girls with an account of her travels, including the outward voyage on the 'Queen Mary' and the return on the 'Queen Elizabeth'. Music was well represented by a recital of folk songs, a flautist and a performance on the 'cello by Mme. Alvin held at the Boys' Grammar School.

Music making, too, had a busy year, when the school choir continued the tradition of singing at St. Mary's and performed the 'Messiah', in two parts, at the school. The first was in conjunction with the carol concert and the second at Easter.

The boarders performed 'Peter Pan' and the Drama Club tackled 'The Ghost Train', both in the spring term.

Many visits were made in the year, notably those close to home. Mr. Bowman at the Station Flour Mill talked about the working of one of Hitchin's oldest industries, and this was logically followed by a visit to Stevens' bakehouse in Walsworth Road to see bread being made. Miss Aillie Latchmore guided a party round Ransom's Distillery, samples of their drugs being taken back to the school to be displayed in a glass case in the Geography Room. Hitchin Museum was also visited as was a 'Leisure Hours' exhibition staged at the Town Hall.

Games enthusiasts went to Wimbledon and to the England v. Scotland International Hockey Match, won by England 6–2. Doreen Drake and Irene Charter reached the semi-final in the Senior section of the Harpenden Schools Tennis Tournament where they were beaten by the pair who eventually won the tournament.

Election fever which gripped the country in February led to the enthusiasm for holding a mock election at the school. Party political meetings at the Boys' Grammar School were attended before three days were spent by the girls' candidates on their own election campaigns and subsequent balloting. Shirley Osborne, the Liberal candidate, wrote at the time:

> 'A great deal of canvassing and declamation of the rights of man had preceded this. The School had been unusually gay with posters urging one to vote for the Liberal, Labour or Conservative candidate and red, blue and yellow ribbons decorated many juvenile tunics. One Communist poster exhorted the proletariat to boycott the bourgeois, imperialist elections. As was expected, the Conservative candidate obtained a majority 76 votes, but the Liberals surprised everybody with 53 votes and so defeated Labour with only 35 votes!'

The School Council discussed the forfeiture of lost property. This practice had led to enormous amounts being gathered in and having to be stored. Instead, it was agreed that girls who transgressed should deprive their form of points in connection with the 'Tidiness Picture' and the culprits should be required, in some way, to help in cleaning the school.

The previous year the girls asked to say 'Amen' at the end of prayers instead of singing it. They now asked to reverse this decision, a move which was accepted by Miss Badland with the proviso that she would not be prepared to change it again in another six months!

1950–1951 Betty Preston

Deputy Head Girl: A. Kirby.
Prefects: J. Hales, S. Overton, K. Howard, J. Walsby, S. Beach, A. Kaufmann, B. Crabbe, S. Evans, W. Kirby, M. Cole, A. Robertson, S. Mauger, J. Darby, G. Boorman.
Games Captain: A. Patrick.
Swimming Captain: S. Beach.

The Festival of Britain provided the highlight of this year in which the Queen came to visit 'Hitchin's Historic Pageant'. Yvonne Else, Ia, described the Queen's arrival, 'I had never imagined her to be so lovely! She was wearing a powder blue hat with darker blue feathers in it. Her skin was of the rosiest colour and her dark brown hair peeped beneath her hat. The royal car passed and that was the last I saw of her'. Some pupils from the school appeared in the pageant dressed in stiff collars, with black ties and straw boaters, which the earliest pupils at the school were expected to wear.

The first G.C.E. Examinations were taken in the summer of 1951 and the school magazine was changed in size to a half size 'pocket edition'.

Just before Christmas, the boarders moved from the main school building into Highbury House and enjoyed their new quarters in 'this beautiful house'. In the spring term the pupils were still taking their meals in the main dining room and suffered greatly from the weather as a result. This was rectified and all boarders' meals in the summer term were served at Highbury House. Fourteen seniors slept there; the remaining eighteen boarders who slept in the dormitory at the school, spent the rest of their free time at Highbury House.

Interest in lectures appears to have declined and only one, 'Hertfordshire Place Names', was given. Interest in music was maintained with two piano recitals and a further one with violin. English and French folk songs were performed at the school and visits made to 'Let's Make an Opera', and to a Concert and Gym Display at Barclay School, Stevenage. The Drama Club presented 'The Zeal of Thine House' – an ambitious undertaking about the building of Canterbury Cathedral which required elaborate sets and, at times, many players on the stage. Since four of these were angels resplendent with impressive wings, and the space was somewhat restricted, it was not easy to stage, but the difficulties were well mastered. Jennifer Hale is mentioned as having taken the chief acting honours as the cathedral architect, though all the players performed well.

There were the usual school theatre visits – 'The Merchant of Venice' at Bedford, 'Bartholomew's Fair' at the Old Vic and, nearer home, the Thespian production of 'Bitter Sweet'.

Apart from Wimbledon and the Hockey International in March, England v. Wales, the year seems to have been dominated by the Festival of Britain and the local pageant, since no other school trips were made. There was a visit to the school in the summer by 'the Mothers from Rotherhythe' – presumably parents of the children helped by the Mission.

1951. Old Girls' Tea in the Courtyard
(Esther Speed (Brayshaw)]

The Science Club had its inaugural meeting at the start of the autumn term and fulfilled an ambitious programme during the year, including a visit to Russell's Leather Works in Bancroft – 'fascinating, though a little smelly', thought J. Walsby – and to Hitchin Gas Works.

In June the school held an Open Day in conjunction with the Flower Show. On the appointed day, after prayers, all the competitors set to work, in the courtyard, before carrying their efforts into the Hall where they were to be judged by Mrs. Ena Harkness. During the afternoon the Junior school pupils gave dancing and eurythmics displays, followed by the Seniors doing gymnastics. Next came the form running races when IIIb won the Junior Trophy and VI the Senior. Vases were presented to the two forms with the most points in the Flower Show – IVb in the Senior School and IIIb, their second success of the day.

At the end of July, the O.G.A. held its usual summer gathering. It was, however, an unusual and special day because the window, commissioned in memory of Miss Gosnell, was about to be unveiled above the main school entrance. Miss Seebohm had been invited to have this honour but a bout of illness confined her to her home. In her place, Miss Pennefather, niece of Miss Gosnell, performed the ceremony before the visitors had a special tea, served in the courtyard.

1951–1952   Ann Patrick

Deputy Head Girls: A. Kaufmann, B. Crabbe.
Prefects: S. Evans, A. Robertson, S. Mauger, J. Darby, I. Charter, R. Goldmark, S. Johns, A. Marchant, M. Sumner, P. Dowell, A. Harris, B. Lovett, J. Loveday, J. Clarke, J. Butlin, E. Stoddart, C. Newsom, J. Horrell, S. McConochie.
Games Captain: W. Kirby.
Swimming Captain: J. Meek.

The death of King George VI overshadowed the spring term, and a memorial service was held in the school Hall at which two of the King's favourite hymns were sung.

The school lost one of its oldest friends in December when Miss Esther Seebohm died. She had taken a great interest in everything connected with School, and pupils were always welcome at her lovely house in Benslow, which she left to the Hitchin Rural Music School.

Workmen had been busy building in what had been Miss Badland's sunken garden, and now a new domestic science room and two new form rooms were brought into use. The old domestic science room (now Room 20) was converted into an extra wing of the dining room, while the Museum was restored to its place in the corridor.

The school calendar reported, for the first time, a 'Meeting of Third Form Parents' and it is reasonable to assume that this was the first year it took place.

The Staff minutes recorded, 'school has responded well to the recommendation that clothes should be changed for games and gymnastics'. Up to this time, normal school clothing had to be worn for games; knickers and normal blouse for gymnastics.

109

The boarders, in their first year at Highbury House, were unfortunate in losing both the House Matron, Miss Potter, and her assistant, Miss Bird, both of whom had been at the school for four years.

After its first burst of enthusiasm, the Science Club suffered from waning interest. Those who did attend had a return visit to Russell's Tannery and were given specimens of parchment and dyed leather which were put into the school museum. Mr. Greville Young, a surgeon from Lister Hospital, gave a talk 'Round and about the Life of Lord Lister' – a useful preliminary to a visit made to the hospital later in the summer. The Council for Education in World Citizenship (C.E.W.C.) also complained of lack of enthusiasm and support. Perhaps the formation of a Debating Society was an indication of the wish to participate rather than be a passive audience. There was one lecture, on the work of the United Nations.

There was a recital of 'Babar the Elephant' and one by a Woodwind Quartet from the Royal Philharmonic Orchestra. Owing to the very bad weather, two instrumentalists arrived very late so the programme began with only the clarinet and flute. The school orchestra increased considerably in size and added more violins, a viola and two clarinets, whilst the 'cellos increased to four. The choir gave a concert of secular and sacred songs for the Parent–Teacher Association (P.T.A.) meeting in the newly opened village school in Little Wymondley.

A school visit was made to hear the Archbishop of Canterbury, Dr. Fisher, preach on 'Vocation' at St. Alban's Abbey, and parties went to Cambridge to see 'Julius Caesar' and to the Phoenix Theatre in London for 'Much Ado About Nothing', whilst the school's own production was 'Lady Precious Stream'. This Chinese comedy with its sophisticated humour is set in a highly stylised convention totally unlike our own. Nevertheless, it was performed with enthusiasm, and tripping on tip-toe, with knees together, was to be seen all round the school for weeks before the performance. It was judged 'a fine production'.

It was a good year for games – the first XI lost only one match (against the Old Girls) and were beaten by Hertfordshire and Essex High School in the final of the Inter-Schools' Hockey Tournament. The 2nd XI were unbeaten except in the tournament, and the Senior Netball team was unbeaten except in the Schools' Netball Tournament.

1952–1953 Anne Harris

Deputy Head Girl: S. Johns.
Prefects: J. Loveday, A. Gee, J. Horrell, B. Lovett, V. Douglas, P. Dowell, P. Gorman, M. Lloyd, M. Morgan, M. Smith, M. Withers, M. Whitworth, B. Hill, T. Rose, D. Sexton, A. Stokes, P. Webb, A. Ashworth, A. Metcalf, D. Biddlecombe, G. Fay, E. Chennells.
Games Captain: Ann Gee. **Secretary:** P. Gorman.
Swimming Captain: Judith Horrell.

After last year's sadness when the King died, this was a year of jubilation with the Coronation of Queen Elizabeth II. On 22nd May, Mr. W. Hill, Chairman of the Urban District Council, presented the school with souvenir copies of Richard

Dimbleby's book, 'Elizabeth Our Queen' and a coronation mug each, before the pupils attended a special service in St. Mary's. This was arranged for the secondary school pupils in the town, and the Rev. Peter Hartley gave an informative address on the significance of the coronation ceremony.

Sweet rationing, abandoned for a short time in 1948, was finally abolished and the 'D' and 'E' coupons became part of history.

The first Harvest Festival took place in October, as agreed the previous year, and the fruit, flowers and vegetables were taken to the Mission in London.

The price of the magazine was reluctantly increased to remain financially viable, and the School Council also agreed that a Ballroom Dancing Club might be held one dinner hour a week during the winter.

The previous year it was agreed to put a seat in the wood; this had now been done. Now there was a request for a litter bin. Without discussion this suggestion was carried out at once!

In the magazine was published a photograph of fourteen of the fifteen girls then in the school whose mothers had also been pupils.

An enthusiastic VIth form put new vigour into the Science Club, which had a full and varied programme: visits to Ransom's Distillery, St. Christopher's Press and Letchworth Museum. At the Royal Festival Hall the members heard Peter Scott on 'A Wild Goose Chase' about a recent trip to Iceland, illustrated by his lightning charcoal sketches of his subject. Dr. Gee came to school to talk about modern research into rubber.

The Current Affairs Club also had a successful year with talks on race relations in South Africa, women in India, and about Nyasaland, Pakistan and Lebanon.

The local M.P., Mr. Fisher, conducted the club members around the Houses of Parliament.

In the spring, a large group of girls went to hear Eric Skipton telling of the attempts to climb Mount Everest and the men who had tried and failed. In 1951 he was asked to lead a reconnaissance expedition with Edmund Hillary to find a route to the South Col and two months after the lecture we all learned that Hillary and the Sherpa guide, Tensing, had conquered Everest just before the Coronation.

A visit of a different kind was made when a party went to the Chelsea Flower Show. On arrival the girls broke up into small groups to make their way round the large marquee and see the exotic exhibits.

The highlight of the musical year was the occasion when the Leonard Hirsch Orchestra visited the school for a concert to which members of other grammar schools were invited.

The school staged its own musical event in the Drama Club operetta 'The Great Bell of Burley', preceded by a short one-act play, 'The Sparrow's Flight', written and produced by Miss Daintree. The task of presenting a play in which all the characters are men and all the actors girls can present problems but was tackled with care and enthusiasm. As a result of the two performances, the school was able to buy a set of curtains which would be of immense value in future productions.

The games report for the year has nothing to distinguish it from many others but the account of the International between England and Belgium deserves mention. The result was a win for England 11–0. Ann Gee Senior Sixth reports 'Belgium may not have won, but they are the team which the crowd of 43,000 will remember. Having lost, they skipped happily off the field and their sportsmanship well earned for them the terrific applause they were given'.

1953–1954 Margaret Lloyd

Deputy Head Girl: Margaret Smith.
Prefects: A. Gee, M. Lloyd, P. Dowell, M. Morgan, M. Smith, M. Whitworth, M. Withers, G. Fay, A. Willsdon, S. Bryant, S. Chapman, M. Kerrigan, C. Fulton, S. Bonsey, S. Sumner, D. Humphreys, A. Craddock, M. Pearce, G. Boorman, A. Silvey, I. Patrick, M. Kavanagh, D. Shaw, G. Poole, M. Selby, A. Gorman.
Games Captain: Ann Willsdon. **Secretary:** Myra Selby.
Swimming Captain: Ann Gee.

Three very good friends of the school died: Mr. Widdows had been a school governor since 1934 and had been chairman from 1946 onwards. Miss Hughes had been a teacher for thirty-two years and even after her retirement was a frequent and welcome visitor. Memorial services to both were attended by some staff and sixth form pupils – Mr. Widdows' at St. Mary's and Miss Hughes' at the Friends' Meeting House. Mrs. Palmer, a governor appointed by Newnham College, had served the school well for ten years and would also be sorely missed.

A great event! The new Domestic Science building was at last completed and the three first forms and Va were moved to classrooms there.

Early in the autumn term a party of old people from the Mission was entertained and, walking round the grounds, greatly admired the view from 'the school on the hill'. After a hearty tea they were given a concert of short sketches and a suitably serious rendering of the Hippopotamus Song! The guests, not to be outdone, responded with a medley of old songs accompanied on the piano by a lady of 80 years. D. M. Kerrigan wrote a detailed account of this visit. Later in the year a party of 'young Mums' from the same source came to Hitchin and saw a production of the play.

It was decided that the names of the form mistresses would be added to the cards showing room numbers, and that all unclaimed and unmarked lost property would be sold at the end of each term and the proceeds sent to the Mission.

The school clubs all showed a marked upsurge in support and fulfilled interesting programmes. Debates seem to have dominated the year starting with 'A Woman's Place is in the Home', at Hitchin Boys' Grammar School, and 'This House Deplores Co-education', at Alleynes. Unfortunately, no record survives of either outcome!

The Pestalozzi village in Switzerland was still a very new concept in 1954 since it was still only eight years since the idea was born of giving orphan children, of all nationalities, a real home together. The girls were very impressed by a lecture telling of the spread and aims of this movement.

Specially memorable visits were those to the Ideal Homes Exhibition and to Westminster Abbey when Dr. Tanner, Keeper of the Muniments – title deeds and charters – gave a special tour of those parts of the building not usually open to the public.

The outstanding theatre visit was undoubtedly that made to the Old Vic, for a performance of 'Hamlet' – Richard Burton in the title part, Claire Bloom as Ophelia, Fay Compton as Gertrude and Michael Hordern, even then playing the part of an old man, Polonius. A memorable peformance indeed!

This must have given a very high standard to aim for in the Drama Club production of 'She Stoops to Conquer'. The Hertfordshire Pictorial wrote at the time '. . . no idle flattery this. I have never seen a more polished performance on any amateur theatrical stage'. Praise indeed.

As always, the games won far exceeded those lost throughout the year. It was decided to sacrifice rounders in favour of junior tennis, though it could still be played for some games lessons. A. Gee was selected to play in the Hertfordshire Junior County Hockey Team and M. Morgan and B. Whaley were chosen as reserves. The school again went to the Hockey International and saw England v. Scotland – the seats were 3/– each and the programme 6d!

It was decided to start a Games Fund, to help defray some of the heavy cost of sports equipment, and voluntary regular contributions were sought from each form.

1954–1955   Christine Fulton

Deputy Head Girls: G. Boorman, M. Whitworth.
Prefects: C. Fulton, M. Whitworth, G. Boorman, M. Kavanagh, A. Craddock, D. Humphreys, R. Frost, A. Gorman, P. Gregory, B. Jenkins, S. Jones, J. Patrick, A. Silvey, G. Smith, A. Venning, S. Horrell, P. Withers, S. Ansell, E. Shelford, T. Trenaman, E. Tyler, S. Fay, S. Livings, A. Aitken, J. Hudson, B. Webb, H. Sexton, J. Nuttall.
Games Captain: M. Kavanagh.
Swimming Captain: S. Jones.

The Queen Mother visited Hitchin, in March, to open the new Girls' High School in Bedford Road, and in May parties from both Grammar Schools were in St. Mary's for a broadcast of a sung Eucharist.

There were many changes in the form room arrangements at the H.G.G.S. – all the first forms had been grouped in the new Building, and the Senior Sixth now had thirty members and moved to the old dormitory (now the library) which they converted into a series of private studies. The dining room had been made more attractive with bright curtains and the addition of pictures produced by the students. An attractive Christmas card was on sale this year showing a photograph of the school under a blanket of snow.

'During the Spring Term all the trees on one side of Highbury House were cut down, which caused much disappointment until we (the boarders) learnt that in their place tennis courts were being made.' Thus reported A. Gorman. The magazine editors showed their approval of the new summer dresses: 'This year we have new summer frocks for girls with normal figures! The old frock – made in one size for first formers and sixth formers alike – is becoming rarer. Possibly it has gone out of fashion to have an eighty inch chest, forty inch waist and eighty inch hips!'

The Current Affairs Club had an active year with several speakers and one debate, 'This House agrees with Commercial T.V.'. This revolutionary concept was soundly defeated. The Science Club, too, had a busy series of talks and visits. They now planned to expand to field work and rambles.

Music was not neglected because, apart from the varied music making always present in the school, a party travelled to the Albert Hall to hear 'Messiah' given by the Royal Choral Society and the London Symphony Orchestra, conducted by Sir Malcolm Sargent. Only three weeks later a joint audience from both Grammar Schools enjoyed hearing excerpts from 'Die Meistersinger'.

Many visits figured in the calendar. One party went to the B.B.C. and, on arrival, saw Ronnie Waldman, well known presenter of 'Monday night at Eight', hurrying across the foyer. Another stayed nearer to home and went to the Hitchin Water Works, in Queen Street, where they learned that a million gallons of water – most of it from Charlton – were used in Hitchin each day, and that the water in the tower on the hill came from the Oughton Head Springs.

Longer visits were made to the C.E.W.C. Conference held at the Central Hall, Westminster, during the Christmas holidays and to Dale Fort Field Centre in Pembrokeshire for a Marine Biology Course. For the more adventurous, a visit to the Yorkshire Dales at Easter presented the opportunity to try the thrill of pot holing.

A party of Sixth formers went to Stratford to see Anthony Quayle as Bottom in 'A Midsummer Night's Dream'. This set a standard to aim for in the school's production of 'The Merchant of Venice'. From the newspaper criticism it seems that they succeeded. 'The gods of diction must have looked down . . . it was beautifully spoken' and 'some very able acting . . . all round measure of success'.

The games report 'ups and downs' were unspectacular in this year. It seems that the visit to the Hockey International had moved into the regular school events. This year England beat Wales 6–1. Inflation raised its ugly head in that seat prices had gone up from 3/– to 5/–!

1955–1956 Patricia Withers

Deputy Head Girls: Eileen Shelford, Bridget Webb.
Prefects: Bronwen Jenkins, Judith Nuttall, Helen Sexton, Gillian Allen, Eileen Shelford, Susan Horrell, Patricia Withers, Ann Marlow, Gillian Smith, Yvonne Tapson, Jill Covington, Betty Eggby, Bridget Webb, Patricia Glenwright, Pamela Sharpe, Sheila Fay, Barbara Woolley, Salley Curtis, Marian Watts, Maureen Rutland, Janet Lloyd, Margaret Davies, Jennifer Munday, Hilary Walker, Yvonne Else.
Hockey Captain: Bronwen Jenkins.
Netball Captain: Ann Marlow.
Tennis Captain: Margaret Kime.
Swimming Captain: Susan Horrell.

The Mission, supported by the school for many years, held its Jubilee Service at the Festival Hall. Four members of the sixth form represented the H.G.G.S. in a choir made up of all the schools present. Princess Margaret received, from each school, a purse containing its contribution towards an old people's centre. Our purse was of white silk, embroidered with the school badge by Miss Fletcher and presented by Patricia Withers.

After only a year in their new quarters, the sixth form moved again, into the old main library. The former dormitory now became the library for the whole school, bringing the books of the main, senior fiction and junior sections into one large room. This seems to have been a popular move with all the students, though there was still the annual plea to return books on time.

The School Council met as usual, and for one meeting, the whole school formed the 'Strangers' Gallery'. It was agreed to sing the Lord's Prayer at some Morning Prayer Assemblies for a trial period.

A conference of the Student Christian Movement, held at the Boys' Grammar School, had an audience from most of the schools in the district to listen to a talk 'Why Vocation?' Following this was a further talk and later discussion groups. Perhaps as a result of this day, the senior pupils were moved to start a branch of the Christian Union at the Girls' Grammar School and held three lunch time Bible Study groups within the summer term.

Another new group to be started this year was a Junior Pets Club, which debated hunting, held a quiz and heard several talks by the members about their own pets.

The Current Affairs Club heard of the Law System and the Law Courts, the Press and its activities and how Hitchin Urban District Council ran its affairs. A debate at Alleynes – 'This House believes in National Service for Women' – was soundly beaten. The club held a food sale in the courtyard of apples, chestnuts and groceries and was able to send £6 to the United Nations Children's Fund.

The Council for Education in World Citizenship held its conference, as usual, in London and 2,000 members heard the Rt. Hon. Selwyn Lloyd make his first speech since becoming Foreign Secretary and Earl Attlee in his first public appearance since his retirement as Leader of the Opposition. The most entertaining speaker was Ritchie Calder, Science Editor of the 'News Chronicle'. With the rise of interest in current affairs, the Science club was in the doldrums with only four visits in the autumn term and nothing since.

The musical highlight was a visit to Covent Garden to hear 'The Magic Flute', with Geraint Evans as Papageno. In school the Hirsch String Quartet played for the senior school and the fourth form went to the Boys' School for a similar concert. The school Choir performed Bach's 'Christmas Oratorio' and a visit was made to Cambridge for 'Let's make an Opera', by Britten.

A group of girls went to see 'The Rivals' in which John Clements, Athene Seyler

1st and 2nd XI hockey teams. Captain and goalkeeper of the 1st XI is Bronwen Jenkins on the far right. Maureen Rutland, 2nd XI goalkeeper, is on the left next to Pat Glenwright, Captain 2nd XI, standing back left.   [Maureen Rutland (Conlon)]

and Laurence Harvey appeared. Not wishing to waste any time, they left Hitchin at 7 a.m. and spent the morning sight-seeing and visiting the National Gallery before a picnic lunch in St. James's Park!

The school production was 'The Importance of Being Earnest', a comedy enjoyed by audience and cast alike. In the magazine, even the 2nd forms wrote with enthusiasm about the play.

Games reports were as usual though we must note that after both practical and oral examinations, two pupils qualified to umpire school matches and were awarded their whistles – A. Marlow for netball and C. Hancock for both netball and hockey.

1956–1957   Janet Lloyd

Deputy Head Girl: Elizabeth Pugh.
Prefects: J. Lloyd, E. Pugh, J. Atkinson, C. Brown, M. Clements, J. Covington, M. Davies, Y. Else, P. Kay, B. Lawton, J. Manning, A. Marlow, Y. Richardson, J. Vaughan, M. Watts, G. Keeble, D. Cole, A. Varallo, J. Dunn, G. Cropp, R. Jillings, J. Burman, F. Wilkins, B. Allen, P. Bradsell, M. Tarry, S. Griffith, G. Sims, A. Manners, M. Gibbens, J. Bye, M. McCarthy, S. Farris, J. Pooley, J. Davison, P. Wheeler, J. Pepper.
Hockey Captain: Patricia Kay.
Netball Captain: Ann Marlow.
Tennis Captain: Patricia Kay.
Swimming Captain: Joan Pooley.

'The past twelve months have seen momentous changes in world affairs and at home, but at school little has occurred to vary the even pattern of the days. Some pleasant new window curtains have been provided in the Hall and the swimming pool has been repainted in a vivid shade of pale green. Moreover the price of school dinners has gone up from ten pence to one shilling.' This was the review of one of the magazine's joint editors.

It was decided by the School Council to use hand-bells for fire alarms in place of the former whistle; and that a Schoolgirl's Diary would be sold bearing the school crest on the front.

The number of boarders diminished considerably for there were no new girls in September, but two Hungarians joined them and settled in well. These were refugees of the Hungarian uprising earlier in the year.

After many years as the H.G.G.S. Company, the 1st Hitchin Guides disbanded when Miss Hasler, the guide Captain, left the school. It would be re-registered, as an open company, in the town.

Hitchin held its first Music Festival in May and many of the girls took part. The choir, both orchestras and the choral verse-speaking group all distinguished themselves. The choir, competing against ladies' choirs, won their class and also shared the President's Trophy; the choral verse-speaking group came second in their class. Both orchestras also competed and played well but were the only musicians in their groups.

The pattern of lectures, debates and concerts continued, and it was notable over the past few years that more and more activities were taking place in conjunction with the Boys' Grammar School. A Valentine's Dance had been the social high-light for some years and at Easter this year there was a joint expedition to Snowdonia. It is reported in the magazine as a 'climbing' holiday but it seems to have been more tough mountain walking than the 'rope and crampon' variety. It was a visit much enjoyed by all those who went.

There was a musical return visit by old friends of the school – Jack Brymer and the Hirsch Quartet.

The Science and Current Affairs Clubs both complained of poor attendance at their meetings.

The Drama Club production this year was 'Romeo and Juliet' which had a very mixed reception. Pauline Dolden, in Ia, thought 'Romeo was fairly good but did not show emotion well . . . rather stiff, but Juliet was brilliant, though when she stabbed herself, it was too sudden'. Ann Eggington of the same form thought, 'the sword fights were not as good as the rest of the play' but concluded 'I truly had a good half-crown's worth!'

1957–1958 Christine Brown

Deputy Head Girl: Billie Lawton.
Prefects: C. Brown, J. Burman, J. Bye, C. Boyd, S. Muir, M. Bowker, B. Lawton, B. Allen, M. McCarthy, J. Harrison, M. Shaw, A. Thrussell, S. Griffith, J. Pepper, M. Hendry, J. Thompson, Y. Richardson, M. Gowers, M. Pepper, J. Whitehorn, J. Dines, R. Wheeler, A. Staffell, M. Brown, D. Barsby, F. Muir, M. Chamberlain, J. Hemmings, M. Ashby, M. Knight.
Hockey Captain: Christine Boyd.
Netball Captain: Ann Tyrer.
Tennis Captain: Jennifer Whitehorn.
Swimming Captain: Christine Boyd.

Asian 'flu decimated the school population in the autumn term and, at one time, half of the pupils were absent. Recuperation was not aided by the failure of the heating system though, in consequence, the Middle School was given an unexpected day's holiday.

Hitchin had now established links with their twin town, Bingen, and the school played its part in corresponding with school girls there, at the Hildegardisschule. A party from Bingen came to Hitchin and toured the school. Miss Badland later joined a party which went out to Germany.

There were great changes made, with an extension of the dining room under construction, two new art rooms completed and a further two music rooms – the latter being placed strategically well away from the form rooms!

Along with the other staff changes, it was especially regretted that Miss Radway would be retiring after being at the school 'for such a long time'. Miss Badland joined the boarders in Highbury House at the end of the autumn term, and five new grass courts were brought into use there for the tennis season.

There was only one general lecture in the school programme – a talk on France for the sixth form pupils, prior to a visit to stay with families in Orleans.

After last year's successful trip with the Boys' School, it was decided this year to have a joint venture to the Yorkshire Pennines where the party was based at Newfield Hall, near Malham.

The second Hitchin Music Festival was as successful as the first and again the school did well in several areas. This time the Choral Verse Speaking Group won two major awards and Mrs. Bowes-Lyon presented Janet Carling and Angela Saunders, on their behalf, with a cup. The school choir were second in their group and the orchestra third.

Apart from the established clubs, there were several new entries; a Junior Drama Club was mentioned for the first time; a Chess Club proved very popular and a Gramophone Club listened to a wide range of music. The Science Club went to the Lister Hospital where, in the Pathology Laboratory, they saw tissue slides and bacterial cultures before seeing the Lord Lister museum exhibits and visiting the nurses' lecture rooms. 'The Atom – 1957' was an exhibition visited by the sixth formers, illustrating the practical, industrial uses of radiation and radioisotopes, before they were given details of careers in this field.

Theatrical visits included a performance of 'King John' and another of 'A Midsummer Night's Dream' at Cambridge, and to see John Gielgud, at Drury Lane, in 'The Tempest'.

The Drama Club did not stage a full production this year but gave three play readings instead, of which 'The Happiest Days of Your Life' seems to have been greatly enjoyed.

Games results were rather disappointing due, in part, to the younger, inexperienced teams. Greater things were anticipated next year. There were, however, successes in the Schools' Umpires' examinations, and Elizabeth Sainsbury and C. Pettit passed the netball test and Frances Muir the hockey, whilst Ann Tyrer passed to umpire both netball and hockey.

1958–1959   Frances Muir

Deputy Head Girl: Marion Knight.
Prefects: F. Muir, M. Knight, M. Bowker, J. Dines, R. Wheeler, J. Hemmings, E. Grigg, B. Saunders, H. Whitworth, C. Tuckwell, B. Mills, R. Day, V. Coaker, A. Morley, C. Cox, S. Gardner, L. Calver, J. Scott, B. Wheeler, J. Greig, R. Turney, P. Vivian, J. Boorman, J. Conway, M. Chapman, R. Jarvis, S. Herbert, A. Thompson.
Hockey Captain: Angela Morley.
Netball Captain: Rose Wheeler.
Tennis Captain: Helen Whitworth.
Swimming Captain: Angela Morley.

After seemingly interminable building work, the school returned to its former peaceful atmosphere. The dining room was now completed, as were the kitchen extension and the new entrance hall. The Senior Sixth would be granted the privilege of using this entrance to the school.

The growth of and increasing danger from road traffic had led to the Cycle Proficiency Test and, with so many girls cycling to school, it was pleasing that so many of the girls passed and proved themselves accomplished road users.

Miss Stovin and the Choir. [Miss R. Stovin]

Film shows were a new phenomenon and replaced many of the former lectures. There was only one talk, about 'The Times' newspaper, and two films were shown to the whole school. They saw a ballet, 'Romeo and Juliet', with Yalina Ulanova dancing the title part. Susan Mogridge, IVa, reported '. . . when closeups were shown, Ulanova appeared middle-aged (she was in fact forty-eight), and not beautiful . . . dancing quite wonderful . . . she seemed quite natural . . . young and gay'. The second film was instructional, on the techniques of netball; it was well received and set a high standard for which to aim.

Films are mentioned, too, in the new Film Society which, though it offered a wide range and variety of programmes, complained of very poor support and in consequence, would not be able to continue. A Photographic Club, also newly formed, complained of lack of support and feared it too would cease. Both the Science and Current Affairs Clubs changed their approach during the year, relying more on members' involvement in their planning and functions. The Science Club formed small groups to pursue specific projects: one group printed photographic negatives, one made a crystal set; others did flame experiments, finding their own horse power and studying crystal gardens. With all these activities they had only one speaker, from de Havillands. The Current Affairs Club tried to be more democratic in involving representatives of all age groups to take much more responsibility in the organisation of their activities. This programme also featured a film – on the work of the International Voluntary Service.

A Chamber String Orchestra was formed of the most advanced pupils from several schools in the district, including three girls from H.G.G.S., and a concert was given. The conductor was Mr. Gasparian – well known to the girls as a violin tutor. The choir took part in a concert at St. Mary's where they sang Mozart's 'Ave Verum'. They also took part in the joint schools' choirs' concert at Hitchin Town Hall and sang Part 3 of 'Messiah' and a Ralph Vaughan Williams chorus. Several of the orchestra members went to a schools' Music Course held at Welwyn Garden City which concluded with a student concert.

A Christmas dance at the Boys' Grammar School was publicised in the calendar and the usual Valentine's Dance took place. The joint Easter expedition was to the Lake District where, based by Coniston, the boys and girls spent a happy, strenuous week, tramping the fells and lakesides.

The Junior Sixth form sat in on a debate in the House of Commons where the third reading of the Mental Health Bill was approved. A later debate was on whether the Scottish B.B.C. Orchestra should be disbanded – a proposal regretted by the M.P.s.

The Drama Club, after several play readings, including 'The Boy with a Cart' by Christopher Fry, decided to make this their production for the year. Barbara Sillence as the boy was especially commended as identifying herself completely with the part, while Christabel Sharp was very convincing as his mother.

1959–1960 Jacqueline Conway

Deputy Head Girl: Sheila Gardner.
Prefects: J. Conway, S. Gardner, C. Cox, J. Boorman, H. Whitworth, A. Thompson, B. Wheeler, R. Day, A. Simpson, P. Beckwith, M. Felstead, A. Thomas, H. Price, J. Drummond, R. Taylor, P. Goldsmith, S. Disbrey, E. Sainsbury, L. Fay, J. Phillips, V. Pearson, E. Malcolm, J. Ellis, M. Cruse, J. Simmons, A. Will, J. Sheppard, J. Whitworth.
Hockey Captain: Rosemary Day.
Netball Captain: Elizabeth Sainsbury.
Tennis Captain: Sally Disbrey.
Swimming Captain: Ann Thompson.
Games Secretary: Patricia Beckwith.

This was World Refugee Year and most forms in the school had special fund-raising efforts to support it. These ranged from the ever popular food sales and fairs to jive sessions and a treasure hunt. The staff served coffee after the school play and Miss Badland played her part in organising a competition. The money raised by all this activity was a handsome £156.

The school had two extra days' holidays this year; the first for election day and the second to mark the wedding of Princess Margaret.

At the end of the school year, the last five boarders, including the Head Girl, left Highbury House, though two returned in the autumn as day girls.

Other changes were minor. In the dining room, to relieve congestion at the serving hatches, one person from each table would in future collect both meat and vegetables. Latecomers, for a trial period, had been excluded from prayers but the possibility of leaving space at the back of the hall would now be investigated. A Uniform Committee was established to discuss all matters of dress, though it was agreed that most faults were not in what was worn so much as in how it was worn!

Lectures now seemed out of favour and none are recorded though the sixth form had a film show.

Music was maintained with a recital by the Kerry Camden Quintet, and two concerts plus a recital by the students. Several members of the orchestra attended the Mid. Hertfordshire Youth Orchestra meetings at Hatfield School, and the choir took part in the concerts arranged by the Hertfordshire Rural Music School.

Extra-curricular activities had a most eventful year with the Current Affairs Club, active for many years, being disbanded at Christmas and the decline and fall of both Chess and Gramophone Clubs as well. The Science club complained of fluctuating attendances for its varied programme. Visits were made to Bay Tree

Cycling Proficiency Awards. *L. to R.:* Carole Cox, Susan Rotheray, Mrs. Shirley Williams,   ?   ,
  ?   , Helen Robinson.   [Herts Pictorial]

Press in Stevenage and to Hitchin Telephone Exchange. Mr. Turner, a local veterinary surgeon, described his work. The Pets' Club reported being 'in full swing' and busy compiling a 'Pets' Scrap Book' with contributions from the members.

Visits were, as always, very varied – from Hitchin Gas Works to a fashion show! At the Gas Works the girls were shown how the coal was heated to extract the gas and other by-products used for plastics, dyes and medicines. Miss Fletcher took a party to the Kayser Bondor factory, at Baldock, to see a collection of colourful cotton dresses as well as the lovely lingerie for which the company was famous.

The joint Grammar Schools' expedition at Easter went to North Wales where some energetic members climbed to the top of ten mountains more than three thousand feet high.

A party from Bingen came to Hitchin in May, and girls of the folk dancing troupe stayed with school pupils who hoped to visit their new friends in Bingen at a later date. A dance was held in the school in honour of the visitors, and pupils from other schools in the district were invited.

There was an upsurge in theatre visits: 'King Lear' at Stratford, 'Macbeth' at the Boys' Grammar School, 'Great Expectations' at the Mermaid and 'Brittanicus' at the Savoy. There were also two theatre trips to Cambridge; to 'Le Bourgeois Gentilhomme' and to 'The Winter's Tale'.

The latter provided a standard to aim for in the school's production of the same play, an unusual choice for a girls' school. Jennifer Sexton of the sixth form reported '. . . every girl was acting for every second while on stage . . . this was an impressive performance'.

This was not a good year for sport and there was only one success in the Umpires' Test when Susan Potter qualified to umpire netball.

The Cycling Proficiency Test was again taken by a number of girls and the local Labour M.P., Mrs. Shirley Williams, presented the certificates.

1960–1961   Rosemary Taylor

Deputy Head Girl: Elizabeth Sainsbury.
Prefects: Rosemary Taylor, Elizabeth Sainsbury, Mary Cruse, Janet Sheppard, Jean Whitworth, Ruth Everett, Martha Fulton, Julia Johnson, Patricia Knight, Angela Parker, Janet Spicer, Janet Varey, Mary Lawman, Jennifer Lawson, Elizabeth Thomas, Janet Whiter, Lesley Dove, Julie Green, Janet Poulton, Pamela Masson, Sandra Jones, Susan Mogridge, Anne Rogers.
Hockey Captain: Janet Sheppard.
Netball Captain: Jennifer Lawson.
Tennis Captain: Elizabeth Sainsbury.
Swimming Captain: Jennifer Lawson.

The school had a new external coat of paint and, as if to complement it, the magazine had a new, modern cover. This showed half a Fleur-de-Lis (part of the school badge) and the letters H.G.G.S. and the year.

Miss Chrystal, a teacher at the school for twenty years, left to become Deputy Headmistress at Rayleigh and Dr. Winifred Symonds retired as the Medical Officer, her place being taken by Dr. Burgess.

The library was augmented by a large number of books, on permanent loan from the County Library. There were also facilities to buy new books and have old ones re-bound at subsidised rates. A separate Music Library was established, with books and scores to be stored in Room 20.

Two extra grass courts were opened at Highbury House, and in consequence it was not necessary to convert the top hockey pitch for this use at the end of the Easter term. Padder tennis was started on the lower field, an innovation which, it was hoped, would be valuable.

A heavy duty, plastic cover was bought for the swimming pool to help conserve a little heat in the water. It took four girls to fold it back each day, but this was an effort deemed worth while if the temperature could be held a little higher than formerly.

Music making took on a new meaning when the students tackled the Benjamin Britten opera about Noah and his Ark, 'Noye's Fludde'. In this modern work, apart from the more usual instruments, are such things as Chinese blocks and slung mugs to make alternative sounds. Everyone seems to have had a wonderful time and the proceeds went towards the purchase of a French horn for the orchestra. Though this was a more conventional instrument, the first attempts to play it were variously described as 'a cow elephant in pain' and 'the fog horn of a ship'. The choir sang in 'The Bridal Day', produced for the school in the autumn, and performed special pieces for the carol concerts.

The Drama Group had a very busy year with several play readings which continued even when the group was decimated by girls taking part in the opera.

1961. Noye's Fludde. *L. to R.:* Susan Wearmouth, Janet Haywood, Lesley Dove, Patricia Knight, Margaret Liptrot. *Front:* Susan James. [Miss Stovin]

The Science Club made two popular local visits – to Ransom's Distillery and to Simpson's Brewery. They also enjoyed several films, ranging from 'Oxygen' to 'The History of Colour'. The Pet Club had now widened its horizons to embrace all animals and felt that a change of title should be considered. They had a wonderful day at Whipsnade, mostly dashing about the zoo to catch the various animals' feeding times and stopping only long enough to feed themselves!

A party of Fifth Form girls went to Cambridge to see 'Hamlet' with Jeremy Brett in the title part and the fourth year pupils saw 'Twelfth Night' at the same theatre. The 'A' level Sixth Formers went to the Mermaid and sat through the three hours of the 'Wakefield Mystery Plays'. Reaction was varied, but most felt this was an experience not to be missed.

The highlight of the hockey season was the success in winning a match against Herts. and Essex School – the first time Hitchin had beaten these opponents. The 1st XI also won their section in the Hertfordshire Inter-Schools' tournament and lost to Watford Grammar in the final. Susan Potter and R. Taylor were selected to play for the County 2nd XI and J. Sheppard the Reserve XI. The tennis teams suffered from losing most of their players at the end of the previous school year, but a week's tennis coaching at Easter gave forty-eight girls a chance to improve their game.

1961–1962   Janet Spicer

Deputy Head Girl: Julia Johnson.
Prefects: J. Spicer, J. Johnson, J. Whitworth, P. Knight, P. Masson, S. Mogridge, A. Rogers, S. Horrocks, J. Carling, S. James, B. Porter, B. Smith, L. Abbott, P. Dolden, D. Luck, J. Hester, P. J. Talbot, A. Thomas, M. Vines, A. Melot, B. Brazier, J. Povey, M. Dyer, A. Fovargue, C. Gentle, S. Will.
Hockey Captain: Susan Potter.
Netball Captain: Susan James.
Tennis Captain: Susan Potter.
Swimming Captain: Penelope Jill Talbot.
Games Secretary: Janet Carling.

The major news of the year concerned two headmistresses. Miss Chambers, the school's Headmistress from 1919 to 1945, died in March, two days after suffering a stroke, and Miss Badland left at the end of the summer term to take up another appointment. There had been many changes and improvements at the school in her seventeen years' service, which would remain as a testament to her life in Hitchin. Since her successor was unable to take up the appointment immediately, Miss Allright was to be acting Headmistress for the autumn term and Miss Britton her Deputy.

The School Council decided that a suggestion box should be available throughout the year, and that meetings would only take place when there was sufficient business to justify it.

The calendar shows a positive explosion of lectures on all sorts of topics, and it is significant that many were for small groups of one field of study, or age group, which were taken out to hear the talks: the VI History division were taken to the Victoria and Albert Museum; the VI Pure Maths to the Royal Institute; Regent's Park Zoo was visited by the Zoology group and the English students went to the Planetarium. Lectures on the school premises were by a W.A.A.F. Squadron Leader and a lecturer from the Sorbonne University; by a New Zealander and a speaker on Russian education. Recreation was not neglected and Ballroom Dancing classes were started at the Boys' School.

Two horns and a set of timpani were added to the orchestra – a change reported by V. Offner and H. Mould in Va as having 'made a great deal of difference to the sound of the orchestra though it is questionable whether they enhance it!' These two budding timpanists, with as many as thirty bars rest between bouts of activity, had plenty of time to hear the playing of the remaining instruments: 'on the whole, what we hear is good'. The orchestra entered Hitchin Music Festival and played for a school concert. The choir had many new members and sang well in the Non-Competitive Class of the same festival.

The Science Club had only one visit, to the Lister Hospital, and a restricted programme of talks. It was obviously suffering from poor support, perhaps due to the new attractions of the Debating Society and Discussion Group. They had several debates, amongst which they decided 'That men should always wear the trousers'. The Pet Club found itself in trouble and the magazine printed an amusing plea, by Nina Brammer and Sylvia Pratt, to help save this endangered species with an injection of new blood.

A series of Cycle Proficiency Lectures, followed by the test, resulted in eleven girls passing, six of whom got more than 90% pass mark and were therefore awarded a pennant.

There was an inter-school Road Safety Quiz held in Hitchin Town. The

Intermediate team came third and were awarded 2/6d. savings stamps each. The Senior team was second in its group and won 5/– savings stamps each. Two junior school girls entered as individual representatives in the Hitchin Road Safety Cycle Rally – Merralyn Pollock was 1st and won 15/– and Mary Williams was 3rd and won 5/–.

Six of the girls travelled, with a large contingent from the Boys' School, to visit Bingen and enjoyed sampling German life. School began at 8 a.m. but finished at 1 p.m., and the English girls had difficulty in coping with the quantities of German meals. The highlight of the visit was a dance, held on a Rhine river boat, and a visit to the Wine Festival.

Though school hockey was disappointing, six girls were chosen for County Teams. Susan Potter was awarded County Colours and was chosen as an Eastern Counties Junior Reserve.

G. MARGARET WARWICK
Headmistress 1962–

Margaret Harrison was born and brought up in the small Yorkshire village of Rothwell and attended Wakefield High School. She took an Honours degree in Geography at London University (Bedford College) and then went on to study the violin, under Robert Masters, for a further three years at the Royal Academy of Music in London.

Her first teaching appointment was at Cheltenham Ladies' College. This was followed by ten years at Bradford Girls' Grammar School, first as Head of Geography and then as Assistant Headmistress.

There was a break with tradition when Miss Harrison married widower Kenneth Warwick. This made her the first – and to date, the only – married headmistress at Hitchin Girls' in over seventy-five years! Their marriage took place at the Cathedral and Abbey Church of St. Alban in June 1965.

Kenneth Warwick, a Chartered Engineer, was the Director of Projects at Geo. W. King's in Stevenage. He was also very active in local and church affairs in Hitchin.

When he retired from King's, in March 1970, Mr. Warwick became a Consultant Engineer, intending to devote more time to technical writing. He had long-term plans to enter the Anglican Church, but sadly, these had to be abandoned because of increasing ill-health. Mr. Warwick died in February 1977, leaving his wife to bring up their nine-year-old daughter Claire, who went to Selwyn College, Cambridge, in 1986 to read Classics.

Mrs. Warwick has always been very conscious of her responsibilities as Headmistress, and one of her most important aims has always been to ensure that her pupils do not specialise in particular subjects at too early an age and so 'lock' potential career doors. To that end, pupils have always been actively encouraged to follow a liberal, well-balanced curriculum that allows them to develop all-round interests.

Mrs. G. Margaret Warwick, B.A.Hons.(London), G.R.S.M. Headmistress 1962–

Her period as Headmistress has been marked by some of the most wide-ranging educational changes of the twentieth century, and it has fallen to Mrs. Warwick to implement them within the School. There have been new examinations: the Certificate of Secondary Education (C.S.E.) (1965) and the General Certificate of Secondary Education (G.C.S.E.) (1986); new curriculum initiatives such as Technical and Vocational Education Initiative (T.V.E.I.) and Certificate of Pre-Vocational Education (C.P.V.E.) (1985); re-organisation: the loss of Grammar School status with the introduction of 'all ability' schooling in 1973; the North Hertfordshire 16–19 Consortia; the 1986 'Secondary Review'. The School itself has also changed considerably over the years with greatly increased numbers of both staff and pupils and three new, purpose-built subject and accommodation Blocks (Science and Gymnastics (1971); the Lower School (1978); Music (1982)).

Throughout all this, Mrs. Warwick has always tried to remain true to that same fundamental belief that she expressed in 1962: that it is only possible for a Head to do what her Staff will allow her to do. That is why, wherever possible, she has always tried to act in accord with staff wishes, even if she has not always agreed with certain policies.

No one could ever claim that this Headmistress lives in an ivory tower in some inaccessible corner of the School, doesn't know the name of any member of staff below the level of Departmental Head and needs at least a week's notice before discussing the most simple of matters! Her room is next-door to the staff room and there is frequent contact between Headmistress and staff throughout the day. Sometimes an official appointment is necessary, but should staff wish to discuss something with her, a knock on her door is often all that is needed.

When it comes to her pupils, Mrs. Warwick freely admits that she cannot possibly remember the names of almost nine hundred girls! However, while she may not always be able to put a name to a face, pupils would probably be very surprised indeed to know exactly how much of a personal interest she takes in their progress and achievements! This is one reason why she has always tried to have at least one or two teaching lessons a week, in spite of her very busy administrative schedule, in order that she does not become too distanced from the efforts of the ordinary teacher.

Music and gardening are amongst Mrs. Warwick's interests. She is an accomplished violinist and for a time she conducted and played in the School Orchestra. She has also been spotted playing the violin – complete with decorative tinsel! – in the orchestra for the carol singing on the last day of the autumn term. She also plays the organ at her local Church. Gardening is a 'very therapeutic' exercise and weeding, in particular, allows her the luxury of organising her thoughts without distraction!

STAFF APPOINTMENTS DURING MISS HARRISON'S (MRS. WARWICK'S) TIME 1962–

1962–	G. Margaret Warwick, Headmistress	
1962–1965	Frances E. Cobley	Head of Chemistry
1962–1964	Susan A. Jones	Physical Education
1962–?	Ann M. Parkhouse, Mrs. (+summer term '71)	Mathematics
1962–1965	Judith Robinson	Geography
1962–1964	Marjorie V. Whiting, Mrs.	Mathematics, Sciences

1963–1967	Y. Ireland, Mrs.	Domestic Science
1963–1968	Margaret Rees	Head of History
1963–1966?	Margaret Robson, Dr.	Sciences
1963–1965	Jennifer Tily, Mrs.	Mathematics
1964	Mlle. Andouard	Language Assistant
1964–1973	Rosemary J. Bennett	French, Careers
1964–?	? Carter	?
1964–1982	Terry Gilbert, Mrs.	Chemistry, Head of Chemistry '65, Head of V Year, Careers
1964–1967	Mavis M. Hinde	Religious Education
1964–1972	Doreen Irving (Mrs. Edwards)	History, Head of History '68
1964–1968	Virginia Lee, Mrs.	English
1964–1967	Frances Muir (head girl '58–'59)	Physical Education
1964–1971	Jean? Reid, Mrs.	Art
1964	Herr Richter	Language Assistant
1964	Senorita Santos	Language Assistant
1965–1967	B. Mary Bailey	Geography
1965–1968	Shelagh M. Cox, Mrs. (+'79–'82 part time)	Chemistry
1965–1966	Anthea Edenbrow	English
1965–	Anne Hendy, Mrs.	Mathematics, Head of Mathematics '71, Savings, Senior Teacher '81
1965–?	? Slator	Biology
1965–1968	Anne C. Whittington, Mrs.	Biology
1965–1966	Patricia A. Willmott, Mrs.	Swimming (part-time)
1966–1970	Juliet A. Alton (Mrs. Pennington)	English
1966–1967	Evelyn Gair, Mrs. (from USA)	English
1966–1972	Gillian Heller, Mrs.	English (part-time)
1966–?	Anne Lambert-Lambert	German, French
1966–	John N. McCutcheon, Deputy Head '81–	Physics, Head of Science '68, Timetable '68
1966–1970	Joyce Redman, Mrs. (+'74–'76)	Head of R.E.
1966–1968	Vivienne Robinson, Mrs.	Physics
1966–1973	Christine H. Robson (Mrs. Baylay)	Physical Education
1966–1967/8	Patricia Turner	English
1966–1971	Evelyn Walsh	French
1966–1968?	Margaret Wiggs, Mrs.	History (part-time)
1967–1973	Christine Aspinwall, Mrs.	Head of Physical Education (Captain England Hockey Team)
1967–	E. Margaret Beddard Head of Lower School '78–'84 Deputy Head '84–	Latin, Head of Latin '70–'88
1967–1969	Christine Bridges (Mrs. Hinch)	History
1967–1969	M. Brown	Biology
1967–1972	Marianne G. Devereux	Physics
1967–1971	Roger Gomm	Social Sciences, History
1967–1969	W. G. Hosie, Mrs.	Domestic Science
1967–1975	Peter B. Lord	Head of Biology, Environmental Studies, Careers
1967–	Robert W. Mottershead	Head of Geography, Environmental Studies, Head of IV Year, Examinations Officer, Senior Teacher '82
1967–1971	Jenny M. Withers	Geography, Geology
1968–	Ann Biddle, Mrs.	English, Head of English '79, Drama, Magazine

1968–1974	Gillian F. Colkin	Mathematics, Magazine Treasurer
1968–1970	Susan Cook, Mrs.	Swimming (part-time)
1968–1972	Judy M. Hawkins	History
1968–1973	Christine M. Isherwood, Mrs.	Biology
1968–1973	? Kipping, Mrs.	Biology
1968–1969	Annette Kowarsky, Mme.	Language Assistant
1968–1972	Eilish A. Moore	Domestic Science, Needlework
1968–1970	Philip M. Roskelly	Chemistry
1969–1971	J. Sian Goldsmith, Mrs.	English, Drama
1969–1971	Mary J. Kalaugher	Latin
1969–1974?	F. Max W. Lee, Rev.	Head of Religious Education
1969–1972	Patricia M. Salmon, Mrs.	Music
1969–1972	Carol A. Walsh	Chemistry
1970–1975	Linda J. Dixon, Mrs.	English
1970–1971	Chantal Langevin	Language Assistant
1970–1972	Pauline A. McCormick, Mrs.	Mathematics
1970–1972	Samshe? Mundray, Mr.	Economics, Mathematics
1970–1976	Winifred Sheldon, Mrs.	French (part-time)
1970–1976	Gillian K. Stroud, Mrs.	Sociology, Economics
1970–?	A. J. Williams, Mr.	Art (part-time)
1971–1982	Madeleine Butchart, Mrs.	Extra English (part-time)
1971–1972 (+'55–'67)	Marian E. Clarke	VI Latin, General Studies (part-time)
1971–1982	Pauline Davies (Mrs. Brooks '77)	Classics, Head of III Year '80
1971–1975	Susan D. Evans	Domestic Science
1971–1975	Sandra A. Jenkinson, Mrs.	Geography
1971–1972	Chantal Lamy, Mlle.	Language Assistant
1971–?	Claire Mansfield	French Student
1971–1974	Katherine M. Stones	French
1971–	John D. Wallace	Head of Modern Languages, Head of VI Year '84
1972–1978 (+'84)	Helen M. Bundy (Mrs. Ide)	Environmental Studies, Biology
1972–1973	George Burnham	Economics, History
1972–1975	D. Ian Chalmers	Chemistry, Mathematics
1972–1977	Jack Covington	English, Latin, Library (part-time)
1972–1975	Andrew Hallett	Physics, Mathematics
1972–1976	Jennifer M. Hartnell (Mrs. Hesketh)	History
1972–1975	Susan Kepple (Mrs. Moore)	Physical Education
1972–1976	Margaret E. Nuttall (Mrs. Johnson)	Music
1972–1978 (+'83–)	Zoe M. Powers, Mrs.	Modern Languages
1972–1975 (+'66–'70)	Joyce Redman, Mrs.	Religious Education
1972–	James C. Robertson, Dr.	Head of History, Senior Librarian '79
1972–1987	Penelope J. Smith (Mrs. Bucknell 1982)	Mathematics, Gifted Children Project
1972–1977	Andrew A. Tillett	Head of Music, Choir, Orchestra
1973–1975	Hilary A. Bithell	Art
1973–	Marie Bonner (Mrs. Mead 1983) Head of Lower School '85–	Mathematics
1973–	Priscilla M. Douglas, Mrs.	Domestic Science, Head of IV/V Year 1983
1973–1984 (+'52–'57 as Miss Barker)	Barbara Graebe, Mrs.	English
1973	Fräulein E. Hahn	Exchange Teacher

1973–1975	Karen Kaye, Mrs.	Biology
1973–1975	David A. Price	Head of Art
1973–1978	Marion Shirley (Mrs. Drew)	Head of Physical Education
1973	Dominique ?	Language Assistant
1974–1980	Patricia Ashworth, Mrs.	Chemistry, Badminton Club
1974–1975	Rosemary A. Cole	English
1974–1986	Joyce James, Mrs.	English, Classical Studies, Head of I Year, Head of II Year
1974–1977	Hilary M. Locke, Mrs. (Pupil, H. Taylor '56–'63)	French
1974–1979	Jane C. Maggs (Mrs. Pacy 1977)	Economics, Careers
1974–1976	Pamela M. Sellix, Mrs.	Head of Religious Education, English
1974–1977	Anne Shield	Mathematics, Careers
1974–	Rhoda Smith, Mrs.	Mathematics (part-time)
1975	Rosamund E. Catlin	English
1975–1979	Patricia M. Cousans (Mrs. Healy)	Biology
1975–	A. Margaret Cowley, Mrs.	Physical Education (part-time)
1975–	Robert H. Graham	Head of Biology, Head of V Year '82/'83
1975–	Frances Green	Domestic Science, Head of Domestic Science 1984, Head of III Year '85
1975–1988	Ivor D. Miskelly	English, General Studies, Drama, Junior Library '76–'84, C.P.V.E. tutor. Seconded to Homerton College '86–'87, Business Education
1975–1981	Elizabeth A. Smith, Mrs.	Physics
1975–1986	Susan G. Smith (Mrs. Walker)	Art, Head of Art '81, Printing
1975–1984	Una Stock	Geography, S.C.F.
1975–1981	George Szirtes	Head of Art, Printing, Drama (Prize-winning Poet)
1976–1980	Ann Cunliffe	Latin, English, Head of II Year
1976–1985	Elizabeth E. Gurr	Head of Religious Education
1976–1981 (+'86–'87)	Deborah Lal, Mrs.	Modern Languages
1976–	Gail A. McCormick (Mrs. Jones)	English, Drama, Classical Studies, Head of I Year '84, Junior Library '84
1976–1978	Margaret Ollard (Mrs. Riches '77)	Music, Junior Choir
1976–1978	Patricia M. Pacey, Mrs.	Mathematics
1976–?	Jeanette Ponsford (Mrs. Jenkins)	Mathematics
1976–1980	Judy Russell (Mrs. Dayer-Smith '77) (Pupil '65–'72)	Physical Education, Head of Physical Education '78
1976–1978	Elizabeth Stewart	History
1976–1983	Peter Westwick	Head of Sociology and Economics, C.S.E. Examinations Officer '79
1976–1984	Dorothy Whiteley, Mrs.	Geography, History, Head of V Year '82
1977–1980	Irene Evans, Mrs.	Modern Languages
1977–1984	Christine M. Greenfield, Mrs.	Mathematics S.C.F.
1977–1980	M. Ann Jones, Mrs.	Modern Languages
1977–1981 (+'84–'85)	Joanna Lewis, Mrs.	Biology
1977–1980	Faith Morgan	Religious Education, English
1977–1984	Dilys Pollard, Mrs.	Music (part-time)
1977–1981	Pascaline Polti (Mrs. Frame)	Modern Languages
1977–	Paul A. Rooke	Head of Music, Choir, Orchestra
1978–1986	Pauline Boylan (Mrs. Barnett '79)	Biology, Physical Education

1978–1980	Rosemary J. Garwood, Mrs.	History, English
1978–1981	Sarah Hardy (Miss Tanqueray)	History
1978–1980	Arlene M. Jones, Mrs.	English
1978–	Rita Mottershead, Mrs.	Needlework, Textiles (part-time)
1978–	Sarah Nettell (Mrs. Hulman '84)	Physical Education, Head of Physical Education '80–'86
1978–	Ann E. Neuff, Mrs.	English, Drama (part-time)
1979–1985	Hilary F. Bond (Mrs. Cannon '82)	Chemistry, Assistant Examinations Officer
1979–1982 (+'65–'68)	Shelagh M. Cox, Mrs.	Chemistry, Physics (part-time)
1979–	Christine McCutcheon, Mrs.	Biology (part-time)
1979–1986	Judi M. McMullen, Mrs.	Needlework, Domestic Science (part-time)
1979–1981	Marie-Christine Morrot	Language Assistant
1979–1983	Jayne Morse (Mrs. Treasure)	Classics, English
1979–1981	Marie-Dominique Pinier	Language Assistant
1979–1980	Julia A. Simmonds, Mrs.	Music
1980–1986	E. Ann Barker (Mrs. Percival)	Biology
1980–	Elizabeth M. S. Duignan	History, Careers, Personal & Social Education, Cycling Proficiency
1980–	Joy Hillman, Mrs.	Modern Languages, Personal & Social Education '85
1980–1985	Linda Hopley, Mrs.	Religious Education, English, Head of III Year
1980–	Betty Jackson, Mrs.	Mathematics, Special Needs, Assistant Examination Officer
1980–	Susan Molyneux (Mrs. Streets '85)	Physical Education, Head of Physical Education '86
1980–1984	Paul Timms	Music, Choir
1980–1983	Louise M. Turner	Sociology, Economics, Physical Education, Dance
1980–1984	Angela J. Wilde	Modern Languages
1980–	Elizabeth Wilkins, Mrs. (Seconded from N. Herts. College)	Sociology, Careers (part-time '80–'83, full-time '83–)
1980–	Deborah Wilson	English, Classical Studies, Lacrosse, C.P.V.E. '86/'87, Duke of Edinburgh Award
1981–1986	Marjorie Allock, Mrs.	Computer Sciences (part-time)
1981–1983/4	Julie Bond, Mrs.	Physics
1981–	Anita J. Collis	Modern Languages
1981–	Stefania Creighton, Mrs.	History, Head of IV/V '83
1981–1984	Jennifer P. Harrison	English, Gifted Children Project
1981–1986	Billy Kerr, Mrs.	Art (part-time)
1981–	Carol J. King, Mrs.	Biology, Duke of Edinburgh Award
1981–	Gillian Miller, Mrs.	Art, Head of Art '86
1981–1982	Hilary J. Murley	Modern Languages
1981–1986	Colette M. Quirk	Modern Languages, S.C.F.
1981–1986	Jane A. Whitbread, Mrs.	Physical Education (part-time)
1982–	Phillip Jackson	Head of Chemistry, Christian Union
1982–1983	Jane Robson, Mrs.	Modern Languages
1983–1984	Hazel Bolus, Mrs.	Science
1983–	Linda Elliott, Mrs.	Physics, Gifted Children Project
1983–	Peter Fitzgibbon	Economics, Social Science
1983–1985	Anne Hilson	Classics (part-time)
1983–	Janet Molloy, Mrs. (Seconded from N. Herts. College)	Business Education (full-time '85)
1983–1986	Carolyn Parkinson	Classics, Gifted Children Project

1983– (+'72–'78)	Zoe Powers, Mrs.	Modern Languages (part-time)
1983–1984 (+'87–)	Joyce Smith, Mrs.	Geography (part-time)
1983–1985	Christine Trory (Seconded from N. Herts. College)	Business Education (part-time)
1984–1986	Susan Donnelly, Mrs.	Modern Languages
1984–1986	Elizabeth A. Freeman, Mrs.	Mathematics
1984–	Susan Garnett (Mrs. Lamb '84)	Geography, Economics, Duke of Edinburgh Award, Gardening Club
1984 (May–August)	Janet Gascoigne, Mrs.	Science (part-time)
1984–1985? (+'72–'78)	Helen Ide, Mrs.	Biology (part-time)
1984–1985	Lynda Lee, Mrs.	?
1984–1985 (+'77–'81	Joanna Lewis, Mrs.	Biology (part-time)
1984–1987	Elizabeth Margarson	Geography
1984–	Gwyn Poole, Mrs.	History, English, Classical Studies, Special Needs
1984–1985	Alison Potterton, Mrs.	Mathematics (part-time)
1984–	Wes Smith, Dr.	Head of Physics
1984–1988	Kathryn Wallace (Mrs. Daszkiewicz '88)	English, Classical Studies, Magazine
1984–	Romola Ward, Mrs.	Mathematics (part-time)
1984–1988	Mary Wheeler (Mrs. Richardson '85)	Music, Head of I Year '87
1985–1988	Susannah Bartlett	Latin, English
1985	Pamela Brown, Mrs.	Head of Religious Education, Head of II Year '86
1985–	Veronica Gardner, Mrs.	Biology (part-time)
1985–	Brenda Haines, Mrs.	Home Economics (part-time)
1985–	Karen Harris	Mathematics, S.C.F.
1985 (1 term)	Cyril Hughes	Chemistry (part-time)
1985–	O. Cynthia Myers, Mrs.	Modern Languages
1985–	Jane Preston, Dr.	Biology, Personal & Social Education
1985–	Lynda Watts, Mrs.	Science (part-time), Mathematics (full-time) '87
1986–1987	Lesley Byrne	English
1986–1988	M. Linda Caley	Art
1986–1988	Sarah Foster	Latin, English
1986 (Aug/Sept)	Elizabeth Gent	Art
1986–	Sarah Giles	Chemistry
1986–	Dawn Hilson	Physical Education
1986–1988	Debra Horton	Modern Languages
1986–	Anne Jarman, Mrs.	English
1986–1987 (+'76–'81)	Deborah Lal, Mrs.	Modern Languages (part-time)
1987–	Barry Cooper	Head of Technology
1987–	Jennifer Dewhirst, Mrs.	Mathematics
1987–	Susan Montague, Mrs.	Special Needs (part-time)
1987 (Jan–July)	Susan Nixon, Mrs.	Mathematics (part-time)
1987– (+'83–'84)	Joyce Smith, Mrs.	Geography

1962–1963   Lyndsay Abbott

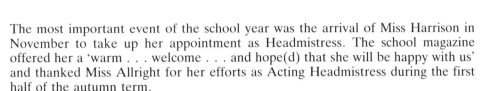

Deputy Head Girl: Carol Gentle.
Prefects: Lyndsay Abbott, Carol Gentle, Pauline Dolden, Diana Luck, Anne Melot, Maureen Dyer, Ann Fovargue, Jane Pryor, Gail Reffell, Moira McNab, Brenda Woods, Maureen Huff, Sally Pritchard, Meryl Brown, Ruth Fountain, Mary Price, Margaret Roberts, Susan Wearmouth, Marjory Hester, Elizabeth Gurney, Elizabeth Tooke, Jennifer Wakefield, Glenda Froy, Hilary Jenkins, Daryl May, Mary Eyles.
Hockey Captain: Anne Melot.
Netball Captain: Maureen Dyer.
Tennis Captain: Maureen Dyer.
Swimming Captain: Moira McNab.
Games Secretary: Moira McNab.

The most important event of the school year was the arrival of Miss Harrison in November to take up her appointment as Headmistress. The school magazine offered her a 'warm . . . welcome . . . and hope(d) that she will be happy with us' and thanked Miss Allright for her efforts as Acting Headmistress during the first half of the autumn term.

Classroom rearrangement in the Main School meant that the Music Department now found itself 'relocated over the road' in the more spacious surroundings of Highbury House. Unfortunately, Miss Stovin's illness meant that neither of the school orchestras played during the autumn term, and Mr. Winram found himself in sole charge of both the Junior and Senior Choirs at the carol concert. Members of both orchestras played in the Mid-Hertfordshire Youth Orchestra course at Welwyn during the Christmas holidays under their famous guest conductor, Muir Mathieson. The choirs and orchestras were pleased to welcome Miss Stovin's return in January. The school concert took place at the end of May. Sheridan's 'The Rivals' was the choice for the school play and, according to pupils, friends and the local Press, 'it seemed to be a success'.

The Senior School enjoyed talks on the Mission and the International School and, for the Sixth Form leavers, there was the chance to listen to a representative of the Yardley Cosmetic Company speaking about a possible career in the beauty business. The Hirsch Chamber Players and Mavis Elmett gave a recital for the Senior School at the beginning of December. The Theatre Centre came in the summer to give the juniors a 'captivating' performance of 'The Struggle', a rather avant-garde play based on Bunyan's 'Pilgrim's Progress'.

There were numerous outings to a variety of places, including Wembley Stadium to watch England play Wales – and lose! – at hockey: '. . . despite the rain we cheered loudly and joined in the community singing, much to the discomfort of Miss Waddilove who was sitting in front of us!' One representative from each form also attended the annual Mission Service in Southwark Cathedral. The Sixth Form did particularly well, attending courses at Offley (University Entrance), Juniper Hall (Geography) and Westfield College (Science) as well as visiting the House of Commons and the Science Museum. The A Level French groups were lucky enough to attend a ten-day course held at the Sorbonne in Paris. Two Sixth Formers took part in a four-day conference in London on ways of dealing with the perennial problem of hunger. There were theatre trips to Cambridge to see 'As You Like It' and 'Oedipus the King' and to the National Youth Theatre for a modern-dress version of 'Julius Caesar', complete with Teddy Boys and crowd-scene extras doing the Twist!

Close links with Hitchin Boys' School were maintained through a meeting of the Bingen Society, the joint Sixth Form Christmas and Valentine's Day dances – for which the Sixth Form dancing classes at the Boys' School during November proved to be a necessity for many! – and a combined Junior Sixth Geography Field Trip to North Wales. There were also the traditional hockey and tennis matches between the two schools and, for the first time, joint dramatic interpretation and discussion through the Inter-Schools Play-Reading Society.

The various school clubs and societies continued to meet during the year and, although there could have been more Fourth and Fifth Years involved, it was generally agreed that there was much enthusiastic commitment shown by members.

Both hockey and netball were affected by bad weather during the autumn and spring terms and, although morale and inter-form tournaments did not suffer, there were few fixtures played against other schools. The hockey teams were also unable to practise much of what they had learnt from a Course given by Peggy Potts, the England Hockey Coach. However, good weather during the summer term led to an enthusiastic response and pleasing standards in both tennis and swimming.

1963–1964 Sally Pritchard

Deputy Head Girl: Hilary Jenkins.
Prefects: Sally Pritchard, Marjory Hester, Glenda Froy, Hilary Jenkins, Daryl May, Phyllis Evans, Margaret Follett, Jean Brittain, Margaret Clark, Shena Fulton, Rosemary Spicer, Wendy Watts, Susan Wyper, Paula Hendley, Susan Jenkins, Wendy McNab.
Hockey Captain: Phyllis Evans.
Netball Captain: Marjory Hester.
Tennis Captain: Hazel Stapleton.
Swimming Captain: Hilary Jenkins.
Games Secretary: Mary Everett.

The highlight of the academic year was the celebration of the seventy-five years that had passed since John Mattock's seventeenth century Foundation had been 're-interpreted' in favour of girls. A week of lectures, films, exhibitions, concerts and other activities was arranged to 'enlarge . . . experience beyond the limits of the normal curriculum' and culminated in an exciting performance of Britten's 'Let's Make an Opera'.

The year also saw the reorganisation of the school Prefect system: 'there will still be a small committee of prefects responsible for administration . . . (but) it is to be recognised that all members of the Sixth Form have duties and responsibilities as leaders of the school'.

There was also an important uniform change – the Junior School, like the Senior School, were now allowed to wear navy skirts instead of tunics. However, the Panama still reigned supreme, having won the annual battle with its arch rival, the Boater!

The decision was taken, in the interests of road safety, not to allow any First Years to cycle to school unless they had passed their Cycling Proficiency Test. This emphasis on safe practice when using the highway was amply rewarded when the

1964. Mrs. Daisy Aves and Miss Harrison. Mrs. Aves (Daisy Chalkley) was one of the original seven pupils at Bancroft. She is pictured with the Headmistress at a reunion to mark the School's 75th Anniversay.

[Mrs. G. M. Warwick]

school's Senior Team won the Rotary Shield in the Inter-Schools road safety quiz.

There were talks during the year on such diverse subjects as Russia, the Mission, a career in the W.A.A.F. and the problems of South-East Asia as well as repeat visits from the Hirsch Chamber Players and Mavis Elmett, and the Southern Children's Theatre Guild.

Once again, the Sixth Form gained most from all the various outings on offer – they went on courses at Offley and Juniper Hall, listened to lectures on computers and on the use of radar in meteorology, and watched performances of 'Hamlet', 'St. Joan', 'A Midsummer Night's Dream' and 'Troilus and Cressida'. The Second Year went to the National Youth Theatre in London to see 'Julius Caesar', while the Thirds saw a production of 'Jane Eyre' in Cambridge. Some of the Fourth and Fifth Years attended a London conference on Italy.

A joint party from the Girls' and Boys' Schools went to the Lake District in April to spend a week at a Holiday Fellowship Youth Camp. By the end, everyone – with their blisters – 'was sad to leave the little camp . . . and return to a mundane existence in the Hertfordshire "levels"'. Later that same month there was an exchange visit to Bingen when fifteen pupils from the Hitchin Grammar Schools went to stay for a week with their pen friends.

There were mixed fortunes for the school clubs. The decision was taken to close the Camera Club 'as there seems to be no demand for (its) continuation'. However, this did not stop the club from being inundated with items to sort out for an exhibition of school life. 'This photographic record,' wrote a member of the Club, 'will no doubt be just as amusing to pupils of the future when they are preparing for the Centenary celebrations!' A very popular Pets' Club was introduced for the First Years. The North Hertfordshire Inter-School Sixth Form Society was also established during the year to help foster the spirit of co-operation in social and cultural activities between the various schools in the area. By the end of the year the Society had arranged a film evening, a jazz and folk evening, a barbecue and Grand Dance: 'it is hoped that the Society's popularity will continue after this good start . . .'

135

This year hockey suffered, not so much from the weather but from the re-levelling of the top pitch, which meant that it was out of use for most of the season. This resulted in the lower field 'being in an appalling condition most of the time (through) being so much in use'. Even so, the teams generally did well and two members of the 1st XI were selected to play for Hertfordshire. The netball, tennis and swimming teams also had successful seasons, and there were special thanks to the First Years for being 'such willing and efficient ball boys'.

The Programme for the week of celebrations to mark the 75th Anniversary of Hitchin Girls' Grammar School:

EVENTS OF THE WEEK

Monday, April 27th

Inaugural Address
by
Mr. Alan Bullock, M.A.
Master of St. Catherine's College, Oxford

Tuesday, April 28th

Dr. A. P. Mathias	'The Molecular Basis of Heredity'
Mr. John Armitage	'The Pursuit of Truth'
Film	Scott of the Antarctic

Wednesday, April 29th

Miss Elizabeth Jenkins	'Writing and Real Life'
Miss Elizabeth Jenkins	'Writing a Biography'

Thursday, April 30th

Concert	Leonard Hirsch Orchestra
Soloist	Michael Roll
Hon. Sir Geoffrey Wrangham	'The Family and the Law'

Friday, May 1st

Mr. Edward Holloway	'The Future of the Commonwealth'
Miss E. D. Allright	'Impressions of Nigeria'
Dramatic Society Performance	'Let's Make an Opera' *Benjamin Britten*

Saturday, May 2nd

Reception for Old Girls

Dramatic Society Performance	'Let's Make an Opera' *Benjamin Britten*

1964–1965   Shena Fulton

Deputy Head Girl: Susan Jenkins.
Prefects: Shena Fulton, Susan Jenkins, Margaret Clark, Paula Hendley, Wendy McNab, Rosemary Spicer, Wendy Watts, Susan Wyper, Jean Brown, Margaret Thair, Susan Wingate.
Hockey Captain: Rosemary Spicer.
Netball Captain: Susan Wyper.
Tennis Captain: Wendy McNab.
Swimming Captain: Margaret Parker.
Games Secretaries: Fiona Colbeck, Susan Lewis.

As the school magazine reported, with just a hint of fatigue, illness had taken its toll: 'although weakened by attacks of German Measles, both staff and pupils have almost completed another school year . . .'

The Sixth Form had cause to rejoice when they were given special privileges allowing them to wear suitable blue or yellow dresses and make-up during the summer term: 'the Senior Sixth, however, are rather set in their ways and so far very few have taken advantage of the concessions'.

Miss Allright, the Deputy Headmistress, retired in July after thirty-seven years: 'It will be hard to imagine Hitchin Girls' Grammar School without her' wrote the magazine committee, and the Headmistress was quick to pay tribute to Miss Allright's high academic and personal standards and 'her real compassion for anyone in difficulties'.

It was during the previous month that Miss Harrison had discovered what it was like to be 'at the end of the alphabet' when, on 7th June in St. Alban's Abbey, she had married Kenneth Warwick, an engineer and director of the Stevenage-based firm of Geo. W. King's.

New ground was broken when the school hosted a two-day North Hertfordshire Sixth Form Conference on the theme of 'The Challenge of Industry', 'the first of its kind to be held in a State School'.

The mystery of the sudden appearance of resin on the floor of the stage was solved when several members of the Royal Ballet School came and gave a programme of classical ballet and modern dance. The Fifth and Sixth Form biologists heard an interesting lecture on cell division, and it was agreed that the use of slides to emphasise the important points made the afternoon 'appreciated by all'.

There were a number of musical events during the year. Miss Harrison took over as conductor of the School Orchestra and the music staff gave a recital, in aid of the Bechstein Grand Piano Fund, that provoked much interest among the pupils 'as we rarely get a chance to hear our teachers play in public'. The opportunity to watch the film of 'The Marriage of Figaro' paled beside the real musical highlight of the year – a performance of Bach's 'St. John's Passion' in the local parish church of St. Mary's. It was given by the combined orchestras and choirs of the Girls' and Boys' Grammar Schools which were joined by two professional singers especially for the occasion.

The school year was only a few days old when the Sixth Form set out on the first of many outings and visits. By the end of the summer term they had seen performances of 'Coriolanus', 'The Master Builder' (with Laurence Olivier), 'Oedipus Tyrannus' (in Classical Greek!) and 'Romeo and Juliet'; listened to outside lectures on everything from 'Ice in the Atmosphere' to 'Lasers' and had attended an important conference on 'Education and Peace' (C.E.W.C.). The Fifth

Year went to Stratford-upon-Avon to see 'Richard II' and there was much praise for David Warner's 'able portrayal' of the title role.

The Inter-Schools Sixth Form Society continued to flourish with a dance, play-readings and a theatre visit. The First Years were still enthusiastically involved with preparing scrapbooks and displays for their Pets' Club, and a party from the Senior Science Club were the first group to visit the new natural gas refining station in Walsworth. The cast for the school play – this year it was an 'entertaining' production of 'Much Ado About Nothing' – was chosen from those members of the Drama Clubs not already involved in the 'St. John Passion'. A Cookery Club for Sixth Formers, under the guidance of Miss Fletcher, was started and proved popular with many girls.

In spite of an encouraging beginning, the hockey teams could produce only variable results during the season. By contrast, the netball teams played enthusiastically and won the majority of their matches, even reaching the semi-finals of the County Championship Tournament.

1965–1966   Kathleen Anderson

Deputy Head Girl: Jean Dollimore.
Prefects: Kathleen Anderson, Jean Dollimore, Janice Buxton, Janet Dickson, Myra Jenkins, Katharine Walmsley, Susan Wingate, Judith Lake, Diana Thompson, Hazel Ridgeway.
Hockey Captain: Sally Bardner.
Netball Captain: Janet Dickson.
Tennis Captain: Myra Jenkins.
Swimming Captain: Helen Cruse.

The reorganisation of secondary education meant that, in a few years' time, the four Hitchin secondary schools would become all-ability five/six form entry establishments.

There was a general feeling amongst the school that the Mission was 'outdated' and that a rather more modern 'worthwhile cause' was needed to take its place. January 1966 saw the formation of the Hitchin Branch of the Save the Children Fund, which from the outset was supported by the school.

In November two of the Sixth Form – together with two Sixth Formers from the Boys' Grammar School – went to Norwich to take part in 'Challenge Trophy', a television quiz show. They lost to the eventual winners of the trophy, but not before the four of them were involved in a frantic rush around the studio to find jerseys so that their whiter than white blouses did not dazzle the cameras!

The school organised a careers evening with a difference when each of the eight guest speakers turned out to be an Old Girl. Between them, they held a variety of jobs including a Pathology Laboratory Technician, a Beautician, an ex-Civil Servant retraining as a Teacher, and a Policewoman. There were talks during the year on the life and achievements of Michaelangelo and a first-hand account of life in modern-day Rhodesia (Zimbabwe), which had recently declared U.D.I., and by local M.P. Mrs. Shirley Williams who spoke on the same subject.

The work of Charles Dickens was brought vividly to life when Roger Trafford brought his one-man interpretation of 'The Pickwick Papers' to school in the spring term. T. S. Eliot's 'Murder in the Cathedral' was the Senior Drama Club's choice for the school play, and the production, of what can often be a 'difficult' piece of modern verse drama, was a great success. There was a new instrumental music group in school when the First Form Recorder Group met regularly during the dinner-hour, even though numbers sometimes dropped 'due to the popularity of . . . tennis playing'. The rehearsals for the ever-popular school concert at the end of May proved to be very instructive for both choir and orchestra when fraught music staff pointed out that instrumentalists and singers could make a 'significant difference' to their performance if they 'spent less time worrying about the notes and more time in watching the conductor!'

There were visits and outings galore during the year. The Sixth Form went to the theatre, lectures, conferences and field courses. The difference between the Geography and Biology Field Courses was neatly summed up by one pupil who went on both: 'Whereas cold feet were the commonest complaint at Juniper Hall, Surrey (Geography), it was frozen fingers and sodden gloves at Malham Tarn, Yorkshire (Biology).'

The very successful Pets' Club metamorphosed into the Animal Club, and membership was extended to include the Second as well as the First Years. There were talks, films, project work and fund-raising events, including a Fair and Food Sale where one bizarre novelty competition involved balancing dog biscuits on top of each other! A new Art Club and Literary Club were formed during the year.

Fortunes were rather mixed for the hockey teams, with 'enthusiastic' players providing rather unfortunate and 'disappointing' results. However, performances in netball, tennis and swimming were rather more encouraging, even though the swimming display on Founders' Day had to be abandoned halfway through because of a thunderstorm!

1966–1967 Judith Lake

Deputy Head Girl: Diana Thompson.
Prefects: Judith Lake, Diana Thompson, Annette Guyatt, Janet Kemp, Maureen Staddon, Patricia Talbot, Gail Wooderson, Creina Richards, Jennifer Sothcott.
Hockey Captain: Mary Snowden.
Netball Captain: Gail Wooderson.
Tennis Captain: Patricia Talbot.
Swimming Captain: Sylvia Driscoll.

The start of the autumn term saw the School doing its best to cope with the 'crowded conditions . . . and inevitable discomfort' that resulted from having a record 590 pupils, including 112 in the four First Year Forms and 80 in the Junior Sixth. However, Mrs. Warwick was able to offer some hope by announcing that consultations were being held with the county architects to build a new gymnasium and science block.

It seemed, in the words of the Headmistress, 'quite impossible' that the 'vivacious, agile (and) elegant' Miss Lamb should have reached retirement age. As a past Deputy Headmistress, Senior Geographer and Careers Mistress, Miss Lamb had left her mark on the School with 'generations of well-educated Geographers and Sixth Formers'.

The school magazine underwent a major change. From now on, it was to be published in the autumn term rather than at the end of the summer term, so as to 'allow all results and reports to be up-to-date for the school year just completed'.

It was a successful year for school activities. There were talks on the Roman Empire, the Mission and China, and the now retired Miss Squire spoke about life at H.G.G.S. in the early 1940s.

The Choirs and Drama Club combined to present Malcolm Williamson's opera, 'The Happy Prince'; Mrs. Warwick conducted the orchestra in the march from 'Carmen' at the end of the school concert; the Senior Drama Club performed Goldsmith's 'She Stoops to Conquer' and the Junior Drama Club produced 'The Reluctant Dragon'. However, it was the performance given by the Monomaniac School of Dramatic Art in 'The Merchant of Florence' that really caught the school's attention! This was hardly surprising as the Monomaniacs were really the Staff: 'it is just as well that there were no talent scouts present . . . or the staff shortage would . . . become extremely worrying', commented the reviewer in the school magazine!

There were outings and visits to art galleries, historical and geographical sites, the Zoo and, above all, to theatres in London, Cambridge and Stratford-upon-Avon. It was at Stratford that the Sixth Form saw David Warner give a 'contemporary . . . and exciting' performance as Hamlet in Peter Hall's much-acclaimed production for the Royal Shakespeare Company. Some of the Sixth Form were also lucky enough to go to Germany at Christmas to attend an international conference. The consequences of political action were made only too clear when the party visited the Berlin Wall and, looking at the watch-towers and minefields, 'realised how difficult escape (to the West) would be.'

The various Junior School clubs continued to have strong support from their members, and there was even a revival of the Stamp Club which had last met in 1948 – to help with Save the Children Fund (S.C.F.) fund-raising. The Senior School societies were active during the year, making a great contribution to music and drama productions. The whole school also enjoyed the facilities and instruction offered by the Athletics Club in the summer term. This replaced the 'very popular' Dance Club that had been held in the winter and spring terms to teach the intricacies of English and Scottish folk dancing!

The games reports for the year make rather disappointing reading. Not only did it take some time for 'team spirit' to develop in both hockey and netball, but the girls also had to cope with both 'invaluable' members of the P.E. Department leaving at the end of the year. The news was better in swimming where the school did very well in the North Hertfordshire Gala, especially the Senior Team which won the Cup yet again, 'just as they have done ever since it was available for competition'.

1967–1968 Creina Richards

Deputy Head Girl: Penelope Barnes.
Prefects: Creina Richards, Penelope Barnes, Linda Burton, Elizabeth Eely, Victoria Foster, Jennifer Sothcott, Margaret Walmsley, Mary Williams.
Hockey Captain: Margaret Walmsley.
Netball Captain: Linda Burton.
Tennis Captain: Patricia Rimes.
Swimming Captain: Pamela Prickett.
Athletics Captain: Barbara Thompson.

The winds of change and reorganisation continued to sweep through education. Mrs. Warwick took the opportunity to remind everyone that good communication played a vital role in coping with the resultant stress.

There was an occasion for rejoicing in November when Mrs. Warwick gave birth to a daughter, Claire Louise. During her absence, the school was left in the capable charge of Miss Britton, the Deputy Head.

A long tradition came to an end in the spring term when the School Council met, for the first time in six years, to discuss the awarding of trophies. It was agreed that the increasing number of girls being taught in similar ability 'divisions' rather than forms made it very difficult to award either the Work Trophy or the Senior Flex Trophy to a single form and still be fair. The decision was therefore taken that these two trophies, together with the Deportment Trophy, would no longer be awarded.

Project-based library lessons were introduced into the timetable to help pupils understand how the library worked and what facilities it offered.

The school continued to enjoy a wide range of activities and cultural outings. The choirs and orchestras had a busy and successful year. The combined choirs of the two Grammar Schools performed Pergolesi's 'Stabat Mater' and Benjamin Britten's 'Saint Nicolas' Cantata in St. Mary's Church. The Senior Drama Club's production of 'The Shoemaker's Holiday' was well received by both public and press. The Junior Drama Club, full of dramatic potential, also produced an amusing and entertaining pantomime.

The school branch of the Save the Children Fund continued to raise money and knit blankets and vests to help with the Fund's work around the world, especially in Vietnam. Hitchin Girls' also received a plaque from the S.C.F. when it acted as a 'Hostess School' for the S.C.F. regional conference.

Although the results were mixed, both the hockey and netball teams generally played well during the year. The tennis teams had a successful season and lost only three of their twenty-one matches. 'Over-whelming enthusiasm' greeted the introduction of athletics into the games curriculum. Junior and Senior Athletics Clubs were formed and plimsolls were soon replaced by running spikes. The poor weather meant a disappointing year for swimming fixtures, especially with the cancellation of the North Hertfordshire Swimming Gala. However, it did not dampen the enthusiasm of the teams which managed to achieve consistently high standards in spite of everything!

141

1968–1969　Vanessa Hull

Deputy Head Girls: Diana Buxton, Vivien Grimes.
Prefects: Vanessa Hull, Diana Buxton, Vivien Grimes, Grace Barringer, Brenda Evans, Wendy Humphreys, Denise Murphy, Susan Pennington, Julie Winder.
Hockey Captain: Brenda Evans.
Netball Captain: Diana Buxton.
Tennis Captain: Cherry Nixon.
Swimming Captain: Pamela Prickett.
Athletics Captain: Barbara Thompson.

There was expansion of careers guidance within the school, involving provision of a specific Careers Room and the reorganisation of the Sixth Form so as to meet the needs of the individual and ensure that each pupil could take her proper place in society.

The new Sixth Form structure – replacing a two-tiered system with seven Tutor Groups, each with its own member of staff and School Prefect – was a particular interest, and would, it was hoped, 'be successful in . . . ensuring greater co-operation between the Junior and Senior Sixth and between the Sixth Form and the rest of the school'.

Mr. Cooper, the caretaker, retired after thirty years' service to the school.

The choir 'broadened its horizons and became more ambitious', singing at the Festival Hall and Brand Street Methodist Church as well as at the carol service and spring concert. The orchestra also thrived and a School Wind Band was formed in the autumn term. The Drama Club presented a 'very enjoyable' production of 'Romeo and Juliet', all the more welcome because it was one of the O Level Eng. Lit. set books! The Debating Society provided an outlet for self-expression with debates on topics both serious and frivolous: its 'Balloon Debate' in which various members of staff battled for verbal survival was judged to be 'great fun' by all concerned! There was also a new Field Club to encourage interest throughout the School in physical Geography. The highlight of the Club's activities was a day-trip to the Derbyshire Peak District in May. The Animal, Chess and Recorder Clubs in the Junior School also continued to flourish during the year.

The two main charities enjoyed an 'active year' of financial and voluntary support from the school. This support allowed, amongst other things, the Hitchin Room at the Mission to be redecorated, and a large donation – the result of a sponsored walk around the lower hockey pitch! – to be made to the Save the Children Fund in its Golden Jubilee Year.

There was a new 'first' when a party of Sixth Formers went to Austria on a week's ski-ing holiday in April.

All the sports teams had an enjoyable and successful season, particularly the 1st netball team which won the cup at the Hitchin Sports Festival and came second in the county tournament. The school also joined the Blue Lagoon Sailing Club at Arlesey, and there were plans for future races between all the Hitchin schools.

Parents and friends were once again invited to attend Sports Day, just as they had done in the inter-war years: 'the weather was at its best . . . all forms showed enthusiasm and keenness . . . it will now undoubtedly become an annual event'.

1969–1970   Eleanor Brown

Deputy Head Girls: Janice Hughes, Barbara Weeden.
Prefects: Eleanor Brown, Janice Hughes, Barbara Weeden, Annette Banner,
Elizabeth Lancaster, Lynn Perrin, Patricia Rimes, Sheila Smith.
Hockey Captain: Susan Woolley.
Netball Captain: Susan Richardson.
Tennis Captain: Patricia Rimes.
Swimming Captain: Hilary Terretta.

There were two centenaries to celebrate during the year: the foundation of Girton
College, Cambridge, in October, 1869 and the Education Act of May, 1870.
'Girton Day' – or 'Girtenary' as the girls called it! – was celebrated on 16th
October. The School gave a special luncheon at which the Mistress of Girton was
the guest of honour. Hitchin Girls' Grammar School was a very appropriate place
in which to hold such a function, as the first Girtonians had met to conduct their
academic studies not very far away, in Benslow House, Hitchin, a 'safe yet
reasonably convenient distance' from the University authorities in Cambridge, who
were not yet of the opinion that women should have access to higher education!
Earlier that morning Lady Llewelyn Davies, a relative of Emily Davis, Girton's
founder, unveiled a plaque at Benslow House and there was also a small exhibition
in the school Hall showing local links with the college. The anniversary of the 1870

March 1970.   'Off to cheer their Games Mistress!' Excited faces look forward to the Women's Hockey
International at White City where Mrs. C. Aspinwall, Head of the Physical Education Department, was
the England Captain.   (North Herts Gazette]

143

Education Act – a very important piece of legislation which provided for the building of Board Schools paid for by a mixture of government grants and local rates – was celebrated by an Open Day when parents and friends were invited to visit the school and go into lessons.

The production of Benjamin Britten's opera, 'Noye's Fludde', in March involved choir and orchestra (and the MacNaghten Quartet), staff and pupils: 'What makes a work of this kind difficult but most rewarding is the number of people . . . and the variety of different elements that have to be combined.' Two months earlier, some of the Fifth Year had also taken part in a combined production of the musical 'Bertie!' at the Boys' School.

The Sixth Form continued to meet with other Sixth Formers in the area through inter-school societies like the British Association for Young Scientists and the long-standing North Hertfordshire Social Committee. 'Each year the (Social Committee) ventures – dances, barbecues, etc. – seem to be more successful and the society itself is becoming more widely known.'

School activities continued to flourish during the year with concerts, recitals, visits to the theatre and outings. The school play was a 'most amusing' production of 'Cold Comfort Farm' by the Senior Drama Club. The juniors continued to enjoy the facilities offered by, amongst others, the Animal, Stamp and Recorder Clubs.

It was a pleasing year for the athletics teams which retained the under 17 Trophy and won the under 13 Shield at the North Hertfordshire Schools' Championship. The 1st netball team entered the North Hertfordshire League for the first time, won their twelve matches (all played away) and emerged the winners! Some of the keen Sixth Form sailors were also awarded a trophy for making the best effort in the 3Ms sailing marathon organised by the North Hertfordshire and East Bedfordshire Sailing Club.

In spite of very unsettled weather, Sports Day 'went smoothly . . . everything ran to time' and there was a thrilling finish when the Senior trophy was won by just half a point!

1970–1971 Sally Cordwell

Deputy Head Girls: Elizabeth Buckley, Jane Toll.
Prefects: Sally Cordwell, Elizabeth Buckley, Jane Toll, Joanna Haigh, Geraldine Kaliski, Jane Matthews, Jill Nicholl, Joanne Saunders.
Hockey Captain: Jane Pye.
Netball Captain: Anne Kenzie.
Tennis Captain: Jane Pye.
Swimming Captain: Hilary Terretta.
Athletics Captain: Ann Kenzie.

Work began on the 'long-awaited' Science and Gymnastics block during the spring term, and the front of the school found itself having to cope with cranes, scaffolding and all the other apparatus of a major building project.

The beginning of the spring term was severely disrupted when the school had to close for a few days owing to a lack of fuel supplies, itself due to industrial action, and the break-down of the school boiler.

Two long-serving members of staff retired at the end of the summer term. Miss Britton, the Deputy Head and Head of Modern Languages, had been at the school for 22 years during which time she had given 'dedicated service . . . approached life with unbounded energy and enjoyed every aspect of her job'. Miss Bolton, who had joined the staff in 1955, was the Head of Mathematics and one-time Senior Mistress. A teacher with 'meticulously high standards', she left the school a 'permanent record of achievement by establishing Mathematics as a strong and popular subject'.

The flourishing B.A.Y.S. (British Association for Scientists) group in school had something to celebrate when Joanna Haigh, the area secretary, won one of only two annual awards offered by B.A.Y.S. Her prize was the chance to observe the standards of teaching in the Science Department of a selected American University.

The main musical events in 'rather a quiet year' were the carol service and the school concert. No doubt heartened by the plans to turn the old Gymnasium into a Drama Room when the new block was completed, the Drama Clubs had a busy year! The Junior Drama Club gave a spirited performance of 'Toad of Toad Hall' to the school and, for the first time, to parents in the evening. One Second Year, writing in the school magazine, had vivid memories of the rehearsals beforehand: the camp bed that collapsed as Toad lumbered onto it . . . the 'forgotten' umbrella stand being pushed onto the stage by a hidden member of the cast . . . Ratty's tail falling off at a suitably dramatic moment! There was also a Junior Drama Festival in the summer term on the theme of 'Suddenly, Everything Was Quite Different'. Some of the sketches about parties and discotheques were 'so convincing that it made us wonder how the Junior School spend their evenings!' The Senior Drama Club presented Shaw's 'Pygmalion' to over 750 people who came to see what was, by all accounts, a very enjoyable and successful performance.

The Junior Sixth organised an afternoon Valentine's Party in February for the old people in Minsden House. The buttonholes, tea, songs and sketches were a 'great success' and it was hoped that it would become an annual event.

There was a full programme of activities and expeditions during the year, including the annual ski-ing trip to Switzerland and a long weekend in Derbyshire for some members of the Fifth and Sixth Forms. Six Sixth Formers – together with twelve boys and four staff from the Boys' School – also went for a week's holiday to the Lake District at Easter. Their verdict: 'A wonderful holiday in which we had climbed many mountains, learned new card games, made many new friends, seen Wordsworth's daffodils, and last but not least, played football in climbing boots, so injuring certain members of Hitchin Boys' . . . who were playing in plimsolls!'

It was a very successful year for sports. The 2nd XI hockey team shared the Hertfordshire Second Eleven Cup with Francis Bacon School and the senior athletics team won the North Hertfordshire Senior Athletics meeting. The 1st and 2nd tennis teams were also undefeated all season.

1971–1972 Mary Arthur

Deputy Head Girls: Deirdre Gray, Judith Russell.
Prefects: Mary Arthur, Deirdre Gray, Judith Russell, Suzanne Bailey, Gillian Carr, Jane Everett, Alison Groom, Catherine Johnstone, Sharon Presswell.
Hockey Captain: Judith Russell.
Netball Captain: Suzanne Pettet.
Tennis Captain: Judith Russell.
Swimming Captain: Mary Arthur.
Athletics Captain: Suzanne Pettet.

It was hoped that the opening of the new Science and Gymnasium Block, after a year 'dominated by the "music concrete" of the cement mixer', would allow the school to develop 'ideas, techniques and interests in a manner appropriate to modern methods'.

It was Miss Badland who had contributed so much to the evolution of just such a liberal education, and when her death was announced in October, the school paused to remember and reflect on all that she had achieved as Headmistress: '(her) insistence on a broadly based curriculum, combined with high academic standards as an individual goal, remains inherent in the ethics of this School'.

The completion of the new building, with its panoramic views over the town below, allowed the old laboratories (Rooms 17, 18 and 19) to be converted into Geography and History Classrooms. The old Gymnasium became the Drama Room, and the vacated Geography Rooms were converted into Art Rooms. The opportunity was also taken to redecorate the library and refurnish part of it with low seating so as to provide an area for informal discussion and talks.

There was drama when two members of staff narrowly escaped serious injury in two (separate and) unconnected incidents in the summer term. Mrs. Parish was hit by falling plaster as a ceiling in the kitchens collapsed and Mr. Lee, the Head of R.E., had to leap clear as a section of the Staff Room ceiling crashed to the floor. The Staff Room had to be closed for ten days to allow repairs to take place.

This year saw a change in the format of school assemblies to provide a more varied and less formal atmosphere. From now on, Sixth Form volunteers took the service on Monday, there was Sectional Assembly on a Tuesday and Staff led Morning Prayers on a Wednesday and Thursday. Friday remained a Form's 'Mission Service'.

The Music Department felt a keen sense of loss when Miss Stovin left after twenty-five years' service to the school. 'Her joy in making music was memorable and the happy, humorous way in which she coaxed the whole school to sing contributed greatly to the warm atmosphere upon which so many of our visitors comment.'

The Junior Drama Club's 'enthusiastic' production was 'The Land of Green Ginger', and it was obvious that they had made good use of the new Drama Room!

The school began to venture further afield on trips and outings during the year. In the autumn term some of the Sixth Form went for eight 'hot and memorable' days in Italy. Through visiting Rome, Florence and Venice the party learnt much about Italian culture, traditions and way of life and were 'all impressed by the variety of sights and experiences open to us'. The Junior School went ski-ing in the Cairngorms where they were able to enjoy better and more abundant snow-cover than the members of the Senior School who had gone ski-ing in Austria at the same time! Some of the Fifth Year also went on various excursions, including a day-trip to Boulogne.

1971–1972. The 1st XI Hockey Team won the Hertfordshire Schools Tournament outright for the first time when they beat Loreto College 1–0 in the final. *L. to R., back row:* Penny Gilman, Jackie Paddon, Gillian Woolley, Carole Cox, Jill Pickering, Sandra Grimes, Mrs. Aspinwall. *L. to R., front row:* Alison Gordon, Yvonne Checkley, Judy Russell (Captain), Leisa Freeman, Suzanne Pettet.

[North Herts Gazette]

There were also closer links with the Boys' School. A barn dance replaced the traditional Christmas dance and there were joint dramatic and musical productions. A glowing review of the Grammar Schools' Joint Concert, by one Phil R. Monic, ended with the comment 'the abiding impression is that of seeing and hearing so many members of both Schools (conducted by Miss Stovin) taking such obvious joy in making great music'.

It was another eventful year for the Hitchin branch of the Save the Children Fund with, amongst other things, a street collection, a market stall and sales of Christmas cards and gifts. There was also a new venture: a Spring Fashion Show presented by the Dorothy Perkins chain of shops, held in the school hall, with all proceeds going to the Fund. The Mission continued to struggle on, with its shortfall in financial contributions being made up by the generous contributions of the Old Girls.

The summer term saw a concentrated effort to raise funds for the Swimming Pool Heating Fund so that its use would not be so dependent on good weather. There were sponsored swims and walks as well as the sale of engraved biros and combs.

1972–1973   Yvonne Checkley

Deputy Head Girls: Jane Buxton, Patricia Stowell.
Prefects: Yvonne Checkley, Jane Buxton, Patricia Stowell, Carole Cox, Vivienne Dilley, Leisa Freeman, Susan Shattock, Gillian Woolley.
Hockey Captain: Leisa Freeman.
Netball Captain: Fiona Smith.
Tennis Captain: Leisa Freeman.

It was with sadness and 'complete shock' that the school learnt of the death of Mrs. Jill Heller in January. Mrs. Heller, a member of the English Department, had been at H.G.G.S. for six years: 'All who knew her enjoyed her delightful sense of humour and respected the sincerity and grace of her character'.

There were 'reluctant farewells' to staff as well. Miss Naylor retired at the end of the summer term after many dedicated years spent teaching Art. The school also said 'goodbye' to Mrs. Aspinwall and Mrs. Baylay, who between them had done so much for school sporting activities during the previous six years: 'we shall long remember this partnership!'.

A joint production, with the Boys' School, of 'The Beggar's Opera' proved to be a 'great success' at the end of the spring term. Another joint attraction was the Thornton Wilder play 'Our Town', set in North America. It was hoped that such artistic ventures between the two schools would soon become a regular event. Meanwhile, 'Verse 5', a joint Sixth Form five-piece folk and gospel group, continued to give a large number of local concerts and even appeared on television in 'About Anglia'.

The Ballet Rambert gave an 'absorbing display' of ballet techniques and the Juniors also enjoyed a mime demonstration. Just before Easter, the Junior Drama Club gave a theatre-in-the-round production of 'The Lion, the Witch and the Wardrobe'. Later on, two afternoons in July were devoted to a 'thoroughly enjoyable' Drama Festival. An upsurge in interest, particularly from the Junior forms, led to the revival of the Chess Club and a total of thirty-one pupils entered the Knock-Out Tournament organised by the Club. In spite of a very disappointing beginning – no-one, apart from the elected officials, attended the first meeting! – the Middle School Debating Society survived the year and held a number of interesting discussions on contemporary topics.

Twenty-five girls went on the French Exchange to Le Mans and had a most enjoyable time exploring the sights and becoming better acquainted with French cuisine. The party also visited a Renault factory: 'the work seemed rather slack, probably because the workers were distracted by . . . fifty beautiful girls!' Another group went to Florence, where, in addition to fighting their way through the crowds in the art galleries, they also became adept at bargaining in the markets and coping with the erratic schedules of Italian trains! At the same time, there were groups on ski-ing trips: the Seniors went to Norway while the Juniors had to be content with Aviemore. Earlier in the year, the better skiers had travelled to Spain to enjoy more advanced slopes.

It was an active year for the school branch of the S.C.F. which continued with its successful clothing collections and sales of work. The 'Roundabout Club' was also restarted to provide an area of particular interest for Junior S.C.F. members such as sponsored 'knit-ins'.

The Swimming Pool Heating Fund reached its target of £3,500 by the end of the summer term. Over half of this sum was raised through the 'remarkable corporate efforts' of the School, parents and friends, including a highly successful Summer Fete.

Even though the team lost its only match of the season, cricket was a welcome introduction to the school's sporting activities. However, there was a word of warning for the players: 'we hope that their practising will not spoil the top hockey pitch, which has now been fully restored (after all the building work) and is looking at its best'!

1973–1974 Annette Hayes

Deputy Head Girls: Susan Hill, Susan Plowman.
Prefects: Elizabeth Gray, Annette Hayes, Elaine Herbage, Susan Hill, Margaret Lamb, Rosalind McCombie, Susan Plowman, Gillian Randell, Judith Watson.
Hockey Captain: Margaret Lamb.
Netball Captain: Ann Pateman.
Tennis Captain: Christine Danks.

The year – an important 'turning point' in the school's history – began with an increase in numbers. Four-form entry now became a reality, although, 'in an already crowded school, one wonders how the extra pupils and staff will be accommodated in the years to come'. The number of Sixth Form Prefects also had to be increased to nine to allow a Prefect to be attached to every Year.

The death was announced in January of Miss Allright. Now retired after thirty-seven years' service to the school, she had been Head of Science, Deputy Head and Acting Head. In the words of the Headmistress, 'Miss Allright would brook no nonsense yet the apparent severity was a facade masking a true kindliness, a forthright wit and a generosity of spirit that endeared her to us all.'

Dora Wilson, who had been a pupil for three years, died in September. This 'tiny girl', whom staff had initially to carry up and down stairs, suffered from progressive kidney failure and, in the days before transplants, was totally dependent on dialysis for her survival: 'she will long be remembered . . . for her courage and determination and for her broad smile and sense of humour'.

The school held an Open Day at the end of the summer term to which parents and friends were invited. It was well-attended, and there were demonstrations and displays including a 'Fashion Show' where some of the girls modelled clothes they had made themselves in needlework lessons.

During the year the school began offering financial help to a poor Korean family through the auspices of the S.C.F. Sponsorship. This scheme guaranteed the family – a sick mother forced to leave her factory job when her right arm had to be amputated, and her two daughters of ten and eleven – a minimum of £60 a year to help provide school fees and other basics: 'in Korea, nothing is provided by the State, and the cost of living has risen sharply, as elsewhere in the world'. S.C.F. provided regular newsletters and these, together with a photograph of the family, were kept on reference in a folder in the school library. There was the hope that, 'as the years go by, a real friendship will be established' between the school and the two young Korean girls 'so that we can help these children through their schooling till they are able to support themselves and their mother'.

As had been hoped, last year's musical and dramatic ventures with the Boys' School were continued this year. The joint Drama Club chose John Bowen's 'The Fall and Redemption of Man' as their annual production. There was also a combined concert which, in addition to more traditional pieces, also included a work especially written for the two schools by David Butler, an 'Old Boy'. The concert, which was a 'great success', was later filmed by the County Film Unit. The Senior Sixth presented a 'very entertaining' revue to the staff and school at Christmas. It had been many years since the last Sixth Form revue and the hope was expressed that 'perhaps this will be a more frequent event' in the future.

In April, a party of Second, Third and Fourth Formers, together with two members of staff, went on a sixteen day Exchange visit to Luzy in the South of France. For part of the time they joined their Exchange partners in the local school: 'it was rather like being a Zoo exhibit, all the French children stared and pointed, but everybody was friendly and kind to us . . . and we enjoyed being treated like V.I.P.s . . . we taught the children English songs. It was very odd teaching Fifth Years "Baa, Baa Black Sheep" and other nursery rhymes.'

The Inter-Form Gymnastics Competition was held for the first time since 1947! There were six sections and, of them all, the vault seemed to have the best potential for trouble. Not only did the competitors have to perform three different vaults, but they also had to face the distinct possibility that they might land in an undignified heap on the floor rather than gracefully on their feet! The eventual winners of the Competition were a First Form who produced 'a very high level of performance in managing to win against the rest of the school'.

Thanks to the efforts of everyone who contributed to the Heating Fund in the previous year, the school was able to enjoy a heated pool during the summer term.

1974–1975   Edwina Dighé

Deputy Head Girls: Karen Pateman, Elizabeth Seddon.
Prefects: Kim Allum, Clare Bradfield, Alison Cross, Edwina Dighé, Beverley Foster, Joy Hammond, Karen Pateman, Elizabeth Seddon, Patricia Tomlin.
Hockey Captain: Clare Bradfield.
Netball Captain: Deborah Arnold.
Tennis Captain: Beverley Foster.

In September, the school dropped the word 'Grammar' from its official title in acknowledgement of its new 'all-ability' status. From now on, it was to be known simply as Hitchin Girls' School. There were changes too in the administrative departments at both County and local levels. Mrs. Winifred M. Austin, B.Sc., who had been Divisional Education Officer for twenty-one years, retired in the summer, to be succeeded by Mr. Brian J. Frederick, B.A. At Hertford Mr. S. T. Broad, M.A., County Education Officer since 1968, handed over to Mr. D. Fisher, M.A.

It is virtually impossible for any public institution to remain unaffected by national events, and Hitchin Girls' proved no exception to the rule as accelerating inflation overshadowed the year. It soon became clear that the school 'was entering a phase of severe financial stringency' as it tried to cope with rapid price increases in the costs of educational books, materials and equipment. All this was in addition to the problems posed by yet more pupils as the school admitted a five-form intake in the First year for the first time.

For a time, even the building of the desperately needed Junior School block seemed in danger of cancellation when the development plans for the Highbury House site had to be abandoned. However, new plans were eventually approved, even though they required the demolition of the Domestic Science room and meant another period of mobile classrooms and 'musical chairs' for some departments!

The ability of the school to cope with such problems and difficulties owed much to the influence and attitude of the staff, and so it was with sadness that staff and pupils learnt of the death of Miss Lamb in July. 'She was an exceptional person . . . who commanded great respect both as a person and in her professional capacity.' Miss Lambe had retired in 1967 after many years of teaching Geography and giving advice on Careers.

One of the most significant decisions of the year was that taken by the School Council and all pupils to withdraw their support from the Mission and its Peckham Settlement at the end of the academic year. This was the result of a combination of dwindling collections, the knowledge that the Settlement had an 'ever-increasing' bank overdraft and the feeling that the school was becoming 'alienated' from Peckham. It was hoped that a suitable replacement could be found in the Hitchin area for all the charitable work associated with the Mission.

While all this was being decided, the school continued to support the work of the S.C.F. and to collect funds for the sponsorship of its Korean family. The Junior Roundabout Club held a Summer Fair and Fancy Dress Competition and raised £13.

The Junior Sixth were actively involved with starting a new club for the residents of Minsden Old People's Home. Their efforts culminated in a 'grand entertainment' at the end of the summer term where 'dance, drama, Old Tyme songs and musical solos were enjoyed by all . . . to say nothing of strawberries and cream!'

After five months of rehearsals the joint production of 'The Dracula Spectacula' with the Boys' School proved to be 'very successful', so much so that the script, by Mr. Gardiner and Mr. Parr, was to be published. The school also enjoyed a Senior and Junior drama festival during the year: 'most Forms presented plays and these were performed well and were most enjoyable'. The Senior Choir sang carols at Hitchin Hospital in December, 'an occasion enjoyed by both the choir and the patients'. There was a concert in April from the combined orchestra of the Girls' and Boys' Schools at which 'a high degree of musicianship was achieved, particularly by the soloists'. Towards the end of the year, the Sixth Form also gave an informal concert which was so enjoyable that it was hoped it might become a regular event in the school musical calendar.

There were very pleasing successes in games during the year, especially when the hockey 1st XI won the Hertfordshire County Shield. Sports Day proved to be very exciting, with twenty-five records being broken and three equalled, out of a total of forty-four events.

1975–1976   Penelope Plowman

Deputy Head Girls: Claire Bousfield, Deborah Sell.
Prefects: Jane Ballantyne, Claire Bousfield, Sandra Chapman, Hilary Farr, Allyson Hibbin, Penny Plowman, Jackie Porter, Deborah Sell, Ingrid Wehrmann.
Hockey Captain: Deborah Sell.
Netball Captain: Deborah Arnold.
Tennis Captain: Deborah Sell.

There was no doubt that the school was becoming increasingly crowded. This year there were 740 pupils. 'To look down at the assembled school with First, Second and Third forms sitting neatly crowded and enduring discomfort with remarkable stoicism, is to understand that change is taking place.'

The co-operation that the harvest festival required seemed to augur well for the future. 'The Sixth Form and First and Second Forms worked closely together on this occasion . . . (and) the Middle School and Fifth were prepared to support this new venture.'

Mrs. Brazier, who had been a member of the domestic staff for almost forty years, was amongst those who retired in July: 'We thank her most sincerely for her courteous service and her loyalty to the school'.

A new scheme was introduced this year to complement the continuing support for the S.C.F. It was decided that the school would vote to support a different charity each year on a seven year cycle. 'Therefore a girl spending seven years at the School will have helped at least seven different charities.' (For this first year the school supported both the R.S.P.C.A. and the N.S.P.C.C., but in subsequent years there would be only one charity.)

1976. Sports Day. Competitors waiting for Mr. Graham to fire his starting-gun as they line up for the 100 metre race. The mobile class rooms can be seen plainly in the background.

[Mrs. M. Drew]

The school continued to receive regular quarterly reports from the two Korean girls they were sponsoring, together with details of how they were spending the gifts of extra money that were raised by 'special efforts' within Years. One letter said: 'Thank you very much for the gift. We have bought many nice things, like medicine.' Another gift enabled them to have the roof of their house mended.

Those members of the school who belonged to the County Youth Orchestra (Reserve) and Choir went on a tour of part of France during the summer holidays. The busy programme for the hundred strong contingent included concerts in Paris and St. Malo. The performance at the Cathedral of St. Brieuc was the most successful and the musicians were 'applauded for a double encore'. The concert at St. Malo was recorded for transmission by French radio.

The athletics teams had a very successful season. They won both the under 15 and under 18 North Hertfordshire Athletics Shields for the second year in succession and eight team members were also selected for the County Championships. The under 14 swimming team also won the North Hertfordshire Trophy.

Henry, the cat, pads round the school
With a knowing look in his eye.
There's a hint of a smile on his furry face
And this is the reason why:

In a secret hide out under the stairs
He hoards our missing things.
Beside his bed (made of odd, woolly socks)
Lie purses, watches and rings.

So if your games kit's missing
You'll know where it has gone.
Imagine Henry down in the woods
Furtively trying it on!

And if you've lost the bag of crisps
You hoped to eat for lunch.
Henry will be in the bicycle sheds
Enjoying a private munch.

At least if homework's gone astray
There's a ready-made excuse.
Point to the pawprint on the stair,
Say, "Henry's on the loose!"

Someone black and white with a furry tail
Can afford to break every rule
So watch out, watch out for Henry, the Cat –
Burglar of the school.

Mrs. Biddle's (English Staff) 1976 poem in celebration of Henry, the school cat!

153

1976–1977   Mary Dalling

Deputy Head Girls: Theresa Hyde, Carolyn Williams.
Prefects: Kay Barrett, Gillian Cross, Amalia Liguori, Sally Marshall, Susan Scowen, Gillian Sykes, Heather Tomlin, Marilyn Watts.
Hockey Captain: Carolyn Williams.
Netball Captain: Jenny Humphrey.
Tennis Captain: Caroline Fletcher.
Senior Librarians: Judith Kemp, Valerie Underwood.

The school voted to support mentally handicapped children as the year's annual charity. Collections and 'special efforts' meant that the children at Butts Close Special School enjoyed gifts that included two bicycles and an overhead projector. Some Sixth Formers also visited Butts Close on a regular basis to lend an extra hand.

Unfortunately, the sheer size of the school meant that the harvest festival had to be changed this year. Only the First, Second and Sixth Forms attended the actual service, leaving the Fourth Forms to take care of the sale of goods. The money raised was given to 'War on Want', and some goods were taken to Minsden Old People's Home.

The drama production was 'Cauchemar' (Nightmare), a 'delightful' musical play written and produced by George Szirtes, the Head of Art and a gifted, award-winning poet. The music was composed and played by Theresa Hyde in the Senior Sixth.

1977.   The U.15 hockey team, unbeaten in twenty-two games over a four year period and winners of the Hertfordshire Schools U.15 Hockey Tournament. (Some of the team were also members of the U.15 netball team who won the North Hertfordshire League Championship Shield.) *Back row, L. to R.:* *Melanie Arnold, Elizabeth Agg, Julie Maylin, Anne Burges. *Middle row:* Sharon Bishop, Penny Macdonald, Dinah Scott, *Peggy Tyler, Susan Hall. *Front row:* *Sarah Davies, Carnice Thomas, *Sally Mack, *Thelma Blake, Julie Huthwaite.   [North Herts Gazette, Mrs. M. Drew]
*Member of both hockey and netball teams.

The drama festival was held in the last fortnight of the summer term when 'the whole school becomes a flurry of organisation and many a strange sight!'

The celebrations for the Queen's Silver Jubilee reached a peak in the summer term with a school concert in conjunction with the Boys' School in St. Mary's Church. There was also a Jubilee Gala Evening that 'gave much pleasure' to all who attended and resulted in a substantial contribution being made to both the Swimming Pool Fund and Prince Charles's Jubilee Fund.

Some of the Senior School went ski-ing in the Italian Alps during the spring term and, by all accounts, had a 'very enjoyable time!'

It was a very successful year for sporting acehivements throughout the school. The under 15 netball team won the North Hertfordshire League, and the under 14 team represented North Hertfordshire at the county championships. The under 15 hockey XI won the county championship for their age-group, and two of the School Teams were worthy runners-up in an international hockey tournament. The swimming teams won both the North Hertfordshire Senior and Intermediate swimming trophies. The athletics teams also won the North Hertfordshire Senior and Intermediate athletics trophies for the third year in succession!

1977–1978   Jenny Humphrey

Deputy Head Girls: Elizabeth Thrussell, Faith Watson.
Prefects: Sandra Blackaby, Jayne Bunker, Yvonne Hawkins, Emma Humphreys, Stephanie King, Anne Powis, Pamela Tickett, Gillian Walsh.
Hockey Captain: Alison Mitchell.
Netball Captain: Jenny Humphrey.
Tennis Captain: Faith Watson.
Senior Librarians: Caroline James, Rosita Peach, Anne Powis.

The Lower School block was completed in February and three hundred First and Second Years got down to the business of 'settling into' their new environment.

The new building meant the establishment of new traditions. The orchestra began rehearsing in the Lower School Hall, and the sunken garden quickly became another area where the Juniors could relax and let off steam at break and lunchtimes! Fourth Formers sat at the head of the table in the dining area and the Fifths did a lunchtime duty, 'thus demonstrating a feeling of care and concern for others'.

The absence of a caretaker during the spring term brought home in no uncertain way the importance of supporting domestic staff. Had it not been for the help and co-operation given by the caretakers from three other local schools, Hitchin Girls' would have had no option but to close: 'It is very easy to take people for granted and only to become truly aware of the debt we owe for loyal service when there is an emergency'.

When Miss Maggs (Mrs. Pacy) entered a school team for the 'Stockpiler' Competition run by the Financial Times, she could not have guessed that the seven team members, from her A Level Economics Group, would be among the 'Top 20' Schools. The careful investment of their imaginary £20,000 worth of British shares had yielded, in just three months, an amazing 20% profit!

1978.   Gilt-Edged Girls. The successful 'Stockpiler' Team. *L. to R.:* Joy Bentley-Tyler, Susan Cook, Karen Bland, Miss Maggs, Jenny Humphrey, Jacqueline Dawes, Ananda Hawkins; Yvonne Hawkins.
[Jenny Humphrey, North Herts Gazette]

It was now four years since the school had begun its sponsorship of two Korean girls through the S.C.F. Both girls were now in a middle school where they were studying hard and doing well.

The Senior Choir went to Offley Place to sing for the old people, and there was also a local carol singing expedition to raise money for the Prince Charles Benevolent Fund. They performed a work by Holst in St. Mary's Church at Easter while the Junior and Middle School Choirs contributed to a concert in the Town Hall during the week of the Hitchin Festival.

Founder's Day was, for the Middle School, different this year when they entertained the rest of the school with an enjoyable entertainment which included musical elements, dancing, a gym display and an 'impressive' judo demonstration.

The production of 'Wenceslas' in December provided a fitting climax to the winter term and showed once again the fine talents the school possessed in staff like Mr. Szirtes (words) and Mrs. Riches (music). The tale of the murder of the 'Good King' – an early Christian martyr – by his brother for his failure to promote the heathen cause was one of the dramatic highlights of the year.

The Printing Club was started by the Art Department during the year to provide a means of 'publish(ing) new poems and stories with illustrations'. It had two hand-presses, paper, a variety of type, and it welcomed all members of the school who wanted to experiment with printing techniques.

The gym competition was a great success as usual, and both competitors and spectators had a 'thoroughly enjoyable' time. The various teams continued to do well during the year, with the under 17 swimming team retaining both the title and the trophy in the North Hertfordshire Championships and the under 13 netball team finishing the joint winners of the North Hertfordshire League.

1978–1979 Sarah Almond

Deputy Head Girls: Amanda Cates, Alison Day.
Prefects: Stephanie Clarke, Ann Cowley, Kiersten Gibbs, Anne Gillham, Carol Pike, Judy Reynolds, Julie Wescott, Sally Wingate.
Hockey Captain: Anne Gillham.
Netball Captain: Ann Cowley.
Tennis Captain: Anne Gillham.

This was the academic year which included the so-called 'Winter of Discontent' when the Trade Unions rejected the Labour Government's 5% limit on wage increases and a series of national strikes followed. There were also widespread power cuts and technical problems with the school boilers which led Mrs. Warwick to instruct some Years to stay at home on designated days.

There was yet another challenge with the introduction of a first course in Computer Studies.

Miss O'Connell retired in July after many years of 'devoted and unstinted service to the School' in the English and Classics Departments, as Form Tutor, drama producer and member of the S.C.F. Committee. 'Many generations of H.G.S. have reason to be grateful for her patience and skill in teaching . . .'

This year, the Founder's Day Service was restored to its traditional time of 11.30 a.m. Unfortunately, the huge numbers involved and the restrictions on space in St. Mary's meant that, from now on, only the Fifth and Sixth Forms were able to attend. Those left behind enjoyed a visit by the Ballet Minerva whose conspicuous talents attracted a lot of discussion and comment afterwards about their various attributes. In the afternoon, the whole school enjoyed a combined fete and obstacle race which raised over £2,250. The money was divided between the British Olympic Fund for the 1980 Games, the United Nations Appeal for blind children in Bangladesh and the purchase of some sports equipment for the school.

Some of the orchestra were asked to help form part of a larger orchestra to play at the initial service to launch the Restoration Appeal Fund at St. Mary's Church. Following the substantial success of the appeal, the orchestra played before the Queen Mother at the Thanksgiving Service later on in the year.

There was another 'first' when an English Speaking competition was introduced for the Lower School. 'Standards were high . . . clearly the result of much enthusiasm and hard work.' Mr Szirtes continued to write and produce new plays for the school, including 'Bear Dance' which was performed at the end of the summer term. Mr. Szirtes was also a contributor to the informal entertainment presented by the Junior Sixth at the end of the winter term. The drama festival produced 'an impressive display of talent' when all the forms, except the exam-involved Fifth, presented their plays to the school. There was also a new venture with the launching of a joint staff/Sixth Form Play Reading Club.

The new school charity was The Guide Dogs for the Blind Association, and there were generous weekly collections and special efforts during the year. There was a practical demonstration of what help and happiness those contributions could buy when Miss Ava Bush (an old girl of the school) and Odin, her guide dog, came to talk to the Junior School in June.

This was also the year in which the A Level Nuffield Biologists undertook their strongest challenge yet . . . exactly how many daisies were there on the top hockey pitch, and how well did they manage to cope with the twin onslaughts of weedkiller and hockey boots? The answer, after a hard afternoon's counting: 'we deduce . . .

157

that 8,200 invincible daisies still exist, as approximated to the nearest 1,000. This statistically viable result is of no importance whatsoever unless you happen to be a daisy lover!'

The netball teams achieved a number of high positions in both North Hertfordshire and County Tournaments, but nothing could compare with the year's 'greatest victory' when the 1st team beat Dame Alice Harpur, their deadly rivals, for the first time in many years! The under 12 gymnastics team beat 'stiff competition' to win the North Hertfordshire Individual County Finals and Lisa Sales received the gold medal. The under 17 athletics team won the North Hertfordshire Trophy for the third year in succession, and the under 17 team retained the North Hertfordshire District Swimming Championships 'after some very exciting races'.

1979–1980 Sally Mack

Deputy Head Girls: Elizabeth Agg, Julie Maylin.
Prefects: Karen Barber, Julia Barker, Gillian Bell, Caroline Gaskin, Julie Huthwaite, Caroline Meek, Joanne Pearce, Dinah Scott.
Hockey Captain: April Steward.
Netball Captain: Elizabeth Agg.
Tennis Captain: Gillian Bell.

The first 'Five Form' entry reached the Sixth Form, and there were now about 900 pupils and a further 100 in teachers and other staff.

Mrs. Sykes retired in December after being in charge of the kitchen for more than ten years. She would be sorely missed, not only for her friendly and good natured personality but for her ceaseless chatter. One member of staff remarked that if some people's tongues could run away with them, Mrs. Sykes was capable of a marathon any day! She had a good word for everyone and constantly claimed 'I believe in looking after my teachers'. This she did, and the school would never be the same again without her. Her successor was Mrs. Hollings, in the new position of Canteen Supervisor.

School dinners would never be the same again after a new cash cafeteria system was introduced in both dining rooms at the beginning of the summer term. This allowed girls to pay either weekly, monthly or termly for their meals and pay any excess money on a daily basis at the checkout.

Miss Rock, who taught French and German, retired at Easter 'after a life-time of loyal and devoted service to education. Her unending patience and deep concern for other people was apparent in all that she did'.

Several of the Fourths had been visiting the handicapped residents at the Sue Ryder Home, at Stagenhoe Park, on a regular basis throughout the year. 'We enjoy going very much (and) help in various ways. Sometimes we just talk to the people there, but we are also sometimes asked to feed and help at meal times . . . or write letters. We admire these people very much for their courage . . .'

The holding of a special Music Festival competition and concert in July marked an 'exciting new venture' for members of the Lower School. The competition was organised on a Form basis, but the great number of enthusiastic entrants meant that there had to be a day of preliminary rounds to decide who was to go forward to the competition proper. There were eventually over one hundred performances to choose from, and the solo prizewinners in each of the six sections, together with the winning forms, gave a 'warmly applauded' concert the following day. Each prizewinner also received a certificate printed on the school's own press, and the winning Form in each year also received a cup.

If you were interested in dance, then you missed the newly-formed Dance Club at your peril! After practising on a weekly basis throughout the autumn term, the club gave a dance display to parents and friends later on in the year. There were many different dances in a variety of styles and costume, and afterwards members of the club went into the audience to collect money in big black hats! The dancers must have made a big hit, for they collected over £47, which was later used to buy new leotards.

A disallowed goal meant that the 1st XI had to share the County hockey tournament trophy with Hertfordshire and Essex. However, the First netball team won the North Hertfordshire under 18 League without losing a single match! In the North Hertfordshire Athletics Championships both the under 13 and under 17 teams won their sections. In fact, as the under 17 team had won 'every year for as long as anybody can remember', that particular result wasn't really surprising!

1980–1981   Paula Gant

Deputy Head Girls: Sally Banks, Karen Martin.
Prefects: Averil Brown, Deborah Hosking, Elaine Howe, Emma Laurens, Susan Norman, Karen Pettit, Rosalind Temple, Sarah Whitmore, Frances Wray.
Hockey Captain: Mary Hamilton.
Netball Captain: Bettina Vanstone.
Tennis Captain: Julia Edwards.
Athletics Captain: Sandra Leigh.

Miss Blackman, the Deputy Head, retired at the end of the summer term after twenty-three years of 'devoted service' to the school. An outstanding English teacher, she had inspired countless pupils with her own love of scholarship, high standards and generosity of spirit. Mr. Szirtes also left to take up a new appointment, and his many and varied talents – artistic, dramatic and poetical – were sorely missed by the School.

While the Fifth and Sixth Forms were attending the Founder's Day service at St. Mary's Church, the rest of the school were being entertained with a concert given by Julie Felix, the popular folk singer. Some wet weather rather spoilt the afternoon fete, but a considerable amount of money was still collected to support The Spastics Society, the school charity for the year. There was also a sponsored balloon race to try and raise the £1,200 needed to replace the 'ancient and rapidly disintegrating' Assembly Hall curtains.

The first-ever Music Festival for the Senior School was held in early November. Support was 'moderate', but nonetheless there were some very pleasing performances in the different instrumental and singing sections.

The performance of 'Twelfth Night' at the beginning of May by some of the Third, Fourth and Sixth Years was a great success – there were even good notices

159

from the local press! It was 'an ambitious undertaking . . . always interesting, often extremely entertaining and sometimes moving'. The drama festival took place at the end of the 'very long' summer term and once again 'showed the school at its most lively and imaginative'. The plays drew their inspiration from a wide variety of sources and were, in turn, amusing, witty, clever and moving. 4S's parody of a black and white silent film, complete with piano music, and the Sixth Form's account of playing 'Pass the Parcel' – with an old granny as the parcel – were particularly well received.

Both the 1st XI and the under 14 hockey teams won their respective leagues during the year. Sadly, even though the netball teams won the majority of their matches, they were eventually beaten in the league semi-finals.

1981–1982 Sara Evans

Deputy Head Girls: Deborah Brownhill, Elizabeth Hawkins.
Hockey Captain: Morag Niven.
Netball Captain: Bettina Vanstone.
Tennis Captain: Julia Edwards.

This year saw the opening of the award-winning new Music block in the grounds of Highbury House. Highbury House became the home of the North Hertfordshire Music School, and the new building was sited adjacent to it in such a way that the accommodation could also be used in conjunction with the Music School in and out of school hours. The new block, consisting of a large performance room, a music classroom and two practice rooms, was a modern building but designed to blend in with the Victorian aspects of Highbury House through the use of red brick and a slate roof. A new bridge linked the site with the school.

Mrs. Gilbert, the Head of Chemistry and Head of the Fifth Year, retired at the end of the summer term. 'Her faith in young people and her genuine interest in each member of her form or class set marked her out as a teacher of unique qualities.'

The One Year Sixth Sociology group achieved something of a coup when Sir Keith Joseph, the Secretary of State for Education, accepted their invitation to visit the school for a morning and 'sit in' on their sociology lesson. The whole Sixth Form had the chance to meet him later, 'both to hear his views . . . and pose their own questions'.

Both staff and pupils adopted a 'more energetic approach' to Founder's Day this year. 'The success of the afternoon was, without doubt, due to the way the whole school entered wholeheartedly into the spirit of everything . . . fancy-dress, cheerleading, the food and the games. The games were . . . a huge success. Bearing in mind the ingredients – "spacehoppers", food and water – it is not really so surprising!' 'Such a lively event seemed a fitting way of ending an interesting school year in which organisation, co-operation and enthusiasm played such major parts.'

The school's strong musical traditions continued with the annual round of services and concerts. The Junior Choir took part in the Senior School carol service for the first time this year. Another important innovation were the new, elected posts of Senior Choir Prefects and the appointment of a Senior Choir Captain. The

The Headmistress, Deputy Heads, Head Girls and Prefects 1981–1982/1982–1983. *Back row, L. to R.:* Elizabeth Hawkins (Deputy Head Girl, 81–82), Dawn Bolton (82–83), Ruth Sherwood (82–83), Susan Banks (Deputy Head Girl, 82–83), Sarah Burnham (81–82), Elizabeth Antrich (81–82), Deborah Brownhill (81–82), Susan Worbey (81–82). *Middle row:* Vanessa Poole (82–83), Cathy Taplin (82–83), Caroline Smith (81–82), Susan D'Eath (81–82), Sally Green (81–82), Shona Watts (81–82), Amanda Walker (82–83), Angela Sladen (82–83), Deborah Newman (82–83). *Front row:* Joanne Boorman (82–83), Miss Fletcher (Deputy Head), Sara Evans (Head Girl, 81–82), Mrs. Warwick (Headmistress), Penny Le Sage (Head Girl, 82–83), John McCutcheon (Deputy Head), Siobhan Whitehead (82–83). Absent: Sarah Hawkins (82–83). [Buchanan]

Lower School Music Festival attracted a total of 169 entries and lasted for three days! The Prizewinners' concert at the end included the twenty-five best items.

In spite of the participation of a rather 'dubious team of stage-struck staff' the Junior Sixth managed to produce a 'polished and highly amusing version' of 'Snow White and the Seven Dwarfs'. The Junior Sixth were also involved in the Welwyn Youth Drama Festival in the summer term with their production of 'Incident'. The 'beautifully choreographed' dance display, also in the summer term, included 'many well-rehearsed performances. Members of the Dance Club were also asked to take part in the "Arts and Drama Week" at North Hertfordshire College'.

The year's charity was Multiple Sclerosis, and the school heard an interesting talk about the problems that sufferers face and how 'these difficulties can be overcome, or at least eased, through support such as ours'.

It was a good year for athletic successes. Amanda Robinson won the under 14 individual gold medal in the county championships and the under 14 team won the bronze team medal. The First Form team won both the North Hertfordshire Athletics League Trophy and the North Hertfordshire Team Trophy. Their prize-winning performance allowed the school team to win the overall trophy at the meeting. The First Form rounders team also won the North Hertfordshire Rounders Tournament Trophy.

1982–1983 Penny Le Sage

Deputy Head Girls: Susan Banks, Sarah Hawkins.
Hockey Captain: Elizabeth Southern.
Netball Captain: Susan Banks.

The school charity for the year was the Cancer Fund for the Children's Ward at the Middlesex Hospital in London. This was a very poignant choice, inseparable from the name of Helen Porter. Helen, a member of the Fourth Year, had died during the summer holidays after a long illness. She could never speak too highly of the love and affection shown to her by the doctors and nurses on the Children's Ward at this hospital.

The 'dedicated enthusiasm' with which the school threw itself into fund-raising activities during the year was 'absolutely marvellous' and included such diverse efforts as a 'take-off' of 'Top of the Pops' and sponsored carol singing! By Christmas – after just one term – the school had raised almost £1,300. The final total was to be an astonishing £3,341.75.

This year also saw Guides returning to Hitchin Girls' for the first time in many years when the 1st Hitchin Guide Company was 'restarted' by Mrs. Wilkins, together with two 'enthusiastic' Sixth Formers, for the benefit of the First and Second Years.

The introduction of the Duke of Edinburgh Award Scheme, organised by Miss Wilson and Mrs. King, also provided the members of the Middle and Senior School with something positive to aim for in the shape of their Bronze Medal Award. If the Scheme attracted enough entrants, it was also the organisers' intention that pupils should be able to go on to their Silver and Gold Awards in future years.

1983–1984 Kathryn Pickering

Deputy Head Girls: Alison Macaulay, Catherine Walton.
Prefects: Amarjit Bains, Joanna Lawrence, Rachel Pugh, Jane Wilson, Ruth Flavelle, Alison Jones, Geraldine Bannister, Elizabeth Southern.

The Helen Porter Award: Michelle Gilders.
(This is an annual award, given by the family of Helen Porter, to the pupil showing most progress and interest in Biology, which had been Helen's favourite subject at school.)

The Cathy Taplin Award: Judith Agar.
(This is an annual award, given by the family of Cathy Taplin, to the pupil who shows an outstanding aptitude for Art and intends to continue studying art at an Institute of Higher or Further Education. The winner's name is also inscribed on a commemorative plaque in the Senior Library. Cathy Taplin was killed in a road accident in August 1983. She had taken her A Levels and was intending to follow a Foundation Course in Art at St. Alban's.)

Mrs. Gilbert's Chemistry Prize: Amy Sadler.
(This is an annual award, given by Mrs. Gilbert, to the pupil showing the most marked progress in Chemistry. 'How typical that Mrs. Gilbert's retirement should be accompanied by such a forward looking gesture.')

It was with some relief that Mrs. Warwick was able to announce that it had been a 'vintage year' in terms of academic success. Approximately forty Sixth Form leavers received County Awards (grants) to enable them to go on to University, Polytechnic and Colleges of Higher Education. In addition, three girls won Scholarships and Exhibitions to Oxford University and Amanda Walker, a very gifted musician, was awarded a 'rare place' to study the clarinet at the Royal College of Music.

Miss Fletcher, the Deputy Head and Head of Needlwork, retired in July after nearly thirty years at Hitchin Girls'. 'She brought to her teaching and her work as Deputy Head high skills in organisation, meticulous attention to detail, and a response to individual needs . . . Her concern was always for "the good of the school". We acknowledge her gift of pictures for the Dining Room and the spring glory of crocus in the drive with gratitude and delight.'

The introduction of a 'Whole Food Bar' by the School Meals Service at the beginning of the year was an instant success with 'figure and diet conscious' pupils. They could choose from a menu that included such healthy delights as raisin salad, wholemeal quiches, pizzas and melon boats. The demand for meals increased by more than 50% and there were even letters from parents grateful that, at last, their daughter was eating a more balanced diet. However, the Main Dining Room still continued to provide food for those pupils who preferred a more traditional school dinner.

The musical event of the year was the production of 'The Lion, the Witch and the Wardrobe', with words by C. S. Lewis and music by the internationally acclaimed composer and pianist, John McCabe. It was a 'great success and . . . a credit to all who took part'.

The Sixth Forms at the Girls' and Boys' Schools combined to produce a highly

1984. Rehearsal time in the Walton Room for 'The Lion, the Witch and the Wardrobe'. *L. to R.:* Michael Bolton (Bowes Lyon School), Elizabeth Lamb, Penny McGeouwn, David Kitching (Hitchin Boys' School), James Pearson (Hitchin Boys' School), Claire Shephard.   [Mr. P. Rooke]

'successful' 'Elizabethan Evening' of madrigals, dramatic excerpts from Shakespeare and a selection of Elizabethan poetry. There were even authentic sixteenth century refreshments of mead, marchpane and gingerbread available during the interval! The evening ended with the reading, by candle-light, of a very moving passage from Shakespeare. At the climax, the candles were blown out to leave the Walton Room in darkness. All went well, until the performance when one girl's candle refused to be blown out and she got a highly infectious bout of the giggles . . .! The success of the joint enterprise led to some of the actors and actresses forming the Sixth Form Society.

The Duke of Edinburgh Award Scheme had now been running in school for over a year and two of its participants had already earned their Bronze Award.

Collections and 'special efforts' raised over £700 for the British Heart Foundation, the elected school charity for the year.

The school choir entered the Bedford Music Festival for the first time this year . . . and won, 'gaining custody of a beautiful trophy and shield!'

The Guides held a grand party to celebrate their first birthday. The Company had had a busy time undertaking a variety of activities including tracking in the woods, pitching a tent and cooking hot dogs. Going off to camp at Henlow with the 7th Hitchin (Our Lady's) Company and trying out all their skills was the highlight of the year. The Company's only regret – it would welcome a few more members!

A party of girls, led by Miss Wilde, went to Germany at the beginning of September to take part in 'Fest '83', the celebrations to mark the Silver Jubilee of the twinning of Hitchin and Bingen am Rhein.

A small group of Sixth Form historians and four members of staff set off for a week at Easter on the school's first foray into the Soviet Union. The week's

1984. The Staff, Sixth Form and Intourist Guide outside their hotel in Leningrad: Dr. & Mrs. Robertson (back row, left), Mrs. Creighton (back row, right). The ship in the background is the Cruiser 'Aurora' which shelled the Winter Palace with blank ammunition during the Russian Revolution.

[Miss E. Duignan]

itinerary had been arranged so as to complement the A Level course the girls were following, but there were also visits to a Moscow school and to the theatre. The party queued for about two hours, in a biting wind, to see the embalmed body of Lenin in his mausoleum in Red Square. After three days in Moscow, it was time to leave for Leningrad. The overnight train journey – complete with wood-burning stove, samovar and tea dispensed by an attendant in the corridor – proved to be a 'memorable' part of the trip!

1984–1985   Elizabeth Lamb

Deputy Head Girls: Claire Roberts, Vanessa Willis.
Prefects: Kamaljit Bains, Sarah Biggerstaff, Sophie Brett, Suzanne Gill, Joanne Poole, Joanne Thorogood, Tina Walby, Louise Waugh, Emma Williams.
Hockey Captain: Samantha Vaughan.
Netball Captain: Carey Irwin.
Tennis Captain: Carey Irwin.

Hitchin Girls' 'really got itself noticed' when, one frosty December morning, the School was inundated with V.I.P.s and camera crews from Anglia Television. The reason for all this activity was the Whole Food Bar – now known as the Health Food Bar: 'All this publicity was thanks to Mrs. Hollings and her cooks who have made this new venture such a great success'.

December 1984. 'Sampling' the Health Food Bar. *L. to R.:* Mrs. Hollings, Elizabeth Wells, Helena Wilton, Nicola Moran, Carol Lamey, Samantha Field.   [North Herts Gazette]

The Sixth Form Society continued to meet on a regular basis during the year. Members were entertained with talks, quizzes, debates and videos. There was also a barn dance at the end of the autumn term and a weekend trip to Denmark. An outing to the Peterborough Ice Rink sorted out the men from the boys: 'Some people proved more incapable than others at the fine art of skating. . . .'

An adaptation of Dickens' 'David Copperfield' was the choice for a joint production by the Girls' and Boys' Schools in November. Rehearsals were 'lively and frequently hysterical', but much hard work and enthusiasm resulted in an 'excellent performance' and there was special praise for the staff who took part.

The 'shock news' of the year was the 'kidnap' of Orinoco the Tidy Womble. (The 'Tidy Womble' was the prize awarded to the tidiest classroom in the Junior School at the end of each term.) Orinoco disappeared one day towards the end of November . . . only to re-appear the next day, suspended from the gantry of the Water Tower outside Room 19. He was eventually rescued by the Fire Brigade – and the culprit caught and punished – but not before some of the Junior School had shed a few tears at his plight.

The Tidy Womble, Orinoco.

1985–1986   Emma Decent

Deputy Head Girls: Sally Thorogood, Nicolette Zarka.
Prefects: Michelle Andrews, Emma Decent, Julia Grimshaw, Jane Hull, Claire Judge, Ruth King, Helen Ogilvie, Sally Thorogood, Nicola Toon, Veronica Wates, Sally Wilson, Nicolette Zarka.
Hockey Captain: Ruth Dickinson.
Netball Captain: Sally Thorogood.
Tennis Captain: Ruth Dickinson.

1986. At the East of England Show. Members of the Sixth Form helping to arrange exhibits for their Spinning and Weaving demonstration at the Peterborough Show. *L. to R.:* Clare Shephard, Mrs. Wilkins, Sarah Rayner, Sarah Lupton, Helen Menzies, Marcia Smith.   (Mrs. E. Wilkins]

The beginning of the autumn term was heralded by intense activity from the Science Block, the Art and Geography Rooms and the Junior Sixth Common Room as a number of specialist areas were re-organised to accommodate two new courses: Information Technology and Modular Technology; as part of the first phase of T.V.E.I. (Technical and Vocational Initiative: 14–18) to provide a curriculum more suited to the world of work. As the Head Girl lamented: 'In September it seemed as if only the First Years knew where everything was!'

History was made in July when, for the first time, the academic year was ended two days early to allow the staff to be trained for the introduction of the General Certificate of Secondary Education (G.C.S.E.) in the following September.

The success of the Whole Food Bar and the general interest in healthy eating was reinforced when Mrs. Greaves, the school dietician, gave a fascinating talk and slide show to the First and Second Years that stressed the importance of 'sensible' eating. The message – if not the spelling – got across: 'If you eat too much fat you can fur up your archeries,' wrote one of the Lower School in her report on the proceedings!

The One Year Sixth had the chance to follow a new course when C.P.V.E. (Certificate of Pre-Vocational Education) was introduced as a one year course with some lessons being taught at North Herts. College. There was a broad spread of skills to be mastered by the girls, including Communications, Computer Literacy, Numeracy and Science. The success of the exercise was demonstrated when Sir Edwin Nixon (Chairman of the C.P.V.E. Examinations Council) chose Hitchin Girls' as one of the Schools to visit in order to monitor the progress of C.P.V.E.

Ever mindful that 1986 was 'Industry Year', the B.P./Schools Industry Link Scheme was introduced in June to help foster better relations between education and industry through visits, speakers, resource packs, equipment and finance for

1985–1986.   Dance Display. *L. to R.:* Maria Lythgoe, Clare Brandish, Andrea Haynes.

[Mrs. S. Streets]

May 1986.   These Old Girls were members of one class during the 1940s and have remained firm friends ever since. They came back to School for a special annual reunion to celebrate their approaching sixtieth birthdays!

(North Herts Gazette)

educational projects. The 'Young Enterprise' Team took part in a scheme supported by British Aerospace and their project won three out of the five available credits.

A small party of Sixth Formers and Staff went to Russia during the Easter holidays and visited Moscow, Kiev (just a month before the Chernobyl nuclear accident), Yalta and Leningrad. The Black Sea resort of Yalta was 'the highlight of the visit', and proved to be a welcome relief after the cold, damp and mud of Moscow and Kiev!

There was a new subject on the timetable with the introduction of a Theatre Arts A/O Level for the Sixth Form at both the Girls' and Boys' Schools. Members of the group showed off their talents in March in a show which included a fifteen minute version of 'Hamlet'!

The case of young Ben Hardwick, whose life was prolonged by a liver transplant, had caught the attention of the nation, and the school voted to support the Fund set up in his memory. Collections and special efforts during the year raised almost £2,000 for the Ben Hardwick Fund.

The presentation evening for the Duke of Edinburgh Award Scheme was held at school for the first time this year. Mrs. Wearmouth, the Chairman of Governors, presented the awards to participants from the North Hertfordshire area.

The weather had a significant effect on sporting activities during the year as heavy rain forced the cancellation of a number of hockey, cricket and tennis matches. However, this was not enough to stop the under 16 hockey team from winning the Hertfordshire Championships and several members of the school were selected to play in the County hockey, tennis and cricket teams. The gymnastics team was invited to the East of England Show in Peterborough where, in spite of torrential rain, they managed to give a 'tremendous performance'.

1986–1987   Clare Shephard

Deputy Head Girls: Sara Gower, Rosalind Young.
Hockey Captain: Emma Stoker.
Netball Captain: Denise Bichener.
Tennis Captain: Monica Parmar.

The long term future of the school was brought into sharp focus in September with the publication of 'Review of Secondary Education'. This two-hundred-page consultation document was Hertfordshire County Council's response to the problem of falling rolls in the North Hertfordshire area. Hitchin Girls' did not appear to be under any immediate threat of either closure or restructure, but it was obvious that the proposed merger of Bowes Lyon and Hitchin Schools would have an effect in so far as the new school would be at a considerable advantage in terms of funding and buildings.

In spite of widespread reservations about the preparation and organisation of the new examination courses, the G.C.S.E. arrived in September for the new Fourth Year and brought with it far-reaching implications for educational change and reassessment.

Staff and pupils alike spent the first week or so of the autumn term memorising the times of the new eight period day.

The Headmistress, Head Girls, and Prefects, 1986–1987/1987–1988. *Back row, L. to R.:* Nicola Russell (87–88), Samantha Field (87–88), Jane Willoughby (87–88), Alexandra Foster (87–88), Carol Lamey (87–88), Emma Stoker (86–87), Clare Adderson (86–87). *Middle row:* Alison Roberts (87–88), Karen Holmes-Walker (86–87), Caroline Brett (86–87), Sarah Lupton (86–87), Katie Finch (86–87), Barbara Webb (86–87), Krisztina Hussey (87–88), Nicola Homans (86–87), Naomi Easton (86–87). *Front row:* Sara Gower (Deputy Head Girl, 86–87), Rosalind Young (Deputy Head Girl, 86–87), Clare Shephard (Head Girl, 86–87), Mrs. Warwick (Headmistress), Linda Brady (Head Girl, 87–88), Hélène Russell (Deputy Head Girl, 87–88), Andrea Lovewell (Deputy Head Girl, 87–88). Absent: Hannah Loney (87–88), Juliet Taylor (87–88).   [Buchanan]

As it was a very long time since the school had last been decorated – almost twenty years in some places – there was 'a real boost to morale' when the painters finally arrived in the summer term and the staff and girls didn't grumble too much when they had to clear out all the accumulated clutter from their studies and classrooms in order to make way for the 'invading decorators'!

The school became involved with the Sainsbury Trust Scheme in an effort to encourage more able young people to make a career in manufacturing industry. Eight members of the Junior Sixth, divided into three groups, were chosen to follow a year-long 'Engineering for the Future' Scheme, sponsored by the S.D.R.C. and British Aerospace, during which they worked towards the completion of a particular design project, utilising the services and expertise of local industry and the S.D.R.C. where necessary. The standard of the projects was so high that S.D.R.C. and British Aerospace co-hosted a presentation evening to celebrate the Sixth Formers' achievement. Juliet Taylor and Joanna Downing were chosen to represent Britain at a tripartite exercise in Germany where they were to give their presentation in German!

The world of business was opened up for Sixth Former Ami Williams when she

1987. Sainsbury Trust Scheme. *L. to R.:* Sally Bryant, Paula Haynes, Juliet Taylor, Hélène Russell.
[North Herts Gazette]

1986–1987. Evening of Gymnastics: Dimensions. *L. to R.:* Louise Chapallaz, Annik Matthews, Zoe Roberts, Clare Brandish, Emma Nott, Katherine Mann.   [Mrs. Streets]

was selected to 'shadow' the Deputy Chairman of John Willmott Holdings Ltd. for a week. 'Executive Shadowing' meant that Ami was present at board meetings and saw, at first hand, the long hours and wide-ranging activities that a busy executive's work schedule involved. Ami also met the Director-General of the C.B.I., and she was invited to describe her experiences to Paul Channon, the Trade and Industry

171

Secretary, at a reception in London to publicise the success stories of Industry Year.

Paints, brushes, sticks of charcoal, sketch books and an easel were new additions to the entrance hall when Michael Murfin took up his appointment as Artist-in-Residence in October. 'This was a most stimulating experience for the whole school, and the girls were able to observe Mr. Murfin at work.'

The Duke of Edinburgh Award Scheme continued to flourish, and Hitchin Girls' now had the largest number of participants – over one hundred working towards all three Award stages – from any school in North Hertfordshire. By the end of the year a few members of the Sixth Form were expected to have finished their Gold Course, 'the first people to have achieved this since the Scheme was introduced into the school four years ago'. In November eleven girls and two staff went to the service in Westminster Abbey to commemorate the thirtieth anniversary of the Award Scheme: 'it was a lovely occasion which they all thoroughly enjoyed'.

The Centenary Committee was formed to co-ordinate the various events planned for Centenary Year, and it was decided that any money raised by the school should be used to make a contribution towards the cost of a covered swimming pool in the grounds of Highbury House.

Two individual achievements were noted during the year. Catherine Skinner showed herself to be an outstanding pupil. Not content with studying four A Levels, Catherine also edited the school magazine, was awarded an Ashdown Scholarship and was the joint winner of the Poetry Section of the Cadbury's National Exhibition of Children's Art. Her prize was a '5 Star', conducted art expedition to Florence and Venice together with a £500 award for the school. On top of all this, Catherine was also applying to read for a degree at Cambridge University! She received her poetry award from Sir Terence Conran at a special presentation at the Royal Festival Hall. Catherine later presented a book

1987.   The Staff hockey team getting ready to do battle with the 1st XI; the Staff lost 1–0! *L. to R.:* Miss Bartlett, Miss Margarson, Mr. Jackson, Mrs. Elliot, Miss Wilson, Mrs. Hulman, Mr. Fitzgibbon, Mrs. Streets, Mrs. King, Mrs. Reeve, Miss Hilson.   [Miss S. Bartlett]

containing her poems to the Senior Library. Alex Foster was awarded the 'Best Achiever' Trophy for 1987 by British Aerospace for her managerial skills in the Young Enterprise Scheme.

The musical event of the year was the double bill of Benjamin Britten's 'The Golden Vanity' and Gilbert and Sullivan's 'Trial by Jury' in April. The production was a great success and it was 'standing room only' for all three performances.

The hockey teams had a most successful season with the 1st XI retaining their North Hertfordshire title and going on to become the Hertfordshire County Champions. The under 18 netball team also won the North Hertfordshire Championships.

1987–1988 Linda Brady

Deputy Head Girls: Andrea Lovewell, Hélène Russell.
Hockey Captain: Carol Lamey.
Netball Captain: Suzanne Wicks.

End of Year Awards:
- Ashdown Scholarship (A County Award to a member of the Junior Sixth showing academic attainment and promise   Anne Williams
- Rand Award (For service to the School)   Aledandra Foster / Hannah Loney
- Cathy Taplin Award (Art)   Catherine Ogilvie
- Helen Porter Award (Biology)   Vanessa Linnett
- Mrs. Gilbert's Award (Chemistry)   Katherine Woodham

Mrs. Warwick celebrated her Silver Jubilee as Headmistress and received the congratulations of staff, pupils and Old Girls. The Head Girl presented her with a silver box on behalf of the school. The staff gift was a Tazza – a small silver dish on a pedestal. By sheer coincidence, it was later discovered that the Tazza bore a 1962 hall-mark! The 'unofficial' staff gift was a handmade doll, some two foot high, dressed in H.G.S. uniform! However, Gloria Marguerite Williams – for that was the name on the doll's report – proved to be anything but a model pupil and both the comments of her teachers and the state of her uniform left a lot to be desired!

In October a small party of ten Fifth Years, accompanied by a member of staff, went on an exhausting nine day exchange trip to Kongsberg in Norway to investigate the effects of acid rain on the environmnent. Their detailed scientific analysis of various aspects of the local environment seemed to suggest some kind of pollution was indeed occurring, and that acid rain might be the possible culprit. There was the chance to renew old friendships when the party's Norwegian hosts visited Hitchin in February.

Hitchin Girls' swept the board at the presentation evening for the Duke of Edinburgh Award Scheme with 10 Gold, 9 Silver and 13 Bronze Awards. Out of the hundred or so awards presented, the school collected more than any other organisation in the whole of North Hertfordshire!

Meanwhile, the Centenary Committee were busy organising ways of raising money for the new swimming pool. There was a very well-supported cheese and wine evening in November where parents and friends could buy souvenir engraved

173

1988. Duke of Edinburgh Award Scheme: Presentation Evening. *Front row, L. to R.: Gold Award –* Sally Bryant, Joanne Hood, Tania Haigh, Sally Hogg, Joanne Stephenson, Joanna Corby, Richard Meredith-Hardy, —, —, —, Krisztina Hussey, Jane Willoughby, Nicola Goulding, Alison Lord, Andrea Lovewell.

[North Herts Gazette]

glassware, postcards and Christmas cards. The Christmas cards featured Elizabeth Wells' (IV) prize-winning line-drawing showing the school at its Bancroft premises in 1889. The more energetic members of the school took part in a sponsored fun walk in April around an interesting and challenging fifteen mile course. The sale of specially printed T Shirts designed by Nicola Vincent (VI) helped to bring in more money. There were also ambitious plans for a May Ball – 'the social highspot of the year' – to be held in 1989.

Thanks to the generosity of the internationally-famous firm of Harkness Roses, it will also be possible, from the 1990s onwards, to buy a rose commemorating the School Centenary. 'Golden Years' – the name suggested by a present member of staff – is a cluster-flowering bush rose, approximately 30″ high, yellow with a hint of coppery gold and bearing sizeable flowers with lots of petals. It was raised by Jack Harkness and bred from the award-winning 'Amber Queen', the 1984 'Rose of the Year'.

The links between Hitchin Girls' and the Harkness family go back some sixty years to when Betty Moore (later Mrs. J. Harkness), a pupil from 1927–1933, married into the family. Isobel Harkness (later Mrs. Parke) was a pupil from 1945–1950 and Ena Harkness (who gave her name to a world-famous rose) used to judge the flower show at the school's Open Days during the 1950s.

And so the school looks forward to celebrating its centenary and honouring the achievements of its staff, pupils and generous friends and benefactors. Whatever the future may bring, there is the certain knowledge that, in a hundred years from now, 'The School on the Hill' will be continuing to fulfil the Founder's wish by 'instructing the children of the inhabitants of Hitchin in good living and virtuous education'.

1988. Discussing duty rotas. *L. to R.* Miss E. M. Beddard (Deputy Head), Mrs. M. Mead (Head of Lower School), Nicola Jackson (Head Girl 1988–89) with her deputies, Martine Hamilton and Jill Robertson. [Miss E. Duignan]

EXAMINATIONS

1965	C.S.E. introduced
1988	G.C.S.E. introduced

PRIZES & COMPETITIONS

1961–1966   Kayser Bondor Prize for Sixth Form

1966–   Mrs. Warwick's Magazine Prize for the best piece of reporting.
Other Magazine Prizes for original writing.
Cycling Proficiency Awards

1972   Hertfordshire Book Award Scheme

1978   'Tidy' Womble, presented by Miss Beddard, to the tidiest Lower School Form Room

1983–1984   Helen Porter Award for outstanding work in Biology
Mrs. Gilbert's Progress Award in Chemistry
Cathy Taplin Award in Art
Guide Dogs for the Blind Award – a carved wooden labrador (made by Mr. David Price), for the Form collecting most milk-bottle tops

1987   Creative Writing Project – Anglia Co-Operative Association

1987   Prizes for the Third Formers who put out the Assembly chairs

1988   Post Prize for the pupil(s) delivering the Internal Post during lunchtime

Rand Award
Ashdown Scholarship
Governors' School Leaving Scholarship

GAMES, TROPHIES & CUPS: New Awards 1962–1988
(regretfully, the list is not complete)

1968–1973	Junior Hockey Cup presented by C. Aspinwall & C. Robson (Games Staff)
1968	Senior Athletics Cup presented by the Junior Sixth
1985	Form Running Cup presented by the 1985 Leavers
1986	Junior Individual Medley Shield
	Senior Individual Medley Shield
1986	Middle School Athletics Cup presented by Mrs. B. Wearmouth, the Chairman of Governors

*Senior & Junior 'Colours' are still awarded for Athletics, Gymnastics & Games: Hockey, Netball, Tennis, Badminton, Rounders.

THE TEACHING STAFF

In compiling any school history it is difficult to reach the real personalities of those most important people, the teachers. Leaving orations share with obituaries a marked reluctance to show a personality 'warts and all', but certain names and characters recur frequently when talking to the old girls of the school.

First and foremost amongst these was **'Ruby' Read**, also called 'The Reed Warbler'. All recollections of her start with her size; 'huge and awesome with a deep, gruff voice', were words repeated time after time. Perhaps the best description of her was that which said, 'She was very tall with bright red hair. She looked like a Grenadier Guardsman'. She certainly terrified most of the children, 'you respected her all right!' A 'little bird told me things', and transgressors got a sharp whack with the ruler. She had her favourites too: Dick Hawkins was allowed to carry her books and on wet mornings was given a lift to school in her lovely old Wolseley. When the kindergarten closed, in 1950, she retired after teaching in the school for thirty-three years.

Miss Hughes, who taught English, also emerges as a 'character'. She was a marvellous teacher who knew how to keep order and was 'as tough as an old boot. Not the sort you got a crush on.' She was short and plump with eton cropped hair and wore a tailored, grey costume, winter and summer for all the years she was at the school. She once demonstrated the 'fireman's lift' by throwing a girl on her shoulder and saying, 'Three times round the tennis courts or once round me!' She had spent some time in Egypt and was easily diverted on to tales of her days there, the favourite being about the shortage of water meaning that she had to bathe in a

The Mistresses in 1938. *Back row:* Misses Saunders, Beckwith, Allright, Woolverson, Harris, Baker, Pearse. *Middle row:* Misses Read, Bullmore, Console, Flinn, Chambers, Radway, Mortimer, Clark, Forbes. *Front row:* Misses Rees, Cartwright, Squire, Wright, Burnand.

soup plate – the image of which greatly amused her audience. Miss Hughes retired in 1948 after twenty-eight years' service to the school.

Miss Mortimer taught French and left in 1950 after twenty-nine years. She terrified everyone, and could paralyse all with a single sarcastic comment. The best way to survive in her lesson was to keep quiet. She was prone to throw things, especially books, and when one girl ducked, it went right out of the open window.

Sports and Gym Mistresses are often popular, and **Miss Squire**, 'Squirrel', was no exception though she tended to stand in the shadow of her inseparable companion, Miss Chambers. She was reputed to have an incredible memory and could address any girl by her first name though she could rarely remember the second! She was a fine tennis player and played in the Hertfordshire hockey team for several years. **Miss Bavin** played hockey for England.

Miss Owbridge Ward is the only teacher described from the early days of the school. She had a great sense of humour and was a 'fresh air fiend'. A window must always be open, even on a train trip to London when all the passengers were showered with smuts from the engine!

Apart from a few eccentric individuals, the majority of the teachers who made a lasting impression on their pupils were either those of excellence or the few who were dominated by the girls. Only **'Little Miss Forbes'** managed to rate a mention in both these groups; probably because she taught the popular, and practical Domestic Science. This 'Gentle Dragon' could spit fire and brimstone and give order marks to one and all – always withdrawn at the end of the lesson if an apology was forthcoming.

Miss Chrystal was small and precise, with straight hair. She was a wonderful teacher who would stride around the room demanding, 'that we have a millimetre of air', at which a girl would bring the long pole and open a window. If one arrived late or without a necessary book she would cry 'Off with your head'. **Miss Williams** – History – from Miss Badland's time. 'All the knowledge came straight from her mouth. She talked all lesson and we listened. I don't ever remember her having a text book, in the time she taught me'. **Miss Lamb** – Geography – Super and very strict but very interesting. She spent a lot of time in Australia. **Miss Howell**, also an excellent Geography teacher. Could be heard striding down the corridor and would enter the room saying 'Question One'. Well travelled and inspiring the pupils to do likewise, **'Auntie' Allright** was a good teacher and stood for no nonsense.

Miss Radway – 'Radish' – taught Maths and was an 'overall terror, always to be given a wide berth though a very good teacher'. She was devoted to Miss Chambers. **Miss Lloyd Williams** – 'Sloppy' – wore a long, droopy cardigan and had a skirt hem which was always falling down – as was her hair. A very jolly person who was an excellent actress. **Miss Collett** was more famous for her brother who rowed 'stroke' in the Cambridge Varsity boat. Always being pestered for his autograph. **Miss Corrigan** – very elderly and 'airy fairy' – was an intellectual of the old order and taught Scripture with a deep understanding of the original Greek. She wore a seersucker dress winter and summer because she was allergic to wool. **Miss Murray** came to school on a motor-bike.

Lastly, two poor souls who could not control their classes, **Miss Missen and Miss Sandercock**. The former taught Maths and came straight from college. Did not believe in homework and would set one problem which the brightest girl would solve on the black-board and the rest would copy. She didn't believe in discipline either so the class was a riot. Once gave 100 lines and accepted, without comment, one line and ninety-nine ditto marks. Also taught Nature Studies and asked each girl to bring a botanical specimen. Every student brought nettles! Not surprisingly, she stayed for only one year. Miss Sandercock suffered in similar fashion. There was a craze for using long toffee tins as pencil boxes. Each girl would carefully ensure that her own overhung the desk and then one of their number, sitting at the back, would ask for help. As she swept down the aisle, the poor teacher would sweep every box on the floor. There would be an ear-splitting crash and the rest of the lesson would be taken up in clearing the mess.

Patricia Stutley (Aspinal), 1945–47, beautifully summed up the teachers of her day. 'The teachers were so dedicated – the "old school", mostly old maids, at least in my early days. They gave their all and really cared.'

Barbara Dunning (Grant), taught Maths from 1941 to 1947 and gave a fascinating insight on life, from the staff point of view:

'Miss Chambers liked to have the junior members of staff live in. There were three of us, plus Miss Forbes, Ruth Squire and Miss Ryder, the most helpful school secretary I ever encountered. We were always under the eye of Miss C. who kept account of our daily life and as phone calls came through the office, she kept an ear on those as well. Supper was a ritual occasion, with Miss Chambers, presiding and dishing out the wartime fare with great ceremony. If we were to be out for the evening and asked for a meal on a tray, some explanation was clearly expected. There was a lot of fun in our sitting room, no T.V. of course, so it was a place of sewing and handicrafts and mutual support. Miss Squire never sat with us but spent every evening with Miss C, and I think she got bored. Miss Forbes was always ready to tell a tale against herself.

The staff room was a very serious place; not many senior staff had a sense of humour, Miss Squire had, but could be very moody. Both Miss Hughes and Miss Mortimer were seen as threatening to the junior staff. They had exclusive use of the two armchairs in the staff room and expected to give advice to everyone else.

Miss Chambers often made unexpected visits to the class room and brought her knitting with her. If she took out the pattern, we knew that we were in for a long stay. She never hesitated to break in with advice to the teacher or the pupils, and I soon learned that Arithmetic was most likely to attract her interruptions. If I changed to Algebra, she was on less sure ground and soon left.

Because of war-time restriction, report forms had to be ruled and used for three terms. Within these limits we were expected to make constructive comments. Miss C. must have read every one judging from the number of us required to justify our remarks and, in some cases, change them. Miss Hughes had enormous writing and "Very Fair" was about her limit in the space provided. She was not challenged so perhaps Miss Hughes was as formidable to Miss Chambers as she was to us.'

It is interesting that the staff most often referred to were those in the latter days of Miss Chambers' time at the school, and the ones listed here are mostly from that era. It is perhaps fair to note that by the mid-1940s many of them had given a lifetime to teaching and were ready for a well earned retirement. The teachers both before and after them must have also produced their share of excellence and incompetence; 'holy terrors' and 'characters'. We leave these few to represent them all.

THE PROGRESS OF MUSIC IN THE SCHOOL

From its earliest days some music was taught in the school but this was confined to class singing. Piano, violin and singing lessons were optional 'extras'. In 1929 a school string orchestra was formed, but several later references to 'new' orchestras imply that they were regularly disbanded.

Miss Chambers was not greatly interested in music, which was reflected in the lack of prominence given to the subject in the school curriculum. The advent of Mrs. Warwick, herself a musician, gave encouragement to the already expanding musical activities.

Immediately post-war Miss Stovin arrived to take charge of the music, and we are indebted to her for the information she has given.

Each class had just one singing lesson a week; those of the upper school being divided into two large groups. With the approval of Miss Badland, a second 'music' lesson was introduced into the timetable, initially for the First Forms but later continuing up the school. School Certificate (later 'O' level) classes were time-tabled in the dinner hours for some years!

There was a very capable school choir which took part in competitions, which they frequently won, both locally and in North London.

In order to discover prospective violinists and with the co-operation of Mr. Gasparian, a peripatetic teacher, thirty violins were bought. Each First Form had a mass violin lesson in the main school building, much to the horror of the rest of the staff! However, from this drastic beginning a small group of very promising string players was found, and this was the beginning of the first school orchestra which survived.

Helped and encouraged by Mr. Bimrose, the County Music Organiser, the school had visiting teachers of all the orchestral instruments and were able to use Highbury House for the individual lessons. The McNaughten Quartet were employed by the County Council to give recitals and talks throughout Hertfordshire. The Girls' Grammar School was fortunate that the Quartet was based in Hitchin and the members were available to teach their own instruments. The choir and orchestra were then able to combine in the production of several operas.

1963.   [Lyndsay Abbott (Thompson)]

When Miss Stovin retired she was succeeded by Mr. Tillett who, in turn, has been followed by Mr. Paul A. Rooke, the present Director of Music.

Facilities for music studies have improved over the years, first by the provision of the foot bridge over the road to Highbury House and in 1983 by the construction of the purpose-built premises. These are now used for the teaching of all kinds of music and lessons for string, woodwind, brass and percussion instruments.

An abiding and much loved highlight of the school year has been, and still is, the annual Carol Service.

Facilities for listening to music are of the most up to date with the midi hi-fi system and compact disc player. A far step indeed from the wonder created when the school got its first gramophone!

UNIFORM

In the early days of the school there was no official uniform, and for the whole of Miss Gosnell's time it was never compulsory. The first photograph, taken in 1908, outside the new school, shows a preponderance of the pupils wearing dark skirts and white blouses or dark dresses with 'sailor boy' collars, but these may have merely been the popular clothes of the time.

1908. The earliest photograph found of the whole school with Miss Gosnell and the Mistresses.
[Hitchin Museum]

FROM TOP TO TOE

The Hats

There is no record of an early style of head gear being especially favoured for winter wear though the straw boater was certainly worn in the summer. In the mid-1890s the black or navy blue velour hat made its first appearance, worn with a blue hat band, (later with a yellow banding), and the school badge. With some minor changes in the size, and the addition of the cheaper felt hat, this remained the winter uniform until the Second World War. The hats then became difficult to obtain and it became optional to wear a navy blue beret. This bore the school badge in the centre, under-edge, and had to be worn straight and pulled down so that the badge was displayed. From 1982 the beret was no longer compulsory winter wear though the first formers still had to buy one since it remained essential for any school trip. In the early 1980s, the first year juniors were allowed to wear white woolly hats – known as 'tea cosies', to make them more conspicuous to motorists.

The photograph, taken in 1925, of a boarder wearing her Sunday winter uniform, is the only one we have which shows the winter hat.

The Panama hat was first worn early in the century and survived as part of the school uniform for more than seventy years. It bore the same hat band as that worn in winter, and the only real change, in the whole of that time, is that both crown and brim got smaller as the years progressed, and a hat band with the reversed colours was introduced for wear by the prefects. The hat was always most unpopular with the girls, who made bitter complaints of the elastic biting into the chin and the straw scratching the head. One poor child was convinced that the hat was wearing away her hair! During the 1930s, the wearing of a Panama hat was compulsory for all girls when playing tennis, following the misfortune of one pupil who got sun-stroke when playing without.

During the Second World War, the hats became difficult and expensive to obtain. The wearing of them was relaxed on normal school days so long as the pupils wore their blazers. On hot summer days the hated hats seemed preferable to a sweltering jacket, and many girls removed them when well away from the school premises. Not a convenient item to carry, they got folded away into satchels where many developed creases impossible to remove. Since they remained essential wear for Founder's Day there was a great deal of steaming and brim ironing required to make them acceptable! By the 1980s hats were no longer required for winter or summer wear.

It is interesting to note that when the Panama was no longer essential uniform, some of the Fifth Formers then chose to wear them for Founder's Day, and many

1925. Dorothy Cobbett wearing her velour hat.
[Joyce Thomas]

1922. Jennie Purdy, Marjorie Simpkins, Kathleen Waldock, Amy Purdy.
[Amy Purdy]

Sixth Formers reverted to variations of the 'boaters' worn by the first pupils in the school.

For many years the boarders had a soft, white linen hat, bearing the school badge, which was worn out of doors on summer Saturdays.

The Coats

Apart from natural developments in the styles, the top coats remained constant. Long, navy blue overcoats and gaberdine raincoats were in use at the turn of the century, the length being determined by the clothing worn underneath. No real change came until the early 1980s, when Mrs. Warwick gave the junior forms the option of a quilted, nylon style – known as 'duvets' to the girls – and the school badge was added to lapels as a distinguishing mark when hats were no longer worn.

Blazer jackets appeared in the early 1920s with the school badge on the pocket. Members of the OGA wore the same blazer with their own badge. This style has survived in the school, unchanged, for more than sixty years since nothing has been designed which improves on its tough practicality. Fortunately, modern fabrics have meant that these can now be washed. It was, for many years, an optional part of the uniform but became compulsory as other forms of identification were discontinued. The boarders always had a special Sunday uniform which was for many years a navy blue costume and silk blouse.

Scarves and Gloves

The fringed, navy blue woollen scarf, with its distinctive yellow banding at the ends, has been part of the uniform for more than sixty years. Not until the hats fell into disfavour was the badge sewn on to it. This has never been an obligatory part of the uniform. As part of the centenary celebrations, a scarf with the colours reversed to be predominant yellow was proposed by the girls and was on sale in May 1988.

182

In Miss Gosnell's time no lady was ever seen on the street without her gloves, either in winter or summer. Woe betide any girl, even on the hottest day, who had her white gloves in her pocket!

The wearing of gloves has followed the general attitude in society and though gloves were worn, in summer, on some occasions before World World II, since that time navy blue woollen gloves have been worn only when needed. In the early 1980s fingerless mittens were very popular, but many girls persisted in wearing them during the school day despite rules to the contrary. It was decided that this practice must definitely stop when one girl was found in the Domestic Science room, rubbing fat into flour for pastry – and still wearing her mittens! White gloves and scarves were introduced at the same time as the white hats.

Cardigans, Jumpers and Pullovers

In the late 1920s a plain, stocking-stitch pullover was added to the uniform. Navy in colour, it had a V-neck edged with a gold band. Miss Badland, in her turn, changed this to a cardigan style. In 1958, she changed it again to a plain, high necked cardigan. Soon after she took over the school, Mrs. Warwick reverted to a plain navy pullover, and in the 1980s the navy, sleeveless, 'tank top' joined this as acceptable winter wear. A white, summer cardigan, with V-neck, was introduced in 1970, and then years later a white 'tank top' became an alternative.

The Gym Tunic and the Skirts

The gym tunic, or gym slip, was first introduced as part of the school uniform in 1915. This was a straight, yolked, sleeveless garment with three boxed pleats, held in at the waist with a braided matching girdle. In the 1920s, the newly emancipated women shortened their skirts and adopted the 'boyish' waist-less look. This was reflected in the school, and one pupil remembered that her sash was just six inches

1933.   The Choir with Miss Saunders at the County Music Festival. [Herts Pictorial at Hitchin Museum]

above the hem line! By 1933, when this photograph was taken, it was returned to its normal place.

Soon after she came to the school, Miss Chambers introduced 'deportment girdles' – yellow girdles which denoted good carriage and lady-like behaviour. The list of proposed recipients was posted behind the Staff Room door and if any member of staff disagreed with the choice, the award was not made. Some years later, the original girdle was confined to the senior pupils and a narrower girdle, of the same colour, denoted the junior girls. The gym tunic, always worn with a white blouse, remained full school uniform, winter and summer, for twenty years and was winter wear for twenty more. Made of serge or gaberdine, it could be stiflingly hot in the summer, though the fortunate few had a lighter alpaca gym slip and square necked silk blouses which could be ordered from the school outfitter in Leicester. The length of this garment seems to have been of vital importance, because generations of ex-pupils remember kneeling on the gymnasium floor to have the distance from hem to floor measured with a ruler! Though this measurement varied from two to four inches the method of ascertaining it remained constant.

In 1934, Miss Chambers changed the style from the pleated to a plain tunic at the end of the autumn term. This caused hardship in some homes since 'wearing out' the old tunics was not allowed.

From the autumn of 1964, Mrs. Warwick agreed that the Sixth Form could wear sensibly chosen, navy blue skirts, and by the end of the 1950s the Fourth, Fifth and Sixth Forms were all allowed to wear skirts. It had been noted that the gym slip, bought to 'grow into', and mid-calf in the First Form, had become very shabby and mid-thigh in the third year. Since this was not a cheap item of clothing, there was some reluctance, on the part of the parents, to replace it for so limited a useful life. By 1963, the gym slip passed into history and the whole school wore a navy blue skirt. A regulation, four-gore style with zipped 'safety pocket' became the uniform in the late 1960s.

1930.   IVa[2]   [Amy Purdy]

The Blouses

Throughout its history, the school blouse has always been plain white and has appeared in a variety of styles. Materials have varied with the era but there is no early record of other than long sleeves. In the 1950s, Miss Badland introduced a uniform, short-sleeved blouse with a 'Peter Pan' collar.

The Badges

In 1923, prefect badges were awarded for the first time and were worn on the left side of the gym slip yolk. The first were a metal diamond shape, later to be joined by a shield. Games colours were fabric shields sewn to the yolk. In 1934 rectangular shapes were introduced and now survive in the school in their plastic form.

The 'Butcher Blue' Slip

The advent of this garment caused great excitement in the school with its promise of more comfortable summer days. It was introduced in 1927 and was a simple slip, made in the sewing class. These were usually kept in the cloak room and, when the headmistress decided the weather warranted it, a blue, diamond-shaped card was displayed and the gym slips were replaced. The butcher blue slips were never worn off the school premises, so travelling to and from school remained an ordeal.

The Summer Dress

Within a few years, the cotton slip had given way to a short-sleeved, summer dress. This was made from blue or yellow checked cotton gingham and survived with minor changes for forty years. Only the blue dress has ever been worn for Founder's Day. In the early days it was bought, ready made, from the school outfitter, but later there were several acceptable pattern designs so that they could be made privately. During the Second World War, when clothing was rationed and

c.1934. *Back row, L. to R.:* Irene Allen, Margaret Saunders, Margaret Primett, Jill Gardener. *Front row:* Mildred Roe, Enid Bryant.   [Sheila Ridgon (Wintle)]

in short supply, the required size of check was not so rigidly enforced and a standard pattern, with the cloth, could be purchased from the school by the home dress-maker. In the late 1960s this practice survived and the approved pattern could be hired from the school for the cost of 1/6d. This proved to be an elaborate, brown paper affair with numerous pieces of bias cuffs, pockets and tab front. It was amazing that the finished product could look so simple and some inexperienced dress-makers must have weakened and resorted to the ready-made product, available from either Nicholls or Hidgcock – the two school outfitters in Hitchin. (When both closed within a year of each other, in the early 1980s, the contract went to Hawkins Ltd. and later to John Lewis (Welwyn) as well). In 1967, the firm making the gingham material announced that it was stopping production and an alternative fabric had to be found.

The choice of fabric was most democratic and the parents were circularised to make a choice from three proposed materials. The majority chose a self-colour, light blue Dacron which was made up into a plain 'princess' style with a back zip. The choice was not a success:– thin girls looked thinner, fat girls looked fatter and

1976. Teresa Wright and Pamela Tickett.
[Alison Walker (Whitby)]

the material showed the slightest mark. All sweat stains remained a constant embarrassment to most of the pupils. Many girls refused to wear it and remained in their gingham dresses throughout their school life. This said much for the generously cut style. One girl was able to wear her first form dress for her final Founder's Day – after the belt had been unpicked and let into the back seam!

From 1975 the same blue Dacron was available as an alternative blue skirt and the dress was gently phased out. Since then there have been several changes in the actual material used for the skirts, but the plain, light blue has remained constant.

The boarders wore 'sensible' dresses on summer Saturdays but their Sunday uniform was usually a white silk dress, for many years worn with thick woollen stockings!

Stockings and Socks

From the earliest times, when the sight of a lady's leg was not seemly, they were encased in thick, black woollen stockings. This wear, for both winter and summer, persisted until the early 1930s though the weight of the wool became progressively lighter. With the appearance of the summer dresses beige, rayon, 'Silkestia' stockings were worn in the summer, and on very hot days, white or fawn socks were permissible. At the end of the 1930s, the black stockings were mostly made of 'Lisle' and fawn was allowed as an alternative colour.

By the end of the war, white ankle socks had become the accepted summer wear, and there were no further changes noted until, by the early 1960s, the stockings had been replaced by white, knee length socks.

In the early 1980s, when 'leg warmers' became very popular, the girls were allowed to wear white ones which would ensure warmth and make them more visible to motorists when travelling in poor winter light. This provided the ever ingenious pupils with a perfect opportunity to stamp a personal touch on their uniform, as has been well illustrated!

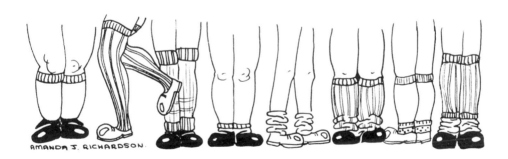

AMANDA J. RICHARDSON.

The Shoes

These varied down the years from black lace-up, to a bar shoe, to brown and then to any sensible style in the permitted colour of the time. Not until the early 1980s, when footwear appeared in a rainbow selection of colours, did Mrs. Warwick allow the wearing of navy, grey, beige, cream and white in addition to the other two colours. In the late 1960s, the girls were allowed to wear the fashionable, long boots for travel to school, though they had to be changed on arrival. In the interests of safety, these had to be white though this was later extended to include black and brown.

One pupil who started school in 1915 was required to provide 'house' or 'ward' shoes, and these may have been part of the uniform much earlier. They were usually made from glacé kid and had a single bar and button fastening. They survived in their general form for at least sixty years until they were allowed, gradually, to lapse; by the mid-1970s only one pair of shoes for both out- and indoors was required.

Sports Wear

The first mention of sports wear of any kind was in the early 1930s, when black plimsolls were required for games and white for gymnastics. The latter had to be pristine at all times and marks could be lost in competing for the Gymnastic Shield. This meant the liberal application of 'Blanco' – and in dire emergencies, white chalk! During the early 1940s, when 'Blanco', still much beloved by the army, was unobtainable, brown plimsolls were allowed.

In the late 1940s it was finally decided to discard the gym slips and do gymnastics in navy blue knickers, which were always worn underneath. This, remembers a pupil who was seventeen at the time, was a source of total humiliation to the older pupils. Shorts – rather long at first – were later part of the uniform until, around 1960, the gym mistress decided that, once again, knickers would be worn instead. The older girls, not so easily influenced as their mothers, staged a 'sit in' and refused to leave the cloakroom! The teacher relented. Christine Hart (Richardson), one of the rebels, says, 'There was some limit to the indignity you can suffer'. A black leotard is now used in the gymnasium. Not until the 1950s was anything other than the gym slip worn for hockey and netball. A short sports skirt was then introduced and survives as a pleated, navy, wrap-around garment with a plain front panel. With this is worn a yellow aertex blouse and navy, knee length socks. The swimming costume has always been plain black, early ones woollen, made by the Stevenage Knitting Company.

Underwear

Rosemary Russell (Cook) – one of the boarders of the 1920s, gave a graphic account of what went on under the uniform in her day. 'We wore a vest and a "liberty bodice" (these were made of cotton stockinette, reinforced with tape bands. They always had rubber buttons for the attachment of suspenders). The Matron liked "combinations" (an all-in-one woollen garment with short sleeves and legs to the knees. They buttoned down the front and had a crotch split, sometimes a back flap too, for necessary bodily functions). Tight, navy, woollen bloomers with cotton linings completed the underwear.'

Later came the navy woollen or cotton knickers which survived as long as underwear was deemed part of the uniform. Many had a pocket, originally intended for a handkerchief, but later adapted, with a button as a safety pocket. Great emphasis was put on the requirement that no 'smiles' should be seen between stocking top and knickers. This seems to have been very important in the 1920s and early '30s!

When the cotton dresses were introduced, the knicker regulations were relaxed slightly to allow the wearing of undergarments to match dress, socks or stockings!

Now the navy blue knickers are worn only with sports wear and the school, wisely, leaves the choice of other underwear to the girls and their parents.

THE PUPILS

THE KINDERGARTEN

In 1896, the Hitchin Girls' Grammar School opened a Kindergarten class for both boys and girls with just three pupils. These numbers grew, over the years, to a peak of about a hundred. Where the lower age seemed indeterminate, the boys were, strangely, required to leave at the age of nine, resulting in some of the earliest pupils having to go elsewhere for two years until they could be 'promoted' to the Boys' Grammar School when they were eleven. This however could be waived in special circumstances, as Miss Gosnell wrote in 1913:

> 'I have had a talk with Miss Wilkins about Stanley and she tells me that he is very well on in arithmetic but that he is backward in reading and she feels he is hardly yet fit for the Boys' School. I do not, as a rule, like to have boys when they are getting big, but Stanley is such a nice, quiet fellow that I am inclined to keep him a little longer. He gives no trouble and is very gentle and well behaved. He may therefore stay until he is fitted for the Boys' School.'

In 1925 Vera Davis came to school and recalled:

> 'You began in the Kindergarten – everyone; babies, Lower and Upper Transition – were in one room (this would be Room 8, the room on the left inside the main school entrance). The "babies" only attended in the morning – the Upper Transition had lessons with the First Form between break and lunch. In the afternoon the Upper and Lower Trans. had lessons such as French, singing and handiwork. In the third term, the

1911. The Kindergarten. Maurice Jeeves standing on the left. Bernard Sanders on Miss Wilkins knee.   [Joanna Sanders (Cooper)]

189

Upper Trans. became (or joined) the First Form if they were academically ready. The "first year" therefore consisted of a year and a term'.

As the Preparatory school grew, the Kindergarten retained Room 8 with its tables of graduated sizes, and the older children moved to the large 'Big Room' which has now been divided to make Rooms 11 and 12. In here, they were promoted to desks for the first time and allowed to use pen and ink. This may not have been altogether wise because a favourite pastime among the boys was, as remembered by Robert Stuteley, to flick their inky pen nibs on the back of the English teacher's jacket!

Miss Finlayson and Miss Bingham were both in charge of the Kindergarten in the 1890s, Miss Wilkins 1907–1915 and Miss Williams 1916–1922. When she left to get married, Miss Mockridge succeeded her for one year before Miss Read took charge of the children in 1924. They remained in her care until the Kindergarten closed in 1950.

The lessons had much in common with other kindergartens though the children did grow a broad bean, on wet blotting paper, which eventually attained nine feet in height though 'unlikely to grow any beans'. Two bird's nests appeared in its 'branches', and it was thought that Watson knew more about this phenomenon than he admitted!

Nativity plays, carols and concerts all had their place, and a number of yesterday's children remember taking part in the play 'Silly Old Alphabet'.

Norman Hyde, in the Kindergarten in the 1930s, claims that 'all the rogues of Hitchin' were at school with him. Play time was taken in the asphalt tennis court and a favourite game was playing chariot racing with the Hawkins twins as horses. Naughty children had to stand in the corner facing the wall and Miss Read, 'a

1935–36. 'Silly Old Alphabet'. Ted Hawkins remembers the rhyme with his letter 'J is for jam you enjoy with your tea, your bread would be dull if it wasn't for me'. *Back row:* Elizabeth Lamb, Phyllis? McCombie, Daphne Foster, Simon Parker or Michael Trench, Margaret Leete, ? . *Second row from back:* Beryl Chalkley, John Sanders, Audrey Cooper, Daphne Sworder?, Mavis Allan, ? , Peter Curnow. *Third row from back:* Dora Edwards, Ann Foster, Jean Ryland or Sonia Upright, Anne Willmott, Pauline Whitby, Rhona Garrett. *Front row:* Jane Barker, Norman Hyde, Ann Barker, ? , Ted Hawkins, Michael Willmott, Isobel Harkness. [Joanna Sanders (Cooper)]

terrifying, large lady, like a battleship in full sail,' struck fear into every heart. He still proudly keeps the yellow 'deportment' tie awarded to him in place of the girls' girdle.

John Sainsbury remembers that a great disadvantage for the boys was that they were never taught any exclusively 'boyish' things. Consequently, they left school unable to play football.

The 1944 Education Act meant that fee paid places came to an end and no more children were accepted into the Kindergarten. From that time the numbers declined steadily as pupils moved up to the school or left to continue schooling elsewhere. In 1950 Miss Read led the last seven of her 'little chickens' into the 'big school' and the Kindergarten closed after being part of the school's life for fifty-four years.

THE BOARDERS

After the almost domestic family life at Bancroft, the move up the hill to the new school brought a great change in the life of the boarders.

The whole of that portion to the right of the main entrance was for the exclusive use of the residents – headmistress, teachers, boarders, matron and maids. This was the 'House' and is still easily identified by the chimney stacks.

In the new building, the girls' sitting room was on the ground floor (now Study E), and their dormitory was at the top of the house, in that portion which is now the school library. Here the room had wooden partitions and a shelf running along under the windows, where each girl had her own wash jug and basin. The younger children slept in one large room opposite the main dormitory.

1925. The Boarders' sitting-room.
[Joyce Thomas]

At 7 a.m. the girls were summoned by a bell to rise and dress before doing their 'three runs' round the hockey field – or music practice – before breakfast at 8 a.m. This was always taken in the dining room at the top two tables and supervised by Matron.

When breakfast was finished, the boarders joined the rest of the pupils in the normal day's activities though they were still segregated at dinner time.

When school finished for the day the girls changed out of uniform into 'afternoon dresses', suitable to the season, before having tea at 4.30 p.m. At 5.30 p.m. the main school bell summoned the pupils to their 'prep', supervised by one of the resident mistresses, which occupied the older girls until supper time. Joan Flex

191

1920s.   A cubicle in the dormitory.   [School Prospectus, Ivy Pettengell (Sainsbury)]

(1925–1928) remembers that Miss Chambers invariably took Evening Prayers and afterwards shook each girl by the hand and bade her 'Good night'.

For some, there was now unfinished 'prep', for others the opportunity to play tennis or read by the sitting room fire, and for the youngest it was bed time. The other girls went to bed at quarter hour intervals according to their ages. On Saturday morning, after breakfast, came 'mending' in the Domestic Science Room, with Miss Forbes. Each girl's laundry had to be inspected and passed before she was released, until dinner time. In the afternoons, outings were arranged which varied from walks in the winter, to picnics in the summer, before each girl could pursue her own interests for the rest of the day.

Many of the mistresses also 'lived in', so the opportunities for undetected mischief were few. Nevertheless some girls, many years after leaving school, admitted to midnight bathing which had never come to the notice of the authorities. This was unlike the midnight feasts which were well known to the indulgent housekeeper who 'turned a blind eye' to them.

All the pupils attended St. Mary's Matins Service on Sunday morning, and walked in 'crocodile' down to the church, escorted by the Matron. For this they wore full school uniform in the winter and an appropriate uniform dress in the summer. During the 1920s this was a white, tussore silk dress, still worn with black woollen stockings and, of course, gloves.

After dinner the boarders always had 'Class' with Miss Chambers; a rather forbidding title covering a pleasant hour in Miss Chambers' sitting room where, after reading from the Bible, the girls knitted or sewed while the Headmistress read aloud to them. This was also the day for writing letters home and an hour was set aside specifically for this task.

The boarders, inevitably, became a close-knit group within the school and 'House' versus 'School' games matches were popular. There was also a Boarders' Choir and they regularly performed concerts and plays which had been prepared in

192

Summer 1928.   The Boarders in their Sunday silk tussore dresses.   [Jean Jackson (Butlin)]

the evenings. An Entertainment was always staged at Christmas, and the boarders had a splendid Christmas party before going home for the holidays.

There is no reliable record of the numbers of boarders in the school at any one time, but it seems there were between twenty-five and thirty of them from the time the new building was erected. In 1915 the fees were quoted as being £45–£60 per annum. By 1945 they had risen to £86–£102.

In December 1950, after more than twenty years in the rather institutionalised main school, the boarders returned to a more homely atmosphere, in their move to Highbury House. This created better surroundings for the girls and released much needed space in the school building. Their numbers were now dwindling as no new boarders were being accepted and, in 1959, when the number of boarders had been reduced to six, Miss Badland moved into a first floor flat at Highbury – the first headmistress to live off the main school premises.

In 1960, the last boarders left the school and with them ended their seventy year history at Hitchin Girls' Grammar School.

'THE TRAIN GIRLS'

The railway was most important to the school, from its earliest days in Bancroft, and remained so for many years. This was the easiest and safest way for girls from the surrounding villages and a few from further afield, to travel. Later, as the school grew, there were more and more pupils travelling by train to the Grammar Schools in Hitchin. Later, when other towns had built Grammar Schools of their own, the numbers declined.

Esther Brooks, who left in 1925, gave a vivid picture of:–

'Hitchin station, swarming with boys and girls, as they arrived for school and left for home. There was great friendly rivalry between the travellers on each of the trains and

193

the "Biggleswade Line" played the "Letchworth Line" at hockey, during half term each year. Even after we left school, the fixture became a Boxing Day event and was held until the outbreak of the war in 1939'.

Joyce Smith (Cole) came to the school in 1930 and travelled from Welwyn Garden City. She remembered:–

'Once on the platform it was strictly boys at one end and girls at the other. We NEVER met – segregation extended to all forms of activity. The only time the boys invaded our end of the platform was when the L.N.E.R. introduced new streamlined engines for the Silver Jubilee of King George V. There was a rush by the boys to keep level with the "Silver Fox" and "Silver Link" as they steamed in. Once seated in the train, supervised by prefects, we usually behaved demurely, but a bout of madness overtook us if the Railway mistakenly included First Class compartments in our batch of reserved carriages. This was a rare treat, to be made the most of. The seats had thick, soft, removable cushions – very bounceable! In between testing them out we relaxed against the white lace antimacassars, savouring our brief luxury.'

Miss Chambers appointed prefects to supervise the behaviour of the travelling girls. It was their duty to ensure lady-like behaviour at all times and to organise the 'crocodiles' winding their way up and down between the station and school. At any sign of trouble, the prefects would be either replaced or reinforced.

When Mr. Tagg, the popular Hitchin Station-master, retired in 1929, the 'train girls' gave him a photograph of the school to remember them by.

THE GIRL GUIDES AND THE BROWNIES

During the Great War, the school formed a 'Corpus Comitum', – which loosely translates as 'a company with a commitment', which was, in essence, very like the Girl Guides. When the corps was disbanded at the end of the war, it seemed a logical progression to form the group into a Girl Guide Company and retain its former leader, Miss Read, as the Captain. This became the 1st Hitchin (School) Company in the spring of 1919.

The Brownies started about the same time, forming the 1st Hitchin Brownie Pack. By the autumn, a senior guide patrol (later known as Rangers) was formed for girls over sixteen, which was supervised by Miss Lamb.

The Guides started with four patrols: White Rose, Fuchsia, Poppy and surprisingly, Robin. Great enthusiasm was shown by the girls and many of them quickly passed their Tenderfoot Test and began work on attaining Proficiency Badges and the Second Class award. Within a year most of them had achieved their aim though the defaulters were the subject of much sarcasm. In this year, they went to a County Rally at Welwyn, which was attended by Lady Baden Powell. The Guides went to a Divisional Camp in the summer of 1920 and were fortunate in the weather for their first experience of life 'under canvas'. They were taken to task by their Captain for the poor standard of Camp Fire entertainments and singing but 'we hope to improve'.

By March 1921 there were thirty-two Guides and three of them were congratulated on becoming First Class Guides and gaining their All Round Cords.

The Brownies were still happily meeting, picnicking at Purwell and making goods for sale at the Hitchin Hospital and school handwork stalls.

In 1922 the Guides was disbanded, to the great regret of Miss Read. Despite Miss Chambers' claim of disinterest, it was a widely held view, that she had intervened because the disappointing examination results of one pupil were blamed on her enthusiasm in pursuing her Guide badges.

1920–22.   The 1st Hitchin (School) Company with Miss R. Read (Captain)   [Mrs. Carling]

A 'Lone Patrol' – Heather, did survive but met off the school premises in an upstairs room at Perks and Llewellyn chemists in the High Street (now Woolworths).

The Brownie Pack survived a few more years before it too was disbanded.

In 1941 the boarders were allowed to revive the Guide Company, under its old name, under the control of Misses Boulton and Ryder. A year later, it became an open school company and had thirty-three members working in five patrols. They took great pride in taking the original company colours to Church Parade on Empire Day and in raising £20 for the Baden Powell Memorial Fund.

In 1942 there was a most eventful summer camp, where the camp site was invaded by cows which developed a taste for the jelly intended for the girls' meal and when a tent collapsed in the middle of the night enveloping the five occupants!

By 1943, the Company had grown to forty-five girls divided into six patrols which won the District Shield. They ran a most successful party for thirty deaf and dumb children, acted as messengers for the Red Cross Sale and distributed and collected envelopes for several Flag Days.

In 1944, the numbers had dropped to twenty-eight in the face of competition from the Girls' Training Corps, a movement designed to train girls for war service. Despite this they came second in the District Hiking Competition the following year and enjoyed a six day camp at Holwell.

In 1948 the Company again competed successfully in the District Shield and planned its first exclusive camp for some years, in Hatfield Park.

1949 was the 30th Anniversary of Guiding in Hitchin, started at the Girls' Grammar School. This year, three hundred guides from the district met in St.

1949. 30th Birthday Party. *In centre, L. to R.:* Miss Lamb (Badge Sec.), Miss Read (began the Company), Miss Errock (Captain), Miss Badland (Headmistress), Mrs. Carling (District Commissioner).
[Marion Wood (Donaldson)]

Mary's Church for Thinking Day, when they remember guides throughout the world. This became an annual event.

The school Guides held a party to celebrate this special birthday to which they invited Miss Read (the first Captain), Miss Lamb (the first Lieutenant), Mrs. Carling (the District Commissioner) and Miss Badland. The Company was now under the guidance of Miss Errock and Miss Hart.

By 1951, the school Guide Company had fifty members and a new Captain, Miss Morley with Miss Farmer to assist her. This was the year that twenty of the guides marched in the Hitchin Pageant.

In 1953, as a Coronation tribute, the Guides tidied and planted the gardens at the rest-houses in Hollow Lane and performed a Czechoslovakian folk dance at a Coronation rally in the Woodside Theatre.

Miss Hasler became the Company Captain in 1954 with Miss Richardson to help her and in 1955 the Company had grown so much that two new patrols were formed, the Thrushes and the Magpies. Guide camps were now taking place further from home and in 1956 there was a Whitsun camp in Essex and a summer one at Bexhill in Sussex.

Two of the Guides achieved their Queen's Guides Award in 1956: Jennifer Whitethorn and Sheila Muir; both were presented by the District Commissioner, Mrs. Carling.

In 1957 some of the older girls went to stay in the Guide House in Baaen, in Holland, in addition to a representative going to the World Centenary Camp, in Windsor Great Park, to celebrate the centenary of Lord Baden Powell.

With the Guide Company in such good heart, it was unfortunate that, in the summer of 1957, Miss Hasler left and, with no-one to replace her, the school company was disbanded, to re-form as an open company in the town. A second

196

revival was attempted in 1982 with Mrs. E. Wilkins as Guide Guider, but the time was not opportune and for the third time, the 1st Hitchin Company of the Girl Guides disbanded in 1985.

THE GIRLS' TRAINING CORPS

The Girls' Training Corps was started during the Second World War to provide some preliminary training before girls went into the forces.

A company was formed which met in the school twice a week. One evening was devoted to first aid, morse signalling and drill. This latter entailed marching, counter marching and slow marching for what seemed like hours! There was also a course on despatch carrying and some girls anticipated practice on a rifle range. The second evening was sometimes taken up more peacefully employed in the Domestic Science room with Miss Forbes, or playing team games and swimming. One girl ruefully observed that the recreational evening could be more exhausting than that devoted to work! The G.T.C. died a natural death with the ending of the war.

HEAD GIRLS

Head Prefect

E. Widdows	M. Woods		S. Turnbull
C. M. Gibson	Hope Fitch		D. Perrott
E. Warren	G. Donson		A. Hillman

1912	Jessie Hall and Gwendoline Bryant (joint)	1913	Doris Armstrong
1914	?	1915	Kathleen Warren
1916	Phyllis Hall	1917	Winifred Taylor
1918	Ruth Mothersill	1919	Eileen Moore
1920	Mary (Esther) Cole	1921	Ida Goldsmith
1922	Gwendoline Dear	1923	Ivy Pettengell

	Head Girl	**Second Head Girl**
1924	Margaret Bell	
1925	Joan Taudevin	
1926	Grace King	
1927	Jean Jackson	
1928	Helen Gray	
1929	Margaret McCarraher	
1930	Janet Mantle	Freda Weedon
1931	Pegeen Keller	
1932	Doris Baker	
1933	Gwen Major	
1934	Grace Mayles	Joyce Thomas
1935	Joan Eddy	Freda Crabb
1936	Margaret Hicks	Janet M. Ferrier
1937	Enid Burgess	Doreen Eddy
1938	Adeline Doble	
1939	Lottie Fraser	Pat Hawkins
1940	Enid Bryant	
1941	Diana Clarke	
1942	Kathleen Bellew	
1943	Pat McCombie	
1944	Anne Willmott	
1945	Gwen Roberts	
1946	Marguerite Delavenay	
1947	Margaret Day	
1948	Joan Wade	

Year	Head Girl	Deputy Head Girl(s)	
1949	Madge Streeter	Margaret Deacon	
1950	Betty Preston	Ann Kirby	
1951	Ann Patrick	Auriol Kaufmann	Barbara Crabbe
1952	Anne Harris	Sheila Johns	
1953	Margaret Lloyd	Margaret Smith	
1954	Christine Fulton	Gillian Boorman	Mollie Whitworth
1955	Patricia Withers	Eileen Shelford	Bridget Webb
1956	Janet Lloyd	Elizabeth Pugh	
1957	Christine Brown	Billie Lawton	
1958	Frances Muir	Marion Knight	
1959	Jacqueline Conway	Sheila Gardener	
1960	Rosemary Taylor	Elizabeth Sainsbury	
1961	Janet Spicer	Julia Johnson	
1962	Lyndsay Abbott	Carol Gentle	
1963	Sally Pritchard	Hilary Jenkins	
1964	Shena Fulton	Susan Jenkins	
1965	Kathleen Anderson	Jean Dollimore	
1966	Judith Lake	Diana Thompson	
1967	Creina Richards	Penelope Barnes	
1968	Vanessa Hull	Diana Buxton	Vivien Grimes
1969	Eleanor Brown	Janice Hughes	Barbara Weeden
1970	Sally Cordwell	Elizabeth Buckley	Jane Toll
1971	Mary Arthur	Deirdre Gray	Judith Russell
1972	Yvonne Checkley	Jane Buxton	Patricia Stowell
1973	Annette Hayes	Susan Hill	Susan Plowman
1974	Edwina Dighé	Karen Pateman	Elizabeth Seddon
1975	Penelope Plowman	Claire Bousfield	Deborah Sell
1976	Mary Dalling	Theresa Hyde	Carolyn Williams
1977	Jenny Humphrey	Elizabeth Thrussell	Faith Watson
1978	Sarah Almond	Amanda Gates	Alison Day
1979	Sally Mack	Elizabeth Agg	Julie Maylin
1980	Averil Brown	Paula Gant	
	Paula Gant	Sally Banks	Karen Martin
1981	Sara Evans	Deborah Brownhill	Elizabeth Hawkins
1982	Penny Le Sage	Susan Banks	Sarah Hawkins
1983	Katherine Pickering	Alison Macaulay	Catherine Walton
1984	Elizabeth Lamb	Claire Roberts	Vanessa Willis
1985	Emma Decent	Sally Thorogood	Nicolette Zarka
1986	Claire Shephard	Sara Gower	Rosalind Young
1987	Linda Brady	Andrea Lovewell	Helénè Russell
1988	Nicola Jackson	Martine Hamilton	Jill Robertson

GENERATIONS OF FAMILY TRADITION

Since the Hitchin Girls' Grammar School opened, there has been the custom of daughter following mother into the school and this photograph, taken in 1964, shows the girls who at that time were following the family tradition.

Of these thirty girls, twelve had a grandmother as well as a parent at the school and one, Victoria Foster, was the fourth generation to be educated there! Her sister, Jane, and a girl whose mother attended, were absent when the photograph was taken.

1964. Daughters and grand-daughters of former pupils. (Names of present girls, with their mothers' and grandmothers' names in brackets. *Back row:* Deirdre West (Gwen Brunt), Elizabeth Cranfield (Joan Sheppard), Karen Cheesmer (Marian Crowe), Helen Cruse (Daphne Crickmer), Sheila Roach (Millicent Grimes), Judith Squires (Doris Taylor). *Standing:* Brenda and Phyllis Evans (Gwen Goldsmith), Susan Day (June Buller), Elizabeth Saville (Mary Robertson), Margaret Jenkins (Eileen McGitchie), Juliet Ball (Brenda Bridger), Mary and Judith Everett (Joan Adams), Christine Sharp (Edna Stanley), Hilary Jenkins (Agnes Sainsbury). *Kneeling:* Brenda Allen (Olive Bowskill), Penelope Lindsell (James Lindsell, father), Jill Sheen (Lucy Stedman, M., Annie Weeden, g.m.), Sarah Theobald (Isobel Farrow, m., Dorothy Tarrier, g.m.), Victoria Foster (Diana Morris, M., Audrey (Collier, g.m., Ethel Jeeves, g.g.m.!), Judith Billson (Doris Miller, g.m.), Rosemary Lawrence (Joy Jervis Hunter), Barbara Rankin (Elsie Binks). *Sitting:* Pamela Philpott (Joan Valentine), Christine Hook (Jean MacLeod), Gillian Stowell (Joyce Powdrill), Susan Woolley (Brynhild Buckler), Sally Bibbings (Betty Gill), Susan Keane (Audrey Handscombe). Absent: Gillian Ball (Brenda Bridger), Jane Foster (Diana Morriss). (School Magazine 1964]

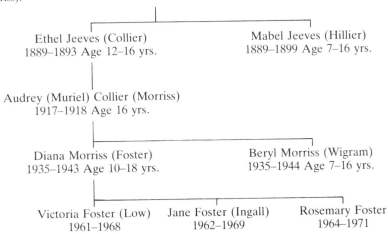

Four generations at H.G.(G.)S.

The two daughters of Jane Foster, who still lives in the area, are still too young to attend the School on the Hill. Perhaps they, too, will follow the family tradition.

THE NON-TEACHING STAFF

Supreme amongst the non-teaching staff was **Ralph Watson**, who was engaged as school Caretaker in 1907. This is somewhat misleading, since his connection with the school went back much further than that.

At the time that the building in Bancroft was purchased, Watson was employed, by Frederic Seebohm, in the grounds of the 'Hermitage'. It is clear, from the recollections of the ex-pupils, that he was on permanent loan to tend the gardens and grounds of the new school. The old pupils agree that he was never seen without his bowler hat when going about his duties in Bancroft, but this must have been in the latter years on that site since he was only seventeen when it opened! At the school on the hill he wore a cap, except on Founder's Day when he showed his respect by donning a trilby.

Watson was always pleased to tell of Mr. Seebohm taking him up to the top of the hill so as to mark, with stakes, the corners of the proposed new building. These vanished overnight and Watson suggested turning a sod of the turf instead. This he did and took great pride in being the first person to start the building of the new school.

In the school magazine issued to mark the Tercentenary of the Foundation he wrote, 'I little thought that I should spend thirty-two years rolling and mowing to make the fields for hockey and tennis courts, but it has been the happiest time of my life; the chatter and noise of the children comes back to me sweeter than any music I have yet heard.'

In the early days, a horse was hired to pull the grass-cutting machine and the roller; for this, the horse wore leather overshoes so as not to mark the turf. Watson was always indulgent when the girls played and bounced in the piles of cut grass. Later came a motor mower – 'the pride and joy of his life'.

He was a father figure to the girls who loved to visit his immaculate, white-washed boiler house, 'just to talk', and his puckish sense of fun endeared him to them. Once when mending a leaking skylight in the gymnasium he made funny faces to make the girls laugh and in the school photograph he nipped from one end to the other so that he appeared twice!

In common with many working men of his generation, he was denied the opportunity of early education but attended Hitchin Adult School regularly, kept bee hives along the Hollow Lane boundary and loved his garden. It was Watson who planted, in 1919, many of the trees still standing in the school grounds. In 1941, at the start of the Easter holiday, ill health forced his retirement. By the time the girls returned for a new term he had died, aged 69. He now rests, quite close to the school to which he devoted his life.

Caretakers and Groundsmen

In 1939, **Mr. Augustus E. Cooper** (known as 'Gus') arrived at the school to assist Mr. Watson and on his death in 1941, became the school caretaker; a post he held for thirty years. Mr. Cooper's solidly constructed stage props, painted by Miss Naylor and her Art students, formed an essential part of several school productions. One groundsman who is well remembered during that time was **Mr. Aprubs**, a Lithuanian, who came to the school after the Russian invasion of his country.

It was appropriate that a bird bath was built in his memory, to stand in the gardens which he tended with such loving care and to attract the birds which had been his friends.

1930.   Ralph Watson and Jimmie.

In 1969, **Mr. Hayes** became the caretaker with an assistant, **Mr. Philpott**. He was quickly succeeded by **Mr. Springham** who left the school in 1971. For the next two years, the post was filled by **Mr. Eames** and in 1973, **Mr. Ashmore** took over and stayed for four years until 1977. During this time **Mr. Jack** became the groundsman and left in 1977. The next caretaker was **Mr. Lovell**, who stayed for one month! Next came **Mr. Gibson** who was caretaker from 1978 to 1985. **Mr. Lyons**, the assistant caretaker, died in 1979 and **Mr. Reg Hall** came in his place until 1984. He has been succeeded by **Mr. Michael Bethell** who is still the assistant and **Mr. Jim Roberts**, who came in 1985, remained as the caretaker until July 1988.

Cleaning Staff

The work of the caretaker would have been impossible without the support of the band of ladies who came in daily to clean the premises after the girls had gone home.

Among these must be mentioned Mrs. Muncy, Mrs. Brazier (about 30 years service) and Mrs. Cooper. Mrs. Armitage cleaned during the 1940s and 1950s to be followed by her daughters Mrs. Cornes and Mrs. Weston who have now been with the school for over 18 years.

Office and Clerical Staff

In Miss Chambers' time at the school, the office was run by some of the teachers who combined this work with some of their teaching: **Miss Mather** taught

Secretarial studies and Scripture (1920–1923); **Miss Bavin** (1924–1927) games. **Miss Catherine E. Ryder** (1936–1952) accompanied the girls on school trips and helped with the Guides; **Gwyneth Lamb** helped with P.E. When Miss Badland came to the school, **Miss Alice Miles** and later **Miss Maude West** were in charge of the office with **Mrs. Lilley** and later **Mrs. Minnie Ambler** to help them.

Some time after Mrs. Warwick arrived **Mrs. Beecheno** took charge of the office and later **Miss Ivy Hare** became the Bursar. Miss Hare was clearly the last of the old school bursars for there was never an electronic calculator to be seen anywhere.

This post has been held in turn by **Mrs. Mary Firmin**, **Mrs. Pat Holland**, **Mrs. Ann Winters** and **Mrs. Diana Reeve**. The bursar deals with all money matters and accounts. If girls have forgotten their dinner money they may borrow it but only once a term as there have been occasions, in the past, when forgetful girls have built up substantial debts.

By 1975, the demands on the office had increased to such an extent that a further post was created to deal with visitors to the school, internal enquiries, the telephone and other duties, not the least of which was to tend sick and injured girls. The first holder of this post was **Mrs. Joan Brasier** who was followed, in turn, by **Mrs. Ida Simpson**, **Mrs. Patricia Wallace** and **Mrs. Jean Sharp**. The sick room can be busy, at times, and the staff render First Aid and then summon parents, doctor or ambulance, as appropriate. Luckily most of the ailments are easily dealt with but Mrs. Simpson recalls having to deal with a pupil who attempted to climb the iron railings and succeeded in impaling herself with a metal spike through the armpit.

Mrs. Jill Smith was Mrs. Warwick's secretary for 15 years until her retirement in 1984 when she was succeeded by Mrs. Simpson. In 1971/72, during Mrs. Smith's absence, **Mrs. Marjorie Vann** ably held the fort, along with Mrs. Beecheno.

Mrs. Warwick's secretary acts as a buffer between her and unnecessary distractions. It is her unhappy task to deal with difficult parents who seem unable to appreciate that the headmistress and her staff cannot be summoned at will. A foreigner once arrived hoping to teach flute playing and was referred to the Divisional Education Officer through whom all appointments are processed.

Typewriters and duplicating equipment have kept up with the times but, surprisingly, the school still has only one telephone line into the premises despite repeated requests for improvement. It is hoped this will happen soon.

Bomb hoaxes were a recurring problem dealt with, initially, by the office staff, as are the perpetual problems caused by 'flashers'. The accurate descriptions given by the girls often lead to arrest of these people but there always seem to be more to take their place. The school's location makes it vulnerable to this kind of nuisance.

The office staff also 'keep an eye' on naughty girls consigned to the space 'under the stairs'.

The Laboratory Technicians

In the early days of the science department, the teaching staff prepared and cleared away their own apparatus but as the number of girls and work load increased, a laboratory assistant was employed. Miss Badland appointed **Elizabeth Cade** who also tended the plants. Soon there was need of more help and, in the mid 1960s, **Mr. Timbury** came as a full-time Workshop Assistant (most other assistants worked part-time). Besides setting up and clearing of experiments, Mr. Timbury also made equipment and his test tube racks are still in use. He was also in charge of the films and projector. Mr. Timbury took a great interest in everything connected with the school; he liked to attend assembly; he ran the Gardening Club and the Bee Keeping Club. When he retired in 1976, after ten years at the school, **Martin Blake** came in a part-time capacity. After the new Science Block was built, **Mrs.**

Deuchar, as her first duty, unpacked all the equipment in the new block. She remained at the school until 1984. **Mrs. Sheila Wilkinson**, who took over in the chemistry lab. in 1975, is still at the school. At that time, **June Fullock** was in the Biology Lab. but she left a year later and was replaced by **Mrs. Brett. Mrs. Ida Doolan** came, in 1979, to help with Combined Science and still does this, in conjunction with part-time duties in the office. Terminology changed in 1979, though the work did not, and the Laboratory Assistants became Laboratory Technicians. In 1984, **Mrs. Diane Morsley** took over in the Physics Lab., where she makes much of the electronic equipment as well as doing the repairs.

The Kitchen Staff

Meals have always been served in the school since, in the early days, the staff and the boarders 'lived in'. These dinners were available to the day girls but tended to be very expensive and many of the pupils brought sandwiches. As the school grew, senior teachers, boarders and senior pupils ate at the top tables in the dining room, junior 'hot dinner' girls at the bottom and the 'sandwich' girls in the Domestic Science room. Here **Miss Forbes** provided hot soup on cold days. Some old pupils remember 'Gum shoe' pudding – steamed syrup pudding which resembled a rubber sole when turned out, and 'vaseline' tart – lemon curd.

During the Second World War, it became an obligation to provide, at modest cost, a hot midday meal for all the children, and **Miss Davies** took charge of the kitchen. **Miss Wesley and Mrs. Hunter** followed in succession by others before the advent of **Mrs. Sykes** in 1968. She was a character and became a well known Mrs. Malaprop since she constantly used the wrong words to the great amusement of her audience. It is said that, fearing she had a ghost in her domain, she invited a visiting clergyman to come and circumcise the kitchen! Nothing was too much trouble for her, and countless girls and members of staff, not to mention visiting Heads and other officials, have reason to be grateful to Mrs. Sykes and her helpers. **Mrs. Parish** and later **Mary McNealy** assisted her in preparing the meals.

On Mrs. Sykes' retirement in 1980, **Mrs. Hollings** arrived and she later introduced the Health Food Bar – a concept so revolutionary at the time that T.V. Anglia came to report on its opening. **Barbara Wareham**, already working in the main kitchen, took over the Lower School meals in 1978. **Mrs. Gates** and **Mrs. Patricia Sarll** (Atherton, pupil 1961–66) have followed in supervising the provision of good, wholesome food.

*　　*　　*　　*　　*

Though not directly employed at the school three other people should be remembered.

Firstly **Mr. Greenwood**, the Welfare Officer (a post which used to be called the Truant Officer). As the title implies, it is he who visits the homes of pupils who are persistent absentees and has statutory powers regarding disruptive children. He can also offer sympathetic help to families disturbed by bereavement and other crises.

Elizabeth Turner is the present school nurse – sometimes called 'the problem nurse', since it is she who makes a weekly visit to discuss any girl's problems in complete confidence. She also attends, with the Medical Officer, regular health checks and arranges for immunisation injections. This duty has come a long way since the title 'nit nurse' described the greater part of the school nurse's duties.

P.C. Roy Benney is the Highbury Neighbourhood Police Officer and liaises with the school in the matter of vandalism, break-in and the persistent nuisance of the 'flashers'. He also deals with petty crime in the school, gives talks on crime prevention and arranges the stamping identification of bicycles to discourage theft.

THE GROUNDS AND BUILDINGS

SUMMARY OF BUILDINGS

1889   In Bancroft.
1892   Cookery Classroom built.
1896   New Assembly Hall and classrooms added.
1908   Hitchin Girls' Grammar School moves to Highbury Road, on top of Windmill Hill.
1920   3 temporary classrooms built. Room 20 fitted out for Domestic Science.
1927   Lower field and woods given but not in use until 1929.
1929   New West Wing built – Rooms 11–15 incl. and claokrooms. Room 10 divided into 2 classrooms.
1933   Swimming Pool opened.
1939   New Hall and Art Room (Room 19) + 3 Laboratories.
1948   3 new hard tennis courts and 3 additional grass courts.
1951   Archways filled in along corridor opposite Rooms 9 and 10.
1952   Lower School Building and Domestic Science room.
1954   First floor of Lower School Building.
1955   Dormitory converted into Library (Senior Library).
1958   Dining Room extended. Entrance Hall enclosed.
1961   The drive was tarmacadamed.
1972   Science Block and Gymnasium completed.
1975   Mobile classrooms on hockey pitch for demolition of lower school.
1978   New Lower School Building and Domestic Science Rooms in use.
1981   Footbridge constructed over Highbury Road.
1982   Music Block completed.

Hitchin Girls Grammar School at Bancroft.   [Pat Gadd]

Hitchin Girls' Grammar School opened with 7 girls, and Hitchin Boys' Grammar School with 24 boys, in 1889 at the site known as 'Woodlands' in Bancroft (now Bells Chemist). It was thought that this site once belonged to John Mattock in 1632 and thus by a curious coincidence what had been his property and probably his own residence came, after two and a half centuries, to be added to his Endowment and become a home for his school.

1892   Cookery classroom built.

1896   New Assembly Hall (now Hitchin Boys' School Scout Hut!) and classrooms added. A good insight into the house may be gained by reading the Auctioneer's guide of 1880, when the house was withdrawn from sale.

1908   An increase in numbers necessitated new buildings for the boys and girls. Frederick Seebohm gave the land on Windmill Hill. On the following pages are copies of the original ground floor, first and second floor plans of the school building. Copies drawn by Amanda Birkinshaw.

1920   The number of girls at the school was approaching 300 and this necessitated 3 temporary classrooms and a cloakroom being built on the site of the kitchen garden near the water tower. These remained until 1939.

1922/23 **The Netball Court** – 'sometimes green, always muddy' was converted to hard (asphalt) on the site of the present Science Block.
         A Sale of Work was held on Wednesday, 22nd November 1922 'opened by Mrs. Pryor, wife of one of our Governors'. The object of the sale – 'to raise money for our new Hard Court' and a fine total of £173. 11s. 3d. was raised.

A good insight into the house may be gained by reading the Auctioneers guide of 1880, when the house was withdrawn from sale.

~~~~~~~~~~~~~~~~~~~~

LOT I

COMPRISES THE EXTREMELY VALUABLE AND COMMODIOUS BRICK-BUILT, TILED, AND SLATED

FAMILY RESIDENCE

CALLED

"THE WOODLANDS,"

With Portico Entrance, and small Piece of Ground in Front, protected by a substantial and ornamental Iron Fence, well situated in the best part of the Town, and near to the Hermitage Road leading to the Great Northern Railway Station.

The House contains Entrance Hall, (extending to Garden), and also a Side Entrance from Yard for Servants and Tradespeople. Oak Staircase.

On the Second Floor are 3 Bed-Rooms and Box Room, a Range of 3 Bed-Rooms with a Second Staircase.

On the First Floor: 4 principal Bed-Rooms, and Dressing-Room, Boudoir with glazed Roof, Bath-Room, with Hot and Cold Water Service, Linen Closet, W. C., and Laundry with Water laid on.

On the Ground Floor: Dining-Room, 17 feet by 18 feet, with Folding Doors, communicating with the Drawing-Room, 23 feet long, including the Bay Window with Folding Glazed Doors opening on to Lawn ; Breakfast-Room or Library, Housekeeper's-Room, Butler's Pantry, Glass-Room, W.C., Large Kitchen with Stone Floor, Pantry, a Passage leading to a large Second Kitchen or Wash-House, Coal-House, and Store Room.

The Basement: Good Cellarage.   A SMALL COURT YARD.

A LARGE ENCLOSED YARD,

With Gate and Footway Entrance from Bancroft ; on the North side of which is a very

SUBSTANTIAL RANGE OF BRICK AND SLATED BUILDINGS,

50 feet long formerly used as Stables and Stores but now used as

A SCHOOL ROOM,

Well lighted and ventilated, adjoining which is a Brick Built and Slated Building, 50 feet by 20 feet used as a CLASS ROOM,

A SECOND SCHOOL ROOM,

(With Entrance from the Yard) and Loft over, at the West end of which is a Potting-Shed with Loft over ; on the South Side of the Yard is a RANGE OF BRICK AND TILED BUILDINGS 68 feet long, used as Boot and Shoe House, Cinder House, large Double Carriage House with Stone and Brick Floor, a second Carriage House with Brick Floor and Loft over, a Washing House, a Range Brick of and Slated W.C's. and Urinals.

A LARGE KITCHEN GARDEN,

Well stocked with Prolific Fruit Trees, enclosed by a substantial Brick Wall, well-built DOUBLE GREENHOUSE or STOVE HOUSE, 30 feet by 16 feet, and LARGE VINERY adjoining, 33 feet by 12 feet, both heated with Hot Water ; two 4-light Cucumber Pits and a 3-light ditto, Coke Shed, Potting Shed, an Inner Yard with a Timber and Slated Shed.

THE PLEASURE GROUNDS,

Which are very extensive and secluded, intersected by Gravel Walks, and adorned with well grown Trees and specimen Shrubs, including

THE HANDSOME LAWN AND PADDOCK ORCHARD,

Approached from the Yard by Pair of Folding Gates, and communicating by a Pair of Folding Gates to the Footpath and Carriage Way at the rear of the property leading from Brand Street to the Fish Pond Closes, with Ornamental Summer House overlooking the Fish Pond Closes, and communicating with which by a Pair of Folding Gates is

</center>

AN ✠ ENCLOSURE ✠ OF ✠ OLD ✠ PASTURE ✠ LAND,

Enclosed partly by a Brick Wall, called

"THE LAWN TENNIS GROUND,"

With Gravel Walk round the same, a Board and Slated Tool Shed. Divided from the Tennis Ground by a Neat Fence is

A SECOND VEGETABLE GARDEN,

With Timber and Slated Tool House. A Covered Subway leads from the Paddock Orchard to the prettily arranged and

EXTENSIVE SHRUBBERIES AND PLEASURE GROUNDS,

Planted with Ornamental Trees and Shrubs in great variety; including

One of the Prettiest and most Valuable Shrubberies in the Neighbourhood,

Forming part of the Pleasure Grounds enjoyed by the late Joseph Sharples, Esq.,

Thickly studded with ornamental Shrubs and Trees, and contains the well-known

FISH POND,

(from which the adjoining Closes derive their name),

Of large extent and through which runs a never failing supply of Water, called "Capswell Stream," (with rustic stone bridge). which is derived from the Spring upon Lot 35 together with

The Ornamental Flint and Shell Building, called "THE GROTTO," with compartments;

Also on an elevated spot in the Grounds is the substantial and ornamental partly Brick-built and Stone SUMMER HOUSE, approached by a flight of steps, overlooking a handsome Lawn and Pleasure Ground, and Fish Pond.

A boarded and rustic SUMMER HOUSE with paved floor, and a FISHING HOUSE.

The Pleasure Ground and Shrubbery are intersected by gravel walks, and form one of the most delightful and retired retreats in the neighbourhood; nearly the whole of the grounds are enclosed on the West and East sides by a substantial brick wall, and towards the North by substantial Boarded Fence.

The Property has a considerable frontage to Bancroft on the East, and to the carriage and footway from Brand Street to the Fish Pond Closes on the West, and is bounded on the North partly by Lots 2 and 7, and on the South by property belonging to Mrs. Curling. The Area of the whole lot is

5a. 0r. 8p.

Subject to rights of footway through the Lawn Tennis Ground as now used by the owners and occupiers of property belonging to Mr. John Durrant, Mr. John Gatward, and Mr. George Jeeves, and by the occupiers of Lot 2.

The above was the Residence for many years of the late Joseph Sharples, Esq. who devoted great attention to making the Residence and Grounds complete in every respect; it is now used as a

FIRST-CLASS SCHOLASTIC ESTABLISHMENT,

Under the management of Messrs. Sharp and Woodhead, who hold it, under a lease, of the term of which two years will be unexpired at Lady Day next, at a Rental of £135 per annum; and admirably placed in the principal Street in the town, facing the Hermitage Road. The Grounds are very extensive, varied, and secluded.

The Compartment formerly used as an Aviary and also the door-way leading into a Potato Pit on the South and West sides of the Building facing the lawn, as also the Window on the North end of the Residence overlooking Lot 2, are to be bricked up by the purchaser of Lot 1, at the expiration of the Lease.

The Greenhouse on the lawn is not sold with the property, the right to remove it is reserved.

The Purchaser to Fence against Lot 7.

The Doorway on the North Side of the Shrubbery abutting upon Lot 7 to be stopped up.

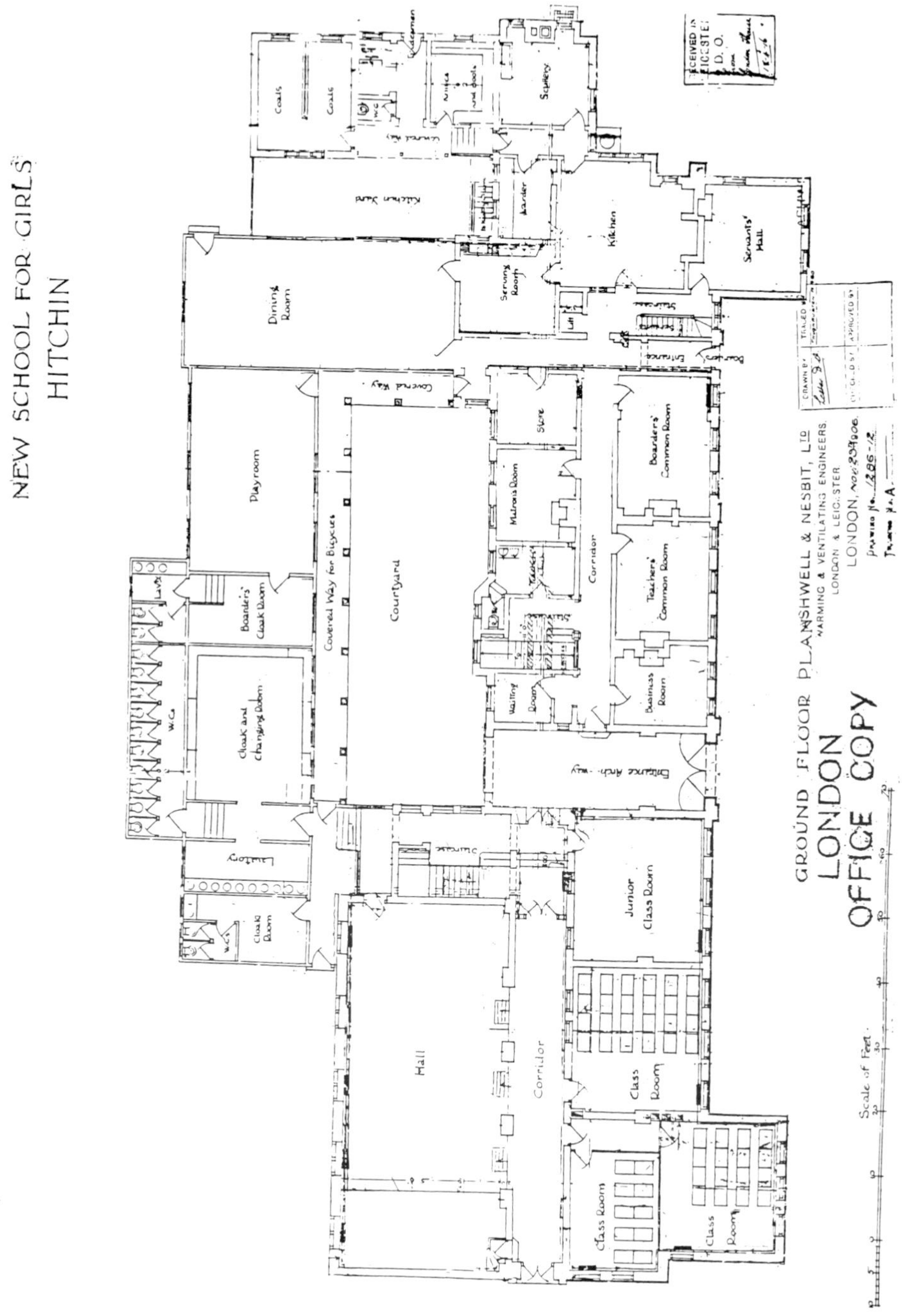

NEW SCHOOL FOR GIRLS
HITCHIN

GROUND FLOOR PLAN
SHWELL & NESBIT, LD
WARMING & VENTILATING ENGINEERS
LONDON & LEICESTER
LONDON
OFFICE COPY

Coats
Coats

Supply

Kitchen Store

Servants'
Hall

Kitchen

Serving
Room

Dining
Room

Boarders'
Common Room

Store

Playroom

Matrons Room

Corridor

Covered Way

Teachers'
Common Room

Boarders'
Cloak Room

Courtyard

Covered Way for Bicycles

Waiting
Room

Business
Room

Cloak and
Changing Room

W.C.

Entrance Arch-way

Lavatory

Junior
Class Room

Cloak
Room

Hall

Corridor

Class
Room

Class Room

Scale of Feet

Class
Room

1906.   Ground Floor Plan.

208

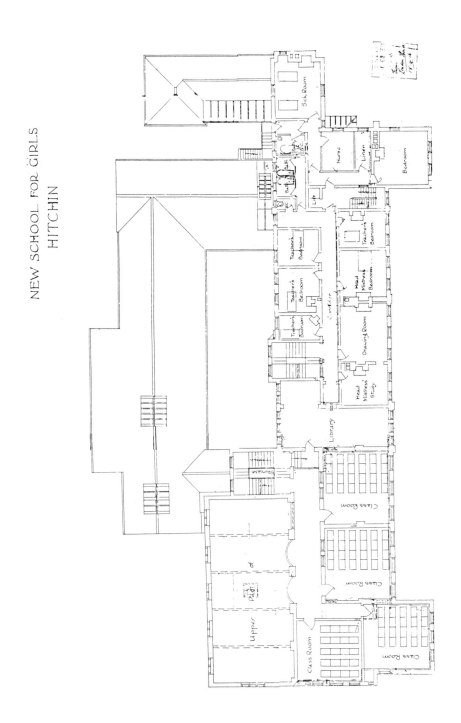

NEW SCHOOL FOR GIRLS
HITCHIN

1906.   First Floor Plan.

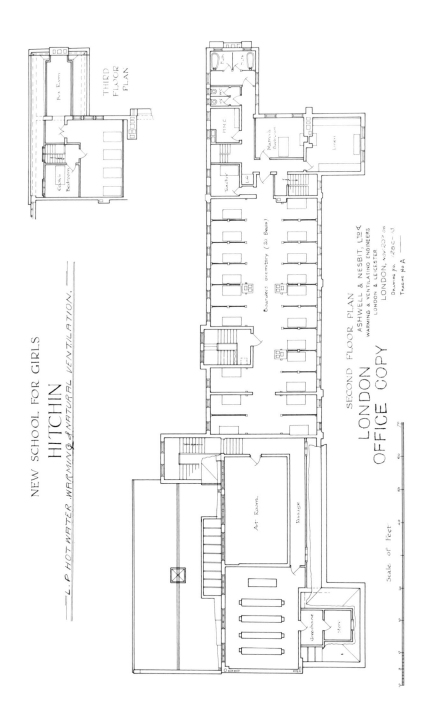

1906. Second and Third Floor Plan.

The choir sat by the pulpit during Assembly, on the forms. The girls sat cross-legged on the floor. The archways open onto the corridor.

The Hall and Gymnasium.   [Jenny Herklots (Nicholson)]

1922   Extracts and pictures from a Prospectus show the school at this time.

'Hitchin is on the L.N.E.R. main line, within easy reach of London . . . a spacious building, facing south and is warmed throughout. It is lighted by electricity . . . received a limited number of Boarders. The dormitory which is warmed in winter is sunny and well ventilated. . . . There is an isolation wing in case of illness. An escort is provided between Kings Cross and Hitchin at the beginning and end of term.'

FEES.

Tuition (for girls whose parents reside in Hertfordshire)   ..   £5 5 0 per Term.

     (for girls whose parents do not reside in Hertfordshire)   £7 0 0   ,,

Hire of books   ..   ..   5 0   ,,

EXTRA SUBJECTS (OPTIONAL):–

Piano   ..   ..   £2 2 0 per Term.
Violin   ..   ..   £2 2 0   ,,
Theory   ..   ..   10 0   ,,
Orchestra   ..   ..   10 0   ,,
Dancing   ..   ..   £1 11 6   ,,
Sketching   ..   ..   £1 1 0   ,,

There is a small subscription to the fiction Library and the Games' Club.

| Boarding Fee | .. | .. | .. | .. | .. | .. | .. | £21 0 0 per Term. |
| Laundry | .. | .. | .. | .. | .. | .. | .. | £1 10 0 ,, |

(Total fees, for a boarder, are approximately £85 to £100 a year). All fees are payable in advance, and a full Term's notice is required before the removal of a pupil and before an extra subject is discontinued.

Next Term begins on

Boarders return the previous day.

THE STAFF consists of highly qualified mistresses with University degrees and specialist qualifications.

Course of Study.

Religious knowledge; English Language, Literature and Composition; History; Geography; French and Latin; Mathematics; Botany; Physics, Chemistry, Hygiene; Needlework; Housewifery; Laundry and Cookery; Class Singing; Gymnastics (Swedish system); Drawing; Painting and Handicrafts; Classes in Gardening, Dressmaking, Book-keeping and Shorthand are arranged for certain girls.

Properly organised Games form a regular part of the School curriculum.

Pupils are prepared for the Universities; for the Oxford School Certificate, Higher Certificate and other suitable examinations. The Examinations of the Royal Drawing Society and of the Associated Board of the R.A.M. and R.C.M. are also taken.

Every care is taken to suit the work of each child to her ability and her special needs.

A list of Clothing, Forms of Admission, and all further details will be sent on application to the Headmistress.

A Class Room.

The Dining Hall.

Vera Davis (1925) remembers that pupils were divided for lunch – the 'hot dinners' sat at the far end and those girls bringing 'sandwiches' (wrapped in greaseproof paper) sat nearest the door. A member of staff sat at the head of each table.

The Laboratory.

Domestic Science Room.

Winnie Prater (Ivory) (1920s) remembers Miss Forbes, with whom she cooked a rabbit. Winnie loved laundry using gophering irons and flat irons. Vera Davis (1925) remembers making brown stew and rice pudding as well as doing Housewifery – this included making furniture polish from wax and paraffin. Barbara Bayes (Pearman) (1927–1933) still has her recipes for Christmas Pudding and Cauliflower Cheese and Margaret Saunders (1937–1942) still uses her recipe for Date and Walnut Cake.

c.1925. Photograph showing the 3 temporary classrooms (on the left of the main building) built in 1920 and which remained until the present hall was built in 1939.

1927   The Misses Seebohm gave the woods and lower field. The field required terracing to provide a games field and three tennis courts which were in use by 1929.

1929   **New West Wing** 'was built where once there had been a tennis court. This gave us the Big Room (Rooms 11 and 12) the small cloakroom (V cloakroom and toilets adjacent) and 3 classrooms over them (Rooms 13, 14, 15). It was all beautifully light and spacious and we took possession of them by processing into them at the beginning of the Summer Term.'

'In the cloakroom there is a drinking fountain which is greatly in demand, and we were delighted to find hot water.' 'We are all very proud of our School which seems completely changed, with so many additions in one term.'

Va report that 'since the new building has been opened we have acquired extra duties. . . . Tap duty has lately been added, which consists of making a tour of the cloakrooms to see that no taps drip . . .'

Room 10 has partition to make it into 2 classrooms. IIIb reporting . . . 'We have a new form room. It was rather dark but now we have glass in the partition which was a lovely surprise and lets us have sunshine in our room. There is another form room next door so we have to be very quiet. Lots of girls keep going through our form room into the next one.'

1933   The Swimming Bath was officially opened on 7th July. Built by John Willmott and Sons.

1939   The New Hall, Art Room (Room 19) and three Laboratories were built and declared open on 28th June.

Queen's Sister Revisits Her Old School at Hitchin

LADY ELPHINSTONE, a sister of the Queen, and an old scholar of the school, opened the fine new buildings of Hitchin Girls' Grammar School on Wednesday last week.

The presence at the ceremony, which was performed in the new school hall, of Miss Janet Gosnell, the first headmistress of the school, and who moved with it in 1908 from Bancroft to the new site on Windmill Hill, gave great pleasure to the very large company which had assembled. In 1919, Miss Gosnell was succeeded by Miss A. M. Chambers, the present headmistress.

The new school hall was "packed" for the opening ceremony.

The hall is 78ft. long by 36ft. wide, and includes a stage and gallery. The hall is very light, with long windows and the light oak panelling to a height of 7ft. 6in. Hall and gallery seat about 450 people.

Adjoining the hall is the new art room, which has a north light, and measures 40ft. by 26ft.

There are also three laboratories— physics and chemistry, biology, and a senior laboratory—which have been fitted by a firm of specialists in that type of work, and a biology conservatory is also provided over the entrance to the new vestibule.

In planning the new additions, which are on the north-west corner of the school, the old art room and science laboratory have been converted into a classroom and geography room, and a new heating chamber, fire escape stairs and cycle sheds have been provided.

The contract price for the work, including re-planning of the heating installation for the existing buildings, was £17,188.

215

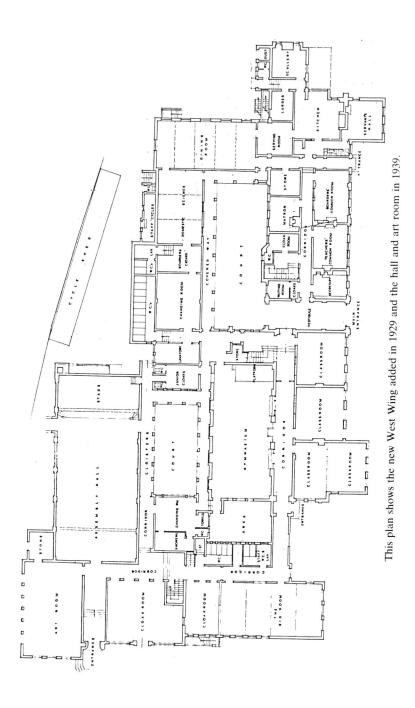

This plan shows the new West Wing added in 1929 and the hall and art room in 1939.

1940   Air Raid Precaution (ARP) trenches bordering top hockey field were filled in.

1948   **3 new hard Tennis Courts** and **3 additional grass courts** were constructed on the top field – the cutting of the tape was performed by Miss Badland and Mr. C. J. Widdows (Chairman of Governors).

1951

Archways filled in between Old Hall and Gymnasium and corridor (opposite Rooms 9 and 10).
Extract from County Plans

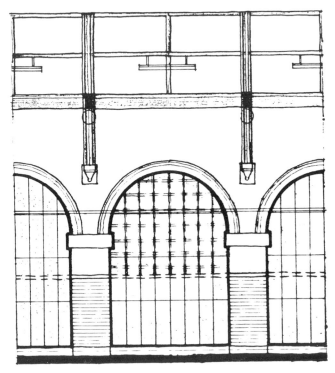

PART OF SOUTH WALL

1952   Renovation of the Domestic Science room (Room 20) and its **conversion into an extra wing of the dining room** were undertaken, making serving and dining easier. A doorway was constructed at the far end leading into Room 20.

1952   **The Lower School and new Domestic Science room** were built on the site of Miss Chambers' garden.

1953/4 Building of the **first floor on the Lower School** completed giving three first forms and Va a classroom each. Miss Badland created a sunken pool.

Miss Badland's garden and the new building.   [School Magazine 1962]

The Lower School and Domestic Science room in winter 1962.   [Aprubs, Goundsman]

218

1955   **The Old Dormitory was converted into the Library.** The main library moved from what became the Staff Room, and the Senior Fiction and Junior Libraries (then in the area next to Room 19) joined it in the spacious newly decorated dormitory at the top of the school.

1958   **The Dining Room** was extended and additions were made to the kitchens. Alterations to Highbury House where Miss Badland moved to accommodation and joined the boarders. Room 20 became a Music Room.

1962. The New Dining Room.
[School Magazine]

Break in the New Dining Room.   [School Magazine]

1958   **Main Entrance Hall** was enclosed.

1952. Miss Hughes in the courtyard by
Room 20 at rear of entrance.
                    [Esther Brayshaw (Speed)]

1985–86. Emma Decent, Head Girl, and her
deputies. Left – Sally Thorogood and right – Nicolette
Zarka.   [Miss E. Duignan]

1969   The Drive was tarmacadamed.

1972   The **Science Block and Gymnasium** were completed. '. . . this will also
        enable the old gymnasium and original Assembly Hall to be converted
        into a **Drama Room** . . .'

1972. Science Block and Gymnasium   [Mrs. H. Cannon]

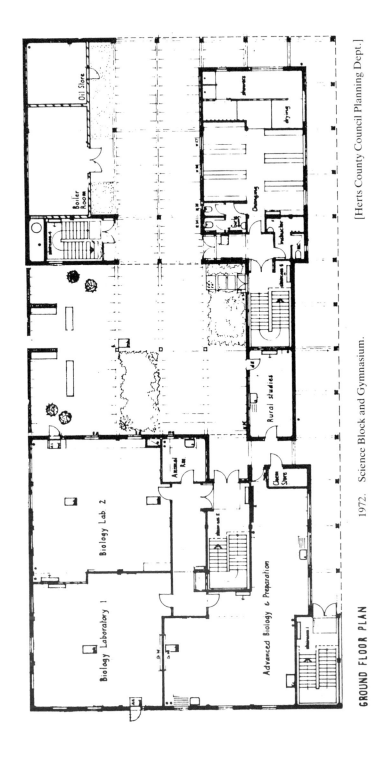

GROUND FLOOR PLAN

1972. Science Block and Gymnasium.

[Herts County Council Planning Dept.]

221

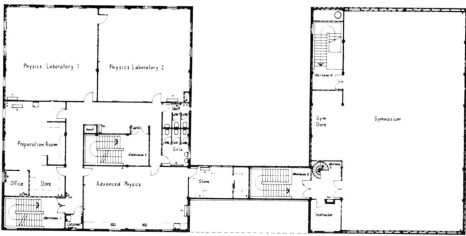

FIRST FLOOR

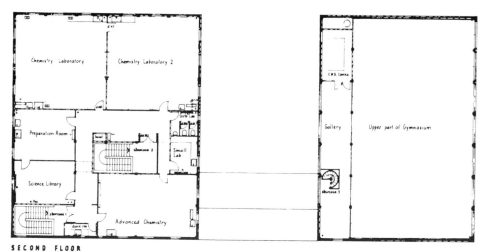

SECOND FLOOR

1972. Science Block and Gymnasium.   [Herts County Council Planning Dept.]

1974   Summer – **Swimming Pool heated** '. . . everyone must be looking forward
        to swimming in the tropical warmth which has long been awaited'.

1975   **Mobile Classrooms** were placed on the edge of the hockey pitch to replace
        the Lower School building and Domestic Science room built in 1952 and
        now to be demolished. Building of the New Lower School and Domestic
        Science Rooms started. Architects Anthony Snow and Michael Jonas.

1978   New Lower School building in use by February.

1978.   Lower School Building.   [North Herts Gazette]

1965. Pathway beside the old
Junior Block on the same site as
the New Building.
        [Miss K. Britton]

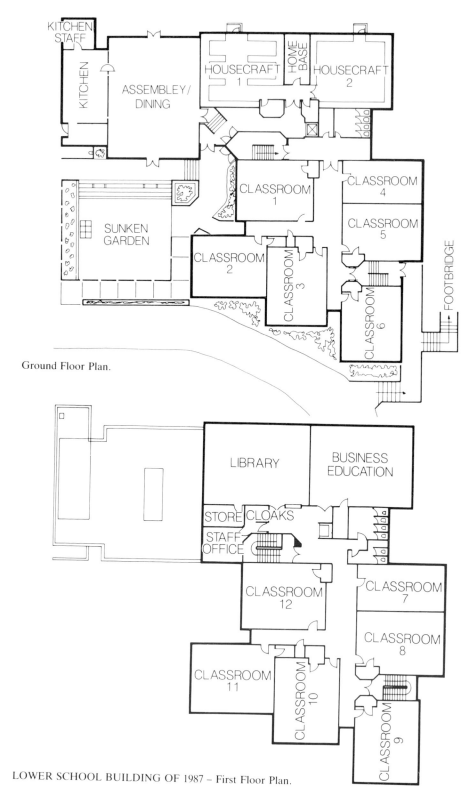

Ground Floor Plan.

LOWER SCHOOL BUILDING OF 1987 – First Floor Plan.

1981   **Footbridge over Highbury Road** to Highbury House, Music Block and tennis courts.

[Miss E. Duignan]

Hitchin Girls' School Music Block – 1981-82

The new Music Block is built in the grounds of Highbury House, a Victorian building occupied by the North Herts Music School and is linked to the main Girls' School by a new footbridge across Highbury Road. The new building is sited adjacent to the Music School in order that the new accommodation can be used in conjunction with the Music School out of school hours.

The new Music Block occupies land which was formerly a stable yard between the old Victorian house and the coach house and cottage. The new building was designed to blend with the Victorian red brick surroundings with slated roofs but retains a modern character expressed by the corner windows and eaves overhangs. Internally, the building consists of a large

performance room for choral and chamber music, with a music classroom and two practice rooms.

It is anticipated that the coach house and cottage will be further developed for teaching and practice rooms.

County Architect's Department
Project Architect **J. Solomon**
Builder **Page & Watts Ltd.**

From booklet 'Hertfordshire County Council Builds'. Photographs by David Houghton.

Ground floor plan for the Music block.

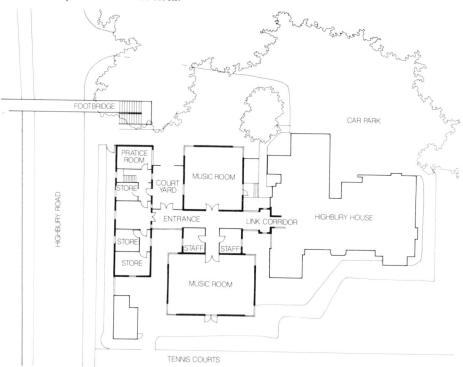

March 1924.   Aerial view of the Grounds and Buildings.   [Aerofilm]

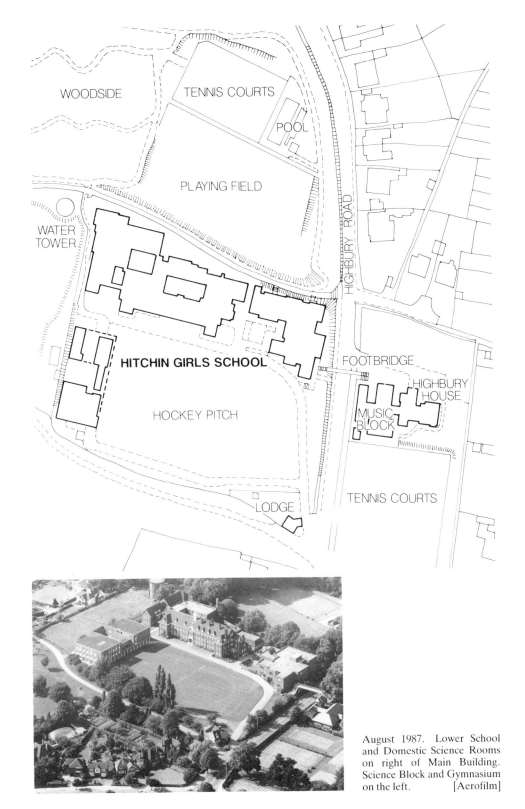

WOODSIDE

TENNIS COURTS

POOL

PLAYING FIELD

WATER TOWER

HIGHBURY ROAD

HITCHIN GIRLS SCHOOL

HOCKEY PITCH

FOOTBRIDGE

HIGHBURY HOUSE

MUSIC BLOCK

TENNIS COURTS

LODGE

August 1987. Lower School and Domestic Science Rooms on right of Main Building. Science Block and Gymnasium on the left.   [Aerofilm]

THE SWIMMING BATH

In the winter of 1932/33, Miss Chambers conceived the idea of building a swimming bath on the lower school field. Mr. Hugh Seebohm, Chairman of the Governors, recalled the Governing body being marched on the coldest day of the year down to the field, where Miss Chambers kept them until they were 'frozen to her purpose'.

It was estimated that the cost would be about £1,500 and, since the County Authority was exercising economy, there was little hope of money from that source. Fortunately, the project seized the imagination of everybody connected with the school and it was not long before all manner of fund-raising events were taking place and donations rolling in.

These efforts were so successful that, by the spring of 1933, £604 had been raised and work was able to start.

Early in June 1933, the whole school was marched down to the pool-side to watch the bath being filled with water for the first time and in a few days more, it was in regular use for swimming lessons.

The new bath was not only functional but very attractive, set as it was surrounded by trees. The natural slope of the ground was used to provide tiered seating where spectators had a good view of all events in the water, and at the foot of the bath was an attractive fountain. Changing cubicles bordered one long edge; there was a diving stage and even a mangle for use on wet, woollen bathing costumes. Nothing had been forgotten!

Mrs. Stansfeld, Principal of Bedford College of Physical Education, performed the opening ceremony on 7th July 1933. As she declared the bath open, the fountain began to play and a student from that College made a perfect dive from

Where Hitchin Grammar School Girls will Swim

"Express" photo)   *(F. Mayo, Welwyn.*

The fine new swimming bath, which is the latest acquisition of the Hitchin Girls' Grammar School. Pupils and parents, members of the staff and friends of the School, have co-operated in building up the Fund which has made the provision of the bath possible. Rands Educational Foundation have contributed £400 towards the cost, £1,070.

1933.   [Hertfordshire Express, Miss Ruby Cannon]

the diving stage to mark the start of a display of diving and swimming by the other students from Bedford.

It was not, in the early days, considered 'ladylike' to race in the water and so the Swimming Competitions were judged for style only; they usually took place on Founder's Day.

Life saving was encouraged and a qualified Lifesaver wore a black cap in the pool; those who could swim the width of the pool wore white. Towards the end of the War, new caps were unobtainable and the old ones were jealously preserved and handed on from girl to girl.

The feature which gave the site its greatest attraction, the trees, also provided its two greatest drawbacks, falling leaves and considerable shade. In an attempt to conserve some of the heat a plastic cover was bought in 1961, 'so heavy that it took six girls to roll it'. Unfortunately, given the vagaries of the English summer, the water still remained so cold that, in 1972, the Headmistress Mrs. Warwick, set up a Swimming Pool Heating Fund. The Foundation Fund provided £500, as did the Hertfordshire County Council. This left the school a further £2,000 to raise.

Once again the school was engrossed in fund-raising schemes and by the beginning of the summer term 1974 the new heating system and boiler house were installed and ready for use.

It is a sad reflection on the times in which we live, that after enjoying, for nearly fifty years, the asset of a swimming pool on the school site, it was closed in June 1980. Increasing vandalism, with filth and broken glass, had rendered the pool unsafe for use by pupils and intruders alike.

In 1987, it was decided as part of the Centenary Celebrations, to launch an appeal for funds to build a six-lane Indoor Swimming Pool on the site at the corner of Highbury and Wymondley Roads.

The wheel has turned full circle and once again a great effort of fund-raising has begun.

1946. Founder's Day.   [Mr. Jesse, School Magazine]

THE SCHOOL MAGAZINE

No school history could be compiled without constant recourse to the school magazines which provide not only information but an abiding flavour of the time in which they were printed. The basics of school life change less than the attitudes to social occasions; the feeling of being 'grown up' in attending a social starting at six o'clock; the pleasure in worthy lectures and the delight in the gramophone and lantern slides; jingoistic patriotism and The League of Nations; the 'flannel' dances and charades; all fix each magazine in its own niche in history.

There are records of a hand written magazine started in 1906 which has, sadly, been lost in time; the first printed copy was in 1910 and with one exception, every subsequent magazine has been traced.

There was one issue each year, until 1923, after which time the magazine was published twice a year until 1939, with the exception of 1928 when the later magazine was not ready in time for Christmas and appeared in the spring.

The covers of the earlier editions were dark brown, changing to dark blue in 1919, and bore the school name and crest. A bright blue cover with silver printing was produced to honour the Silver Jubilee of King George V but remained a 'pocket edition' size of 8″ × 6″. In 1935 the size increased to standard school text book size – 10″ × 8″ – and the colour changed to creamy yellow. A 'Golden Number' celebrated the Foundation tercentenary and the Golden Jubilee of the school in 1939.

During the Second World War, the acute paper shortage was reflected first in the quartered broad-sheet which replaced the usual publication and later in the flimsy, recycled paper and reduction in number of pages.

After the war there was a further change to a bright yellow magazine barely half the size of its predecessor. Other changes in the size and colour followed until, in the '70s and '80s, the magazine grew to be A4 size with a different cover, designed in the school, each year. The magazine reverted to the smaller size in 1986.

There have been only five printers in the history of the magazine:–

J. H. Lawrence of Welwyn	1910–1943
W. Carling & Co. of Hitchin	1944–1959
The Caxton Press of Cheshunt	1960–1966
The Hive Printers, Letchworth	1967–1975
Office Litho of Hitchin	1976–

Though the outward trappings have been altered, as have many of the contents, some things have never changed. Right down the years we hear the anguished cry of the editor asking for more contributions, especially from the Middle School, and for more interesting material.

From this historian goes heartfelt thanks to the many unnamed contributors who have lifted the curtain of time to give a glimpse of the school life of their day.

BIBLIOGRAPHY

The Magazines of Hitchin Girls' Grammar School.
    H.G.G.S. Golden Souvenir Number.
    '75 Years' booklet. Margaret Rees (head of history 1963–1968).
History of Hitchin Grammar School. R. F. Hine.
The History of Hitchin I & II. R. F. Hine.
Hitchin Worthies. R. F. Hine.
The Formative Years of Hitchin Boys' School 1900–1975. Robert Walmsley.
Some Schools in Hitchin History. Robert Walmsley.
Around 1919. Boyhood memories of Hitchin 1979. Robert Walmsley.
A Suppressed Cry. Victoria Glendinning (granddaughter of Hugh Seebohm).
People, Places and Past Times of Hitchin. Aillie Latchmore.
Old Hitchin. T. B. Latchmore and other photographers.
Debrett's Peerage and Baronetage.
Burke's Landed Gentry.
Who's Who
Aerofilms Ltd. Boreham Wood.
British Newspaper Library. Colindale, London.

SUBSCRIBERS' LIST

Subscribers' present names are given; maiden names are in brackets when appropriate. The dates refer to attendance as a pupil unless otherwise stated.

Y. Joy Abbiss, 4 St. Martins Rd., Knebworth. 1943–49.
Susan Abrey (Gilbert), 77 Blackmore, Letchworth. 1959–63.
Patricia A. Adams (Moss), The Fox Inn, Willian, Letchworth. 1948–55.
Pamela Ager (Shelvey), 14, Stanford Rd., Shefford, Beds. 1961–67.
Nina A. Aistrup (Button), 15 Baldock Rd., Stotfold, Hitchin.
Ruth Allen (Spicer), Common Cottage, Milton Common, Oxford. 1963–70.
Helen E. Almond, Flat 2, 2 St. Quintin Ave., London W10. 1968–75.
Beth Anderson, 11 Harkness Way, Hitchin. 1986–.
Jean I. Archer (Hale), 154 Fairview Rd., Stevenage. 1939–44.
Ruth M. Archer (Harradine), 61 Coleswood Rd., Harpenden. 1961–67.
Joan M. Armstrong (Seymour), 106 Bedford Rd., Hitchin. 1936–43.
Mary Arthur, 15 Grove Rd., Dunstable, Beds. 1968–72.
Betty Ashcroft (Beales), 39 Bluebridge Rd., Brookmans Park, Hatfield. 1939–44.
Judith M. Asher (Lake), 184 Beech Rd., St. Albans. 1960–67.
Iris K. Ashton (Dawson), 44 Fildyke Rd., Meppershall, Shefford, Beds. 1942–48.
Christine Aspinwall, Glebe Farm, Shipton Oliffe, Cheltenham, Glos. Staff 1967–73.
Christine Avins (Farris), 476, Uxbridge Rd., Hatch End, Pinner, Middlesex. 1953–59.
Jenifer L. Ayling, 9 Priory Way, Hitchin. 1987–.
Judith E. Aylott (Klempster), 3 Iveldale Drive, Shefford, Beds. 1952–57.
Louise M. Ayres, 39 Orchard Way, Breachwood Green, Hitchin. 1987–.
Lesley Bacon (Veasey), 5 Bladon Close, Lt. Wymondley, Hitchin. 1951–57.
Teresa Bagwell, 50 Fishponds Rd., Hitchin. 1975–80.
Suzanne C. Bailey (Dabson), 'Coppermill', Effingham Common Rd., Effingham, Surrey. 1965–70.
Valerie Bain (Chenery), 161 North End, Bassingbourn, Royston. 1936–41.
Clare Baines (Handscombe), 17 Walnut Tree Rd., Pirton, Hitchin. 1935–40.
Joy M. Baker (Hammond), 3 St. Augustine Close, Hitchin. 1968–75.
Margaret A. Baker (Webb), 18 Bedford Rd., Letchworth. 1953–58.
Christina Baldwin, 'Arundel', Lucas Lane, Hitchin. 1983–.
Elaine Ball, 'Greenwood', 1A Priory Way, Hitchin. 1981–.
Fiona C. Ball, 22 The Paddock, Hitchin. 1982–.
Catherine Ballantyne, Royal Cornwall Hospital, Truro, Cornwall. 1972–79.
Jane Ballantyne, 'Ozleworth', 13 Melrose Close, Kettering, Northants. 1969–76.
Judith Balsom (Terretta), The Old Exchange, The Twitchell, Baldock. 1965–71.
Zoe T. Bankart (Maw), Gosden Cottage, Gosden Common, Bramley, Surrey. 1919–26.
Elizabeth Bankhead, 29 Mexborough St., Leeds, W. Yorks. 1957–62.
Janice E. Barker (Richardson), 25 Oak Drive, Henlow, Beds. 1959–65.
Lesley T. Barker (Gibbs), 44 Sutherland St., London, SW1V 4JZ. 1972–77.
Mary E. Barker, 126 West View, Letchworth. 1987–.
Rachel Barker, Maesbrook House, Vernon Ave., Oxford. 1979–86.
Yvonne Barnard (Checkley), 49 Benslow Lane, Hitchin. 1966–73.
Catherine A. Barnes, 23 Coleridge Close, Hitchin. 1987–.
Deborah E. Barnes, Dr., 35 The Sycamores, Baldock. 1971–78.
Jane A. Barnes, 11 The Mixies, Stotfold, Hitchin.
Susannah C. Bartlett, 46 Townley, Jackmans Estate, Letchworth. Staff 1985–88.
Barbara Baycock (Marks), The Rectory, Chagford, Newton Abbot, Devon. 1948–54.
Angela H. Beak, Lower Cottage, Langley, Hitchin. 1985–.
E. M. Beddard, 24 The Maples, Stevenage Rd., Hitchin. Staff 1967–.
Joan R. Bell (Mayes), 50 Wyche Rd., Malvern, Worcs. 1944–48.
Joanna Bentley, Orchard Cottage, 19 Orchard Rd., Stevenage. 1986–.
Susan Best, 2A Bradway, Whitwell, Hitchin. 1976–81.
Michael Bethell, 15 West Lane, Pirton, Hitchin. Staff 1984–.
Nicola A. Bethell, 4 Old Vicarage Gardens, Henlow, Beds. 1987–.
Elsie Betts (Christopher), 53 Lammas Way, Letchworth. 1925–29.
Joyce H. Binney (Burgess), 55 Fairview Rd., Stevenage. 1938–46.
Jennifer E. Bird, High Meadows, Preston Rd., Gosmore, Hitchin. Governor 1987–.
Victoria L. Birkett, 68 Norton Rd., Letchworth. 1986–.

Kerry A. Birkin, 23 Earlsmead, Letchworth. 1987–.
Amanda J. Birkinshaw, 20 Langbridge Close, Hitchin. 1980–87.
Claire Bishop, 5 Millard Way, Hitchin. 1978–84.
Isabel M. Blackman, 91 Wymondley Rd., Hitchin. Staff 1958–81.
Paula Blowers (Bacon), c/o 5 Bladon Close, Lt. Wymondley, Hitchin. 1976–81.
Gillian F. Boardman (Miles), 74 Gaping Lane, Hitchin.
Lyn Boast (Moore), Cleeve Hill, Cheltenham, Glos. 1957–63.
Elaine M. Bolton, 31 Dacre Crescent, Kimpton, Hitchin. Staff 1955–71.
Gillian D. Bonfield, 39 Barlow Drive South, Awsworth, Notts. 1966–73.
Stella B. Boon, 12 Chelsea Rd., Sheffield. 1927–33.
Evelyn Bosley (Wright), 1 High St., Graveley, Hitchin. 1923–28.
Rebecca M. Bower, 17 Gwendwr Rd., London, W14 9BQ. 1970–75.
Margaret Bowyer (White), 'Whiteacres', Hooks Cross, Watton-at-Stone, Hertford. 1944–49.
Cynthia M. Boyd (Sadler), 38 Bedford St., Hitchin. 1945–50.
Una M. Bracey (Anderson), 'Tremar', Church Path, Lt. Wymondley, Hitchin. 1940–46.
C. M. Bradburn, The Corner House, 110 Walsworth Rd., Hitchin. Governor 1985–.
Kerina J. Bradburn, The Corner House, 110 Walsworth Rd., Hitchin. 1982–.
Vivien K. Bradley (Grimes), 13 Langbridge Close, Hitchin. 1962–69.
Phyllis A. Braybrooks (Tyler), 'Westholme', Oaks Close, London Rd., Hitchin. 1919–28.
Evelyn J. Brazington (Beard), 619 Lordswood Lane, Chatham, Kent. 1951–56.
Margaret Brett, 20 Briary Wood Lane, Welwyn. Staff 1976–.
Molly G. Briars (McClymont), 41 Walkern Rd., Stevenage. 1939–44.
Michelle M. Bridge, The Red House, Whitehill Rd., Hitchin. 1982–87.
Margaret A. Bridges (Elliott), School House, Shimpling, Bury St. Edmunds, Suffolk. 1934–41.
Clair Bristow, 166 Chaucer Way, Hitchin. 1987–.
Kathleen Britton, 34 Wymondley Rd., Hitchin. Staff 1949–71.
Emma & Lisa Broadbent, 121 Coleridge Close, Cottage Meadows, Hitchin. 1985– & 1987–.
Alison M. Brooker (Scarber), 29 Larkins Close, Baldock. 1975–80.
Joyce M. Brooker, 4 Crow Furlong, Hitchin. 1930–37.
Susan E. Brooker (Scott), 13 Allonby Drive, Ruislip, Middlesex. 1973–80.
Esther M. Brookes, 2 Riddell Gardens, The Twitchell, Baldock, 1918–25.
Pauline Brooks (Davies), The Fletchings, 18 Standhill Close, Hitchin. Staff 1971–82.
J. Hazel Broom (Hill), 'Swandean', 61, Church Lane, Colden Common, Hants. 1939–45.
Gillian E. Brown (Melton), 17 Longmeadow Drive, Ickleford, Hitchin. 1967–74.
Janice A. Brown (Dyer), 2 Hoo Farm Cottages, Offley, Hitchin. 1968–74.
Linda C. Brown, Ackworth School, Ackworth, Nr. Pontefract, W. Yorks. 1966–73.
Mary R. Brown (Goodge), 19 The Gardens, Baldock. 1952–58.
Molly Brown (Newbury), 60 Brookmans Ave., Brookmans Park, Hatfield. 1937–42.
Sheridan D. Brown (Pollard), 9 Farthing Drive, Letchworth. 1958–65.
Vera J. Brunton (Nutting), 2 Pound Close, Halesworth, Suffolk. 1932–37.
Anna C. Bruton, 28 Convent Close, Hitchin. 1986–.
Edwina J. Bryant (Bracey), 99A Speldhurst Rd., Chiswick, London W4 1BY. 1972–78.
Julie M. R. Bryant (Bonfield), 29 Sunnydene Ave., Highams Park, London E4 9RE. 1963–70.
Sally M. Bryant, 3 The Beeches, Hitchin. 1981–.
Patricia C. Buckland (Hurley), 39 Girons Close, Hitchin. 1963–65.
Penny J. Bucknell (Smith), 244 Dobcroft Rd., Sheffield. Staff 1972–87.
Hayley & Sophie Bullard, 3 Bladon Close, Lt. Wymondley, Hitchin. 1985– & 87–.
Diana K. Bullen (Grocock), 'Breckland', The Springes, East Runton, Norfolk. 1952–57.
Mr. & Mrs. R. G. M. Bulley, 4 Pirton Close, Hitchin.
Sarah A. Bullock, Abbey Cottage, High Street, Whitwell, Hitchin. 1983–.
Yvonne A. Burges (Else), 50 Benslow Rise, Hitchin. 1950–57.
Melanie A. Burkwood (Gray), 13 Blyth Rd., Ranby, Retford, Notts. 1966–72.
Lynne C. Burnett (Gant), 'Moorfield', Rombalds Lane, Ben Rhydding, Ilkley, W. Yorks. 1964–71.
Janet B. Burr (Moye), 5 Armstrong Close, Wilstead, Bedford. 1968–75.
Linsey A. Butcher, Burford Cottage, Bedford Rd., Ickleford, Hitchin. 1984–.
Jean N. G. Butlin (Jackson), 23 Southfield Drive, N. Ferriby, N. Humberside. 1919–28, Staff 1946–49.
Lorna M. Button (Betts), 15 Arundel Drive, Bedford. 1950–56.
Jane A. Buxton, Dr., 10 Redmiles Lane, Ketton, Nr. Stamford, Lincs. 1966–74.
Elizabeth L. Bygrave (Clarke), 98 Bearton Rd., Hitchin. 1916–21.
Katharine M. Byrne (Wilkinson), 24 Chestnut Drive, Claverham, Bristol, Avon. 1956–63.
Julia A. Cahill, 10 Standhill Close, Hitchin. 1987–.
Rosemary J. E. Campbell (Roden), Fears End, Sandon, Buntingford. 1964–72.
Angela C. B. Cannon (Steel), 85 Rose Lane, Biggleswade, Beds. 1971–79.
Hilary F. Cannon (Bond), 5 Meadow Way, Hitchin. Staff 1979–85.

Joan Cannon, 4 Robert Tebbutt Court, Wratten Rd., Hitchin. 1925–31.
Mavis Cannon (Moore), 3 Whinbush Grove, Hitchin. 1934–39.
Gerard Carling, 27 The Avenue, Hitchin.
Leslie Carlisle (Bunty Whitlock), 10 Dale Close, Hitchin. Ca. 1943.
Penelope J. Carr (Talbot), 'Nelmes', Mill Lane, Birch, Nr. Colchester, Essex. 1954–62.
Shirley E. Carter (Beard), 50 Lyall Close, Flitwick, Beds. 1964–69.
Joyce Cartwright (Marriott), 25 Footways, Wootton, Nr. Ryde, Isle of Wight.
Helen Cashin, 'Thurstaston', Church Lane, Preston, Hitchin. 1976–83.
Eleanor B. A. Cassidy (Johnstone), 'Clearways', Whittlesford Rd., Little Shelford, Cambridge. 1963–70.
Mr. & Mrs. Brian Caswell, 139 Wymondley Rd., Hitchin.
Amanda J. Cates, 36 Otter Way, Eaton Socon, Huntingdon, Cambs. 1972–79.
Andrea M. Chandler, 9 Maytrees, Hitchin. 1982–.
Nancy E. Chandler (Etheridge), 6 Follett Close, Aldwick Grange, Bognor Regis, W. Sussex. 1935–41.
Keeley Cheesemore, 12 East View, St. Ippollytts, Hitchin. 1983–.
Stephanie S. Christie (King), 18 Glenwood Gardens, Lenzie, Glasgow. 1971–78.
Mary Chrystal, Lammas House, High St., Gt. Oakley, Harwich, Essex. Staff 1941–61.
Cecilia D. Clark (Gray), 15 Knowl Park, Allum Lane, Estree. 1937–42.
Daphne M. Clark, Dr. (Humphreys), The Ivy House, Charlbury, Oxon. 1947–53.
Molly Clark, 124 Fairview Rd., Stevenage. 1942–48.
Jean Clarke, 36 Highbury Rd., Hitchin. 1959–71.
Katherine L. C. Clarke, 13 Grays Lane, Hitchin. 1984–.
Margaret J. Clarke (Holliday), 30 Garrison Court, Hitchin. 1937–43.
Marian E. Clarke, 31 Linden Rd., Coxheath, Nr. Maidstone, Kent. Staff 1955–67.
Sharnie Clements, 104 Hitchin Rd., Stotfold, Hitchin. 1984–.
Ingrid M. Cleworth (Metcalfe), 8 Lord Roberts Mews, Waterford Rd., London SW6 2DW. 1964–70.
Rachel J. Clough, 16 Pirton Rd., Hitchin. 1985–.
Linda Coates (Lehain), 'The Kendalls', Milton-on-Stour, Gillingham, Dorset. 1963–70.
Helen R. Cole, 2 Deacons Way, Hitchin. 1981–87.
Joyce M. Cole (Smith), Unit 26, 'Edinglassie', Emu Plains, 2750, Australia. 1930–36.
Trudy M. Cole, 3 Franklin Gardens, Hitchin. 1982–.
Shirley Collins, 'Riddy Hey', 15 The Chilterns, Hitchin. 1953–58.
Anita J. Collis, Stevenage Rd., Hitchin. Staff 1981–.
Gillian D. Cooban (Carr), 109 Hazelwick Rd., Three Bridges, Crawley, W. Sussex. 1965–72.
Rosemary Cook (Russell), 'Longfields', Ledburn, Leighton Buzzard, Beds. 1920–25.
Susan Cook (Walton), 30 Victoria Rd., Hitchin. 1952–56. Staff 1968–70.
Valerie J. Cook (Bunker), 46 Beaconsfield Rd., London W5. 1965–71.
Alissa V. Cooper, 17 Grange Close, Blackhorse Lane, Hitchin. 1987–.
Joanna E. Cooper (Sanders), 10 Wymondley Rd., Hitchin. 1936–49.
Joanna & Rachel Corby, 9 Sandover Close, Hitchin. 1981– & 1983–.
Pat Cousins (Woolard), 25 Great Fen Rd., Soham, Ely, Cambs. 1928–33.
E. Ann Cowley, 20 Howard Close, Daventry, Northants. 1972–79.
Helen M. Cowley, 'Treyarnon', Snailswell Lane, Ickleford, Hitchin. 1980–87.
Margaret E. Cox (Farr), 15 Cross St., Letchworth. 1928–33.
Shelagh M. Cox, 6 Ransom Close, Hitchin. Staff 1965–68 & 1979–82.
Susan Cox (Farris), 40 Trafford Close, Stevenage. 1944–57.
Margaret H. Coxall (Kime), 6 Deva Close, St. Albans. 1949–56.
Kate E. Cracknell, 45 The Avenue, Hitchin. 1984–.
Susan Cracknell (Wearmouth), 45 The Avenue, Hitchin. 1956–63.
Joan C. I. Cranfield (Sheppard), 19 Verulam Rd., Hitchin. 1931–38.
Janet Crichton (Brice), 2 Hazelldell Link, Hemel Hempstead. 1937–42.
Christine J. Croft (Danks), Southern Cottage, Southern Green, Rushden, Nr. Buntingford. 1967–74.
Susan J. Croft, 10 Chaomans, Letchworth. 1985–.
Elizabeth Crook, 9 Kings Rd., Hitchin. 1971–78.
Jennifer Croxford (Dawes), 14 Campbell Close, Hitchin. 1973–80.
Angela Daher (Cooper), 'Ty Gwyn', Standhill Rd., Hitchin. 1944–49.
June D. Daly (Buller), 'Wildwood' Church Lane, Preston, Hitchin. 1937–43.
Cynthia M. Davidson (Smith), 72 Western Ave., Lincoln. 1937–42.
Katharine M. Davies, Dr. (Walmsley), 29 Patshull Rd., London NW5. 1959–66.
Kathleen M. Davies (Bellew), 4 French Mill Rise, Shaftesbury, Dorset. 1935–43.
Diana C. Davis (Phillips), 108 Pixmore Way, Letchworth. 1960–64.
Eleanor J. Davis, 7 Orlando Close, Hitchin. 1986–.
Vera F. Davis, Pirton Grange, Shillington, Hitchin. 1915–25.
Joanna K. Dawe, 8 The Finches, Hitchin. 1979–86.

Judith A. Dawe, 8 The Finches, Hitchin. 1983–.
Sarah J. Dawes, 11 Tennyson Ave., Hitchin. 1987–.
Brenda Dawson (Farr), 16 Marshalls Ave., Shillington, Hitchin. 1969–72.
Brenda I. Dawson (Castle), 63 Royal Oak Lane, Pirton, Hitchin. 1934–39.
Julie A. Day, 22 Kingsdown, Hitchin. 1981–87.
Nicola & Donna Day, 67 Westwood Ave., Hitchin. 1984– & 1987–.
Sara L. Day, 34 Highfield, Letchworth. 1984–.
Elsie R. Dearman (Warner), 'Culver', Police Row, Therfield, Royston. 1942–47.
Sarah E. Derrick, 10 Church St., Welton, Nr. Brough, N. Humber. 1973–80.
Susannah M. Derrick, 10 Church St., Welton, Nr. Brough, N. Humber. 1974–81.
Kathryn L. Dickinson, Rose Cottage, St. Johns Path, Hitchin. 1984–.
Alison & Lucinda Dines, 'Wainwood' Stevenage Road, St. Ippollytts, Hitchin. 1973–80 & 1984–.
Anne B. Docking (Graham), 48 Sollershott Hall, Letchworth. 1932–39.
Linda Dolling, 42 Manton Rd., Hitchin. 1973–79.
Sarah J. Doman, 8 Willoughby Way, Hitchin. 1986–.
Mr. & Mrs. G. Donald, 123 Willian Rd., Hitchin.
Marion J. Donaldson (Wood), 7 Lambourn Gardens, Harpenden. 1941–50.
Lesley P. Donovan (Hall), 'Willow Thatch', 129 High Rd., Shillington, Hitchin. 1955–62.
Catherine L. Douglas, 24 Mount Pleasant Lane, Hatfield. 1984–.
Fiona J. Douglas, 21 Lancaster Rd., Hitchin. 1975–82.
Nicola A. Douglas, 29 Wymondley Rd., Hitchin. 1978–85.
Robert R. Douglas, 29 Wymondley Rd., Hitchin.
Jaqui Dowsett, 44 Antoning Gate, St. Albans. 1977–84.
Phillipa C. Dowsett, 'Trencrom', 50 Horn Hill, Whitwell, Hitchin. 1981–.
Jacqueline M. Drake (Hill), 'Twixtrees', Ewhurst, Cranleigh, Surrey. 1953–60.
Marion Drew (Shirley), 'Hilltop', 63 Highover Way, Hitchin. Staff 1973–78.
Janet Drewett (Carling), Lobbs Hole Farm, Wootton, New Milton, Hants. 1955–62.
Elizabeth J. Drummond-Tyler (Cranfield), 14 Moffats Lane, Brookmans Park, Hatfield. 1959–66.
Rosemary Duddy (Farr), 27 Lister Drive, Northampton. 1969–72.
Betty S. Duignan, 29 Mill Park Ave., Hornchurch, Essex.
Elizabeth M. S. Duignan, 76 Hertford St., Cambridge. Staff 1980–.
Colin E. Dunham, 9 Deacons Way, Hitchin.
Jacqueline L. Dunn (Warner), 51 Arundel Rd., Woodley, Reading, Berks. 1966–73.
Kathleen L. Dykes (Aylmer), 5 Hawkfield, Letchworth. 1926–32.
Barbara J. Dyson (Denniss), 4 St Martins Close, Water St., Stamford, Lincs. Ca. 1920.
Karon W. Dyson (Moye), 18 Woodsett Walk, Conisbrough, Nr. Doncaster, S. Yorks. 1970–75.
Priscilla L. Dyson (Freeman), 71 Browning Drive, Hitchin. 1959–65.
Gillian M. Eades (Newbery), 7 The Green, Tea Green, Luton, Beds. 1962–69.
Doreen Edwards (Irving), 4 The Moor, Melbourn, Cambs. Staff 1964–72.
Joyce, John & Julia Edwards, 40 Harkness Way, Hitchin. Julia 1975–82.
Carol S. Eini (Roth), 3/9 Rehov Ben Zvi, Kiryat Haim 26243, Israel. 1960–67.
Sophie C. Elliott, 14 Mill Road, Gt. Gransden, Nr. Sandy, Beds. 1984–.
Jean Elson, 55 Haygarth, London Rd., Knebworth. 1940–45.
Susan M. Ely (Melton), 41 Grays Lane, Hitchin. 1959–65.
Jane E. Emery (Smith), 16 Balfour St., Hertford. 1927–32.
Julia Emmott, 14 Cranborne Ave., Hitchin. 1985–.
Karen Emmott, 14 Cranborne Ave., Hitchin. 1982–.
Rachel Engjadal (Lachlan) Plataveien 5, 1324, Lysaker, Norway. 1947–53.
Karen Ensbury, 2 Gosling Ave., Offley, Nr. Hitchin. 1982–.
Judith L. E. Evans, 1 Maiden Cottages, Maiden St., Weston. 1966–71.
Joan M. Everett (Adams), 13 Hillshott, Letchworth. 1927–32.
Nicola Everton, 55 High St., Henlow, Beds. 1986–.
Mary R. Ewers (Eyles), 124 Bearton Rd., Hitchin. 1957–63.
Alison L. Faiers, 32A Pirton Rd., Hitchin. 1986–.
Tamsin Faiers, 32A Pirton Rd., Hitchin. 1984–.
Nicola J. Farey, 1 Priory View, Lt. Wymondley, Hitchin. 1975–80.
Deborah J. Farr, 15 Church Lane, Deanshanger, Northampton. 1972–77.
Deborah R. Farr, 3 The Meadows, Breachwood Green, Hitchin. 1985–.
Karen A. Farr (Baker), 10 Meadow Way, Offley, Hitchin. 1964–69.
Penney P. Farrell (Parsons), 72 Tetbury Drive, Breightmet, Bolton, Lancs. 1969–73.
Mollie Farris, 8 Orchard Rd., Stevenage. 1919–25.
Jennifer M. Feaver (Potter), 116 Coleridge Close, Hitchin. 1944–54.
Natalie S. Feerick, 'Ravensview', Hexton, Hitchin. 1985–.
Jean A. Fender (Knight), 34 Romsey Ave., Fareham, Hants. 1956–63.

Margaret D. Fielding (Reeves), 11 High St., Ruddington, Nottingham. 1941–47.
Katherine L. Finch (Katy), 108 High St., Kimpton, Hitchin. 1979–87.
Claire E. Findlay (Bousfield), 14 Stoneway, Hartwell, Northampton. 1970–76.
Joan Fisher (Platt), 'Homecroft', 1A Hensingham Rd., Whitehaven, Cumbria. 1952–59.
Vera Fisher (Dolby), 19 Greydells Rd., Stevenage. 1932–38.
Lynn Fitness (Dunn), 9 Hellards Rd., Stevenage. 1962–69.
Zoe Fitzpatrick, 4 Darley Rd., Breachwood Green, Hitchin. 1986–.
Elizabeth J. Fleet (Sainsbury), 1927 Riverside Crescent, Castlegar, B.C., Canada V1N 3W5. 1954–61.
Patricia E. Fletcher, 74 Sollershott Hall, Letchworth. Staff 1955–84.
Joan E. Flex, Sutledge House, Langford, Nr. Bristol, Avon. 1923–28.
Ruth S. Flex, Willow Cottage, Bridge Rd., Bleadon, Weston-Super-Mare, Avon. 1926–36.
Joan E. Flunder, 34 Woodhall Rd., Wollaton, Nottingham. 1924–28.
Joan A. K. Folland (Latimer), 2 Bickerton Point, South Woodham Ferrers, Chelmsford, Essex. 1937–41.
Elaine A. Fordham (Godfrey), 'Sebago', 43 Bearton Green, Hitchin. 1960–66.
Karen V. Foreman, 24 Broadmead, Hitchin. 1981–86.
Patricia Forsyth (Withers), 26 Meadow Rd., Wokingham, Berks. 1949–56.
Pauline A. Forsyth (Webb), 162 Merry Hill Rd., Bushey, Watford. 1946–53.
Myrtle B. Foskett (Handscomb), 19 Stapleton Court, Aldwick, Bognor Regis, Sussex. 1933–38.
Audrey Foster (White), 80 Strathmore Ave., Hitchin. 1938–43.
Diana Foster (Morriss), Wymondley Hall, Lt. Wymondley, Hitchin. 1935–43.
Enid M. Foster (Bryant), 12 Ratcliffs Garden, St. James, Shaftesbury, Dorset. 1933–41.
Mr. & Mrs. B. Fountain, 92 Greenfield Rd., Flitton, Beds.
Anne B. Franklin (Baron), Pegsdon Common Farm, Pegsdon, Hitchin. 1942–47.
Joyce C. Franklin, 9 St. Andrews Drift, Langham, Nr. Holt, Norfolk. 1930–38.
Julia M. Fraser, 'Penryn', Station Rd., Launton, Bicester, Oxon. 1972–78.
Rosemary M. Fraser (Woolley), 5 Crawford Rd., Milngavie, Strathclyde. 1942–49.
Brian J. Frederick, Divisional Education Office, County Council Office, Grammar School Walk, Hitchin.
Valerie J. Freeman (Beard), 29 Bellevue Rd., Ayr. 1955–60.
Carolyn R. French, 18 Oxford Rd., Breachwood Green, Hitchin. 1986–.
Sally E. Friend, 28 Parkfield Crescent, Kimpton, Hitchin. 1987–.
Alison R. Frost (Mitchell), 23 Folly Path, Hitchin. 1971–78.
Kathleen M. Fryer (Sainsbury), 43 Gaping Lane, Hitchin. 1920–24.
Margaret C. Fyfe, Dr., 129 Seventh Ave., St. Lucia, Queensland 4067, Australia. 1927–37.
Joyce M. Gaddie (Higgins), Goatham Farm, Goatham Lane, Broad Oak, Brede, Nr. Rye, E. Sussex. 1941–48.
Sarah & Charlotte Galer, Acacia House, London Rd., Hitchin. 1983– & 1986–.
Helena S. Galloway (Clarke), c/o 15 Lister Ave., Hitchin. 1963–70.
Pat Garbas (Grimes), 90 Ashcroft Rd., Stopsley, Luton, Beds. 1967–73.
Doreen Gardner (Lewis), 35 Franklin Gardens, Hitchin. 1952–57.
Janice Gardner (Chapman), 'Bancroft', 29 Grove Lane, Bayston Hill, Shrewsbury, Shropshire, 59–64.
Doris R. Garnham (Tomlin), 62 Sandringham Rd., Swindon, Wilts. 1938–43.
Holly Gavaghan, 20 Blakes Way, Welwyn. 1982–.
Pippa-Jane Gavaghan, 20 Blakes Way, Welwyn. 1984–.
Beryl E. George (Tomey), Perth, W. Australia. 1938–43.
Sandra Gibb, 6 Hitchin St., Baldock. 1976–82.
Kirsty A. Gibbons, 53 Royal Oak Lane, Pirton, Hitchin. 1984–.
Katherine Gibbs, 41 West Lane, Pirton, Hitchin. 1987–.
Sarah J. Gibson, 11 Grange Rise, Codicote, Hitchin. 1986–.
Terry Gilbert, 19 Woodstock Rd., London NW11 8ES. Staff 1964–82.
Miriam Gilchrist (Withers), 13 Chorley Ave., Fulwood, Sheffield. 1946–54.
Tina L. Gill, 8 Grange Close, Hitchin. 1978–83.
Elizabeth-Jane A. Girvan, 81 Wymondley Rd., Hitchin. 1986–.
Lorna M. Glenwright, 100 Valley Rd., Codicote, Hitchin. 1978–85.
Grace Gobby, 7 Millbrook, Woodford Rd., London E18. 1926–30.
Patricia Godber (Briston), Park Cottage, 54 Park Rd., Mogerhanger. 1955–60.
Diana M. Godden (Bidwell), 'Silver How', 65 Alzey Gardens, Harpenden. 1966–73.
Elizabeth W. Godfrey, 'Evenlode', 11 Abbis Orchard, Ickleford, Hitchin. 1940-47.
Mary Gooderham (Lawman), 15 Laurel Way, Ickleford, Hitchin. 1954–61.
Emma & Grace Goodey, 3 Waltham Rd., Hitchin. 1982–86 & 1984–.
Carrie-Anne L. Goodwin, 19 Denby, Letchworth. 1987–.
Cecilia M. Gordon (Grice), Lynfield House, Datchworth Green, Knebworth. 1953–59.
Nicola M. Goulding, 6 Codicote Rd., Whitwell, Hitchin. 1981–88.

Sara L. Gower, 193 High St., Codicote, Hitchin. 1980–87.
Barbara Graebe (Barker), Kimpton Vicarage, 11 High St., Kimpton, Hitchin. Staff 1952–57 & 1973–84.
Doris E. Green (Cholmeley), 18 The Grove, Chelworth, Nr. Malmesbury, Wilts. 1935–43.
Jean R. Green (Mitchell), 134 Old Hale Way, Hitchin. 1946–52.
Julie Green, 13 Matthew Gate, Hitchin. 1982–.
Syliva Green (Crabb), 5 Bylands, White Rose Lane, Woking, Surrey. 1929–41.
Valerie Green, 13 Matthew Gate, Hitchin. 1982–.
Gillian E. Greet (Woolley), The Gate House, Dane Hill Rd., Kennett, Newmarket, Suffolk. 1966–73.
Sarah L. Groves, 10 Bowmans Ave., Hitchin. 1978–83.
Doris G. Guest (Franklin), 8 Ivel Rd., Stevenage. 1920–27.
Adrian Haigh, Dr., 33 Chiltern Rd., Hitchin. Last doctor to the Boarders.
Eileen Hailey (Swain), 29 Pryor Rd., Baldock. 1943–49.
Brenda C. Haines, 3 Dene Way, Upper Caldecote, Beds. Staff 1985–.
Linda B. Hakes, 1 Burnt Oak, Wokingham, Berks. 1968–72.
Joan E. Hale, 4 Stanmore Rd., Stevenage. 1938–44.
Shelley J. Hales, Church Farm, Holwell, Hitchin. 1982–.
Anne P. Hall, 5 Green Acres, Lilley, Luton, Beds.
Sarah C. M. Hall, Holy Saviour Vicarage, St. Annes Rd., Hitchin. 1987–.
Margaret F. Halliwell (Bryant), Elmwood, Broomhill, Chagford, Newton Abbot, Devon. 1936–43.
Alexandra Handley, 6 Longmeadow Drive, Ickleford, Hitchin. 1985–.
Audrey F. Harding (Ewing), 21 Stevenage Rd., Knebworth. 1931–40.
Sybil L. Hardwick (Harley), 7 Tudor Court, Hitchin. 1929–35.
Louise M. Hare (Edwards), 10 Browning Drive, Hitchin. 1973–78.
Catherine Hargrave, 6 Cedar Ave., Ickleford, Hitchin. 1976–83.
Elizabeth Hargrave, 6 Cedar Ave., Ickleford, Hitchin. 1974–81.
Betty C. Harkness (Moore), 1 Bank Alley, Southwold, Suffolk. 1927–33.
Ena Harkness, 53 Hawthorn Close, Hitchin.
Lillie Harley, 23 High St., Pirton, Hitchin.
Lucy A. Harley, 23 High St., Pirton, Hitchin. 1987–.
Mary E. Harmer (Throssell), St. Agnells Farm, Redbourn, St. Albans. 1939–47.
Katy Harris, 27 Millard Way, Hitchin. 1984–.
Sophie L. Harrison, 74 Gaping Lane, Hitchin. 1987–.
Carole L. Hawkins, 24 The Paddock, Hitchin. 1986–.
Edith E. Hawkins (Russell), 5 King Georges Close, Bedford Rd., Hitchin. 1915–19.
Elizabeth J. Hawkins, 4 Priory Way, Hitchin. 1974–82.
Freda E. Hawkins, Prof. (Crabb), 1 Rosemary Mews, School Lane, Kenilworth, Warwicks. 1923–36.
Judith A. Hawkins (Carmichael), The Old Meeting House, Chapel Bell, Wymondham, Norfolk. 1949–55.
Sarah K. Hawkins, 4 Priory Way, Hitchin. 1975–83.
Yvonne E. Hawkins, 3 Mount Pleasant, Hitchin. 1976–78.
Jennifer E. Haynes, 3 Canham Close, Kimpton, Hitchin. 1977–84.
Mary F. Heagren-Gibbs (Nicholls), Anvil House, 15 St. Albans Rd., Codicote, Hitchin. Staff 1938–45.
Ethel M. Heap, Halfmoon Cottage, Ansford Hill, Castle Cary, Somerset. 1930–36.
Lindsey P. Hehir (Hancock), 20 Brook View, Hitchin. 1968–75.
Elaine P. Hemmings, 'Whitehorn', Todds Green, Stevenage. 1983–.
Laura A. Henchoz, 6 The Paddock, Hitchin. 1979–86.
Anne Hendy, 5 Sandover Close, Hitchin. Staff 1965–.
Hertfordshire Local Studies Collection, Stock Exploitation Unit, Hertfordshire Library Service, County Hall, Hertford.
Nicola Hewer, 53 Westwood Ave., Hitchin. 1984–.
Christine D. Hewson, 29 Hammond Close, Stevenage. 1972–79.
Maureen E. Hicklin (Robson), 29 Staining Rise, Staining, Blackpool, Lancs. 1967–74.
Margaret E. Higgins (Peggy Mackintosh), 33 Yallop Ave., Gorleston-on-Sea, Norfolk. 1916–27.
Kerry A. Highton, 24 High View, Hitchin. 1987–.
Nicola G. Hill, 3 Stotfold Rd., Walsworth, Hitchin. 1979–85.
Susan E. R. Hill, 29 Kershaws Hill, Hitchin. 1979–86.
Valerie Hill (Jackson), 30 Bury Rd., Shillington, Hitchin. 1953–56.
Joy Hillman, 16 Broadmead, Hitchin. Staff 1980–.
Mr. & Mrs. R. Hillman, 77 Manor Rd., Barton-le-Clay, Beds.
Dawn Hilson, 9 Charlton Rd., Turvey, Beds. Staff 1986–.
Katharine M. Hince (Kirby), Rosewood Forest Drive, Kingswood, Tadworth, Surrey. 1959–65.
Adrienne L. Hippey (Gray), 24 Alexandra Street, Kirkby-in-Ashfield, Notts. 1967–73.
Patricia Hobday, South Africa. 1960–67.
Ivy M. Hoddell (Darkin), 17 Farmdene Close, Highcliffe, Dorset. 1925–28.

Karen & Nadine Hodge, 50 Parker Close, Letchworth. 1983– & 1983–85.
Beth L. Hollingsworth, 143 Wymondley Rd., Hitchin. 1986–.
Heather A. Holloway (Donald), 2 Mount Pleasant, St. Weonards, Hereford. 1968–73.
Phyllis E. Holloway (Sayer), 26 Fontwell Rd., Selsey, Chichester, W. Sussex. 1935–40.
Alison J. P. Holmes, 51 Willoughby Way, Hitchin. 1980–87.
Heather Holmes, 86 Grovelands Ave., Hitchin. 1981–86.
Jackie Holmes-Walker, 1 Beech Way, Blackmore End, Wheathampstead. 1978–83.
Karen Holmes-Walker, 1 Beech Way Blackmore End, Wheathampstead. 1980–87.
Suzanne Holmes-Walker, 1 Beech Way, Blackmore End, Wheathampstead. 1984–.
Joanne Hood, 1 Tithe Close, Codicote, Hitchin. 1981–88.
Sarah A. Hope, Rosemary Cottage, Offley, Hitchin. 1976–83.
Dorcas M. Horne (Molly Hewett), 19 Park Road, Hale, Altrincham, Cheshire. 1935–41.
Margaret M. Horritt (Roden), 64 Downlands, Royston. 1955–61.
Sharon Hose (Bacon), c/o 5 Bladon Close, Lt. Wymondley, Hitchin. 1974–80.
Kathleen M. Howard (Anderson), 47 Carlton Rd., Hale, Cheshire. 1959–66.
Georgina R. Howe, 15 Hampden Rd., Walsworth, Hitchin. 1983–88.
Susan J. Howlett (Carlisle), 17 Baliol Rd., Hitchin. 1975–80.
Alison E. Hubbard (Jones), 118 Chase Hill Rd., Arlesey, Beds. 1977–84.
Helen C. Hubbard (Taylor), 78 Brockett Rd., Stanborough, Welwyn Garden City. 1974–79.
Betty G. Huckle, 'The Cottage', 3 Great Green, Pirton, Hitchin. 1934–38.
Maureen M. Huffer (Moule), Greenslade Farm, Steeple Morden, Royston. 1954–60.
Alison N. Hughes, 14 Westbury Close, Hitchin. 1976–83.
Eleanor M. Hughes (Brown), 'Five Oaks Lodge', Ben Rhydding, Ilkley, W. Yorks. 1965–70.
Lawrence E. Hughes, 14 Westbury Close, Hitchin.
Sarah L. Hull (Welch), 48 Oliver St., Ampthill, Beds. 1974–80.
Audrey Humphrey (Holmes), 47 Grovelands Ave., Hitchin. 1943–48.
Jeanette K. Humphrey, 36 Belmont Rd., Luton, Beds. 1971–78.
Abigail E. Hunt, 19 Wymondley Rd., Hitchin. 1985–.
Isabel J. Hunter (Wallace), Spindle Cottage, Preston, Hitchin. 1921–28.
Kathryn M. Hunter, 14 Beech Way, Blackmore End, Wheathampstead. 1979–86.
Susan R. Hurry, 2 Simpson Close, Maidenhead, Berks. 1971–78.
Ella Hyde (Carver), 'The Rockery', Saxon Rd., Wheathampstead. 1941–48.
Joyce Ilett (Downing), 30 Glenhurst Ave., Bexley, Kent. 1935–42.
Anne & Helen Imrie, 30 Girons Close, Hitchin. 1981– & 1985–.
Carey A. Irwin, 21 The Chestnuts, Codicote, Hitchin. 1978–85.
Kerry A. Ives, 82 West Hill, Hitchin. 1986–.
Betty Jackson, Luton, Beds. Staff 1980–.
Karen E. Jackson, 14 Ashgrove, 140 Burnt Ash Hill, Lee, London SE12 0HU. 1975–82.
Nicola D. Jackson, 12 Ruskin Lane, Hitchin. 1982–.
Sarah & Helen Jackson, The Leathern Bottel, 11 Water End, Cople, Beds. 1983– & 1986–.
Helen E. James, 28 Shillington Rd., Pirton, Hitchin. 1981–87.
Margaret Jammes (Roberts), 37 Weston Rd., Olney, Bucks. 1937–42.
Agnes M. Jenkins (Sainsbury), 66 Bedford Rd., Hitchin. 1921–27.
Audrey M. Jenkins (King), 15 Cranborne Ave., Hitchin. 1942–46.
Hilary Jenkins, 30 St. Paul's Gate, Wokingham, Berks. 1957–64.
Sally E. Jenkins, 15 Cranborne Ave., Hitchin. 1974–79.
Susan M. Jenkins, 15 Cranborne Ave., Hitchin. 1973–78.
Carole Johnson, 87 West Hill, Hitchin. 1987–.
Margaret E. Johnson (Nuttall), 15 Times Close, Hitchin. Staff 1972–76.
Mary Johnson, 61 Walkern Rd., Stevenage. 1940–45.
Wendy G. Johnson (Gentle), 42 Redhoods Way East, Letchworth. 1953–58.
Andrea Jones, 27 Whitehill Rd., Hitchin. 1983–.
Gail A. Jones (McCormick), Putnoe, Beds. Staff 1976–.
Jennifer M. Jones, 34 Harkness Way, Hitchin. 1979–86.
Margaret M. Jones (Boyd), 10 Chiltern Rd., Hitchin. 1955–61.
Muriel J. Jones (Dunn), 14 Pond Rd., Holbrook, Derbyshire. 1952–59.
Alison Judge, 34 Cranborne Ave., Hitchin. 1983–88.
Audrey E. Keane (Handscomb), 51 York Rd., Hitchin. 1937–42.
Debra J. Keane, 51 York Rd., Hitchin. 1977–82.
Olive G. Keen, 3 Hog Green, Elham, Canterbury, Kent. 1936–40.
Sarah J. S. Keene, 28 Wilton Rd., Hitchin. 1981–.
Elizabeth M. Kelly (Goddard), 'Strathearn', 17 Suffolk St., Helensburgh. 1965–71.
Pamela J. Kemp (Proctor), 27 Higher Drive, Purley, Surrey. 1933–39.
Rachel Kennedy, 1 Milksey Cottage, Priory Lane, Gt. Wymondley, Hitchin. 1987–.

Myra C. Kerrison (Jenkins), 67 Bearton Green, Hitchin. 1959–66.
Anne-Marie & Sarah Kidd, 18 Radcliffe Rd., Hitchin. 1985– & 1987–.
Melanie Kindley (Arnold), 8 Spellbrooke, Hitchin. 1973–80.
Betty E. King (Bryceson), Forge Cottage, 65 High St. Warboys, Huntingdon, Cambs. 1925–29.
Brenda King (Royal), 12 Standhill Close, Hitchin. 1944–49.
Carol J. King, 6 Rectory Close, Clifton, Shefford, Beds. Staff 1981–.
Debbie King, 14 Gomer Close, Codicote, Hitchin. 1981–87.
Enid P. King (Pedley), 'Falkland', 70a High St., Buntingford. 1939–43.
Judith King, 14 Gomer Close, Codicote, Hitchin. 1986–.
Ruth King, 14 Gomer Close, Codicote, Hitchin. 1979–86.
Sara J. King, 9 Whitegale Close, Hitchin. 1982–.
Mavis P. Kirby (Mottram), 2 Bramshott Close, London Rd., Hitchin. 1942–47.
Patricia Kirby (Simpson), 2A Beacon Ave., Dunstable, Beds. 1962–69.
Lynn Kirbyshire (Chatman), 47 Turpins Way, Baldock. 1972–79.
Marion Knight (Weare), 421 Don Buck Rd., Massey, Auckland 8, N.Z. 1951–57.
Kim Kokhuis, 19 Round Green, Guilden Morden, Nr. Royston. 1987–.
Janet Lake, 69A Mount Ephraim, Tunbridge Wells, Kent. 1929–36.
Marian Lake, 68 Cecil Rd., Norwich, Norfolk. 1927–33.
Susan Lamb (Garnett), 36 Hampden Rd., Hitchin. Staff 1984–.
Heidi L. Lambe, 5 The Beeches, Hitchin. 1983–.
Carol J. Lamey, 13 Munts Meadow, Weston, Nr. Hitchin. 1981–
Amanda Lamont (Hillson), 11 Bossington Close, Rownhams, Nr. Southampton, Hants. 1967–75.
Emma J. Langstaff, 46 Norton Rd., Letchworth. 1985–.
Victoria C. Langstaffe, 9 The Aspens, Hitchin. 1985–.
Emma C. Laurens, 8 Hitchin Hill Path, Hitchin. 1974–81.
Janet A. Lavallin-Puxley (Mantle), 'Berehaven', Sutton, Sandy, Beds. 1924–31.
Mandy Lavender (Pinkstone), 131 Wymondley Rd., Hitchin. 1965–71.
Joanna R. Lawrence, 10 Matthew Gate, Hitchin. 1977–84.
Valerie A. Leal-Bennett (Walsh), 37 Benslow Rise, Hitchin. 1966–72.
Maureen J. Leather (Kent), 11 Spurrs Close, Hitchin. 1967–74.
Antoinette Lee (Rose), 94 Hadley Rd., New Barnet. 1947–53.
Janet M. Lee (Hemmings), 44 Baldock Rd., Letchworth. 1952–59.
Janet A. Leech (Ritch), 'Long Moor', Meldreth Rd., Whaddon, Nr. Royston. 1939–49.
Kathryn A. Legge, 11 Swangleys Lane, Knebworth. 1985–.
Rachel M. Legge, 11 Swangleys Lane, Knebworth. 1987–.
Edyth R. Leitch (Lock), 12 Lime Ave., Blackmore End, Wheathampstead. 1917–22.
Paula A. Le Roux (O'Dell). 1975–80.
Katherine P. Le Tissier, Guildown Close, Le Villocq, Castel, Guernsey. 1972–78.
Doreen Leuty, 15 Tennyson Ave., Hitchin.
Ann Levy (Whittenbury), 26 Kings Hedges, Hitchin. 1951–56.
Diana E. Levy, H.M.S. Sultan (Wrns. Qtrs.), Military Rd., Gosport, Hants. 1979–86.
Barbara G. Lewellen, 17 South Croft, Henleaze, Bristol.
Kate Lewis, 58 Willoughby Way, Hitchin. 1986–.
Pamela Linder (Tendell), 54 Rosedene Gardens, Ilford, Essex. 1952–59.
Penny Lines (Farris), 10 Oak Lane, Graveley, Nr. Stevenage. 1958–63.
Myra W. Llewelyn (Selby), 15 Keswick Drive, Lightwater, Surrey. 1947–54.
Julie & Anne Lloyd, 5 Grange Close, Hitchin. 1985– & 1986–.
Joan M. Locke (Castle), 14 Chandos Court, Martlesham, Woodbridge, Suffolk. 1934–39.
Rhona Lofts (Pimm), 4 Cedar Rd., Aller Park, Newton Abbot, S. Devon. 1959–65.
Janet M. Love (Ferrier), 4 The Grove, Hartford, Huntingdon, Cambs. 1932–37.
Andrea J. Lovewell, 23 Milton View, Hitchin. 1981–.
Susan H. Lucas (Woolley), Thorny Lee Farm, Combs, Chapel En-Le Frith, Derbys. 1963–70.
Rosemary Luck (Taylor), 5 Walden Place, Welwyn Garden City. 1954–61.
Ann Luke (Tyrer), 5 Hallingbury Close, Lt. Hallingbury, Bishops Stortford. 1951–58.
Sarah Lupton, Royal Free Hospital, Hampstead, London NW3. 1980–87.
Deborah Lysons (Arnold), 2 Sorrel Close, Burghfield Common, Reading, Berks. 1969–76.
Molly A. Madgin (Littlefield), 15 Orchard Crescent, Stevenage. 1941–44.
Wendy E. Males (Pennicott), 66 Balmoral Rd., Hitchin. 1976–82.
Joan Mallett (Cholmeley), 'Conifers', Salmons Lane West, Caterham, Surrey. 1933–40.
June Mallett (Hawkins), 7 Long Wools, Broadsands, Paignton, Devon. 1936–42.
M. Mannion, 79 Pasture Rd., Letchworth.
Frances R. Mardle (Handscombe), 131 London Rd., Baldock. 1935–41.
Maralyn E. Martin (Thomson), 28 Queen Elizabeth Close, Shefford, Beds. 1963–69.
Rachel L. Massey 392, Icknield Way, Letchworth. 1987–.

Sandra Mathers, Fairhaven Cottage, Buttons Lane, Whitwell, Hitchin. 1984–.
Joy S. Matthews, 206 Whitehill Rd., Hitchin. 1987–.
Fiona J. McAllister (Colbeck), 43 Primula St. Lindfield 2070, N.S.W., Australia. 1958–65.
Gillian J. McBride (Hall), 7 Warrenne Rd., Brockham, Betchworth, Surrey. 1949–56.
Marjorie E. McCarley (Pearcy), 8 Grimstone Rd., Little Wymondley, Hitchin. 1948–54.
Mr. & Mrs. J. N. McCutcheon, 15 Maytrees, Hitchin. Staff 1966– & 1979–.
Mandy McGeown, 25 Hensley Close, Hitchin. 1983–.
Penelope A. McGeown, 25 Hensley Close, Hitchin. 1983–.
Marie Mead (Bonner), 84 Ampthill Rd., Maulden, Bedford. Staff 1973–.
Kathleen A. Melot (Pettengell), 49 Offley Rd., Hitchin. 1935–42.
Daphne A. Merritt (Flint), 3 Moormead Close, Hitchin. 1933–42.
Eileen M. Middlemist (Jenkins), Roselea Cottage, Watery Lane, Clifton Hampden, Oxon. 1941–47.
Fiona E. Middleton (Clarke), 1 Talbot Rd., Oxford. 1965–72.
Anne E. Millar, Dr. (Willmott), 8 Mill Lane, Benson, Oxford. 1933–45.
Theresa J. Millar (Marshall), 26 Downlands, Baldock. 1973–80.
Caroline J. Miller, 43 Wymondley Rd., Hitchin. 1986–.
Rosemary S. Millington-Hore (Bunker), 9 Arlesey Rd., Ickleford, Hitchin. 1963–70.
Jennifer M. Milne, 47 New Close, Knebworth. 1955–62.
Leonora M. Minton (Fisher), 57 Orchard Rd., Tewin, Welwyn. 1948–55.
Victoria Minton, 57 Orchard Rd., Tewin, Welwyn. 1982–.
Elizabeth A. Mitchell, 17 The Chilterns, Hitchin. 1978–85.
Gillian Mitchell (Kellett), 8A Old Oak Close, Arlesey, Beds. 1959–66.
Jennifer & Alexandra Mitchell-Cameron, 16 Coleridge Close, Hitchin. 1987–.
Susan K. J. Moate, 85 Penn Way, Letchworth. 1985–.
Pegeen E. Mole (Keller), 110 Pixmore Way, Letchworth. 1926–32.
Moira J. Monk (Birrer), 21 Cranborne Ave., Hitchin. 1945–53.
Claire P. Monks, 7 Parkfield Crescent, Kimpton, Hitchin. 1984–.
Catherine L. Moore, 47 St. Johns Rd., Hitchin. 1976–83.
Irene M. Moore (Tyler), 15 Priory Way, Hitchin. 1919–23.
David W. Morgan, Beech House, 34 London Rd., St. Ippollytts, Hitchin. Governor 1987–.
Gay Morgan, 58 West Hill, Hitchin. 1981–.
Richard A. Morris, Docwra Manor, Pirton, Hitchin. Governor 1985–.
Carol Morrison (Hull), 17 Whitegale Close, Hitchin. 1959–64.
Elizabeth Morrison, 17 Whitegale Close, Hitchin. 1982–.
Diane Morsley, 19 The Elms, Codicote, Hitchin. Staff 1984–.
Lisa Morsley, 19 The Elms, Codicote, Hitchin. 1984–.
Jane E. Moss (Austin), Winsford House, Sherborne St. John, Basingstoke, Hants. 1957–63.
Julia E. Moss (Weston), 43 Hanscombe End Rd., Shillington, Hitchin. 1965–71.
Janet Mothersill, 20 Penruddocke House, The Ridgeway, Tonbridge, Kent. 1920–25, Staff 1949–53.
R. W. Mottershead, 29 Priory Way, Hitchin. Staff 1967–.
Doreen I. Moy (Prentice), 7 The Bit, Wigginton, Tring. 1935–42.
Gwendoline M. Muir (Middleton), 1 Chiltern Rd., Hitchin. 1923–31.
Anne S. Mullen (Burges), 40 High St., Collingtree, Northampton. 1973–80.
Amanda L. Munnelly, Woodbine Cottage, Storehouse Lane, Hitchin. 1985–.
Margaret O. Murray (Lloyd), 'Annandale', Dayseys Hill, Outwood, Nr. Redhill, Surrey. 1931–41.
Cynthia Myers, 1 Walnut Close, Hitchin. Staff 1985–.
Jane L. Neal (Hardwick), Headmasters House, De'Aston School, Market Rasen, Lincs. 1956-63.
Ann E. Neuff, 'Limeacre', Munden Rd., Dane End, Ware. Staff 1978–.
Adrienne A. Newland (Picton), Hillside Cottage, Berrow Hill, Feckenham, Worcs. 1944–50.
Marion A. Newland (Dearman), 9 Deards End Lane, Knebworth. 1916–22.
Deborah J. Newman, 8 Rue Berzelius, 75017, Paris. 1976–83.
Marjorie D. Newman (Sainsbury), 2 Crescent Close, Olivers Battery, Winchester, Hants. 1924–28.
Jennifer C. Nicholson (Herklots), Flat 1, 43 Benslow Lane, Hitchin. 1942–45.
Margaret E. Nickolas (Shaddick), 14748 Darbydale Ave., Woodbridge, Virginia 22193, U.S.A. 1951–56.
Mary J. P. Noble, 66 Ickleford Rd., Hitchin. 1978–81.
Jacqueline R. Norman, 7 Walnut Close, Hitchin. 1979–86.
Mr. & Mrs. L. Norman, 7 Walnut Close, Hitchin.
Naomi J. Norman, 7 Walnut Close, Hitchin. 1983–.
Fiona E. Nott, 17 Bowmans Ave., Hitchin. 1984–.
Jean M. Novell, 31 Marsden Rd., Welwyn Garden City. 1937–42.
Valerie Nye (Groom), 8 Keel Gardens, Southborough, Tunbridge Wells, Kent. 1954–60.
Jean Oates (Brittain), 1 Petworth Close, Stevenage. 1958–64.
Karen E. Odell (Pateman), 8 Storehouse Lane, Hitchin. 1968–75.

Daphne E. Offord (Boorer), 6 Warwick Court, 22 Mount Pleasant Rd., Hastings, E. Sussex. 1928–32.
Margaret Oldham (Waters), 'Little Apples', 25 London Rd., Newark, Notts. 1935–41.
Christine A. Olle (Hook), 6 Oak Tree Rd., Alresford, Colchester, Essex. 1963–70.
Sally O'Neill (Humphrey), 38 Cecil Rd., Queens Park, Northampton. 1973–80.
Jennifer O'Reilly, 6 Taylors Close, Meppershall, Beds. 1985–.
Tracy Osborne, 22 Francis Close, Hitchin. 1985–.
Carol A. Owen (Evans), 25 Needham Terrace, London NW2 6QL. 1951–58.
Janet H. Owen (Hardie), 4 Polayn Garth, Welwyn Garden City. 1937–41.
Jane Pacy (Maggs), 25 Sherborne Ave., Luton, Beds. Staff 1974–79.
Catherine Page (Hodge), 55 Wilbury Hills Rd., Letchworth. 1955–61.
Elizabeth A. Page, 159 Bearton Rd., Hitchin. 1983–.
Grace Page (Tanner), 114 Pixmore Way, Letchworth. 1928–31.
Janet Palmer (Day), 5 Moor End Close, Eaton Bray, Dunstable, Beds. 1953–58.
Linda J. Parish, 12 Francis Close, Hitchin. 1969–75.
Amanda Parke, 'Hilltop', 191 Whitehill Rd., Hitchin. 1981–88.
Claire A. Parker, 21 Bedford Rd., Hitchin. 1987–.
Mr. & Mrs. T. J. Parkes, 11 Swift Close, Letchworth.
Hilary A. Parkman (Farr), 'Mole End', High St., Wymington, Nr. Rushden, Northampton. 1969–76.
Catherine L. Parr, 172 Old Hale Way, Hitchin. 1987–.
Pamela M. I. Parsons (Morris), 59 Burnmill Rd., Market Harborough, Leics. 1938–44.
Rosemary A. Pateman (Spicer), Burleigh Cottage, Burleigh Farm, Hitchin Rd., Codicote, Hitchin. 1958–65.
Dorothy I. Patterson (Nutting), 2 Lochaber Rd., Strathaven, Lanarkshire. 1934–40.
Susan E. Pattison (Lewis) Mortimer Cottage, Westmoor, Mansel Lacy, Hereford. 1958–65.
Una P. Paul (Charlick), Cherry Tree Cottage, 32 Manor Rd., Catcott, Bridgewater, Somerset. 1935–38, Staff 1943–44.
Alison H. Peach, 8 Lakes Close, Langford, Biggleswade, Beds. 1976–83.
Sarah L. Peach, 27 Norton Way North, Letchworth. 1983–.
Margaret Peacock (Walmsley), 63 Cranbrook Rd., Redland, Bristol. 1961–68.
Barbara Pearman (Bayes), 'Viewpoint', School Lane, Offley, Hitchin. 1927–33.
Kate Pearson, 3 Chapel Rd., Breachwood Green, Hitchin. 1984–.
Doreen M. Peck, 25 Trentham Drive, St. Mary Cray, Orpington, Kent. 1924–29.
Patricia J. Peers (Grimes), 29 The Quadrant, Keymer, Nr. Hassocks, Sussex. 1958–65.
Hazell P. Penn (Alvin), 6726 Arbutus St., Vancouver, B.C., Canada V6P 5S6. 1965–71.
Barbara M. Pennicott (Fairweather), 15 Hawthorn Close, Hitchin. 1949–55.
Audrey D. Perry (Richardson), The New House, Gipsy Lane, Knebworth. 1940–46.
Jose Perry (Brinklow), 20 Benslow Rise, Hitchin. 1945–51.
Margaret Perry, 4 Charles Close, The Drive, Sidcup, Kent. 1932–36.
Elsie M. Pestell, 14 Crow Furlong, Hitchin. 1923–28.
Susan Petri (Potter), Orchard House, 21A Lotfield St., Orwell, Royston. 1955–62.
Freda R. Pettengell, 40 Brampton Park Rd., Hitchin. 1938–43.
Susan R. Peyton (Keane), 19 Old Hale Way, Hitchin. 1963–69.
Chloe J. Phillips, 99 Wymondley Rd., Hitchin. 1986–.
Eve Philpott, 14 Greenside Drive, Hitchin. 1957–64.
Averil M. Philpotts (Clayton), 154A London Rd., Knebworth. 1957–63.
Carol A. Pickard (Pike), 8 Ilminster Close, Nailsea, Bristol, Avon. 1971–79.
Margaret A. Pickerill (Wroot), 4 Station Rd., Steeple Morden, Nr. Royston. 1955–62.
Hilda A. Pickett, 53 Parkfield Crescent, Kimpton, Hitchin. 1987–.
Caroline E. Pickstock, 8 Ninesprings Way, Hitchin. 1975–82.
Rosalie Picton, 17 Campkin Court, Cambridge. 1937–40.
Patricia A. Piggott (Wedlake), 17 Moormead Close, Hitchin. 1954–60.
Janet Pigram, 5 The Aspens, Hitchin. 1984–.
Marion Pinnock (Toyer), 48 Higham Rd., Barton Le Clay, Bedford. 1941–46.
Natasha Pitman, 19 Sollershott East, Letchworth. 1986–.
Gillian V. Pollard (Fisher), 10 Foster Drive, Hitchin. 1954–60.
Clare E. Pollington, 10 Canham Close, Kimpton, Hitchin. 1984–.
Ute Pompe, Hildegardisschule, Holzhauser Strasse 6530, Bingen am Rhein, West Germany.
Gwyn Poole, 12 Abbis Orchard, Ickleford, Hitchin. Staff 1984–.
Vanessa & Joanne Poole, 107 Whitehill Rd., Hitchin. 1976–83 & 1978–85.
Patricia Poole (Kenright) & Susie H. Poole, 9 Midhurst, Letchworth. 1962–67 & 1985–.
Hilary Pope (Stapleton), Croft Cottage, 72 Main St., Horsley Woodhouse, Derbys. 1962–69.
Diane Porter, 35 Wellingham Ave., Hitchin.
Janet E. Porter, 58 John Trundle Court, Barbican, London EC2Y 8DJ. 1953–60.
Catherine Poulton, 18 Bury Lane, Codicote, Hitchin. 1983–.

Rachelle Y. S. Powell, 3 Convent Close, Hitchin. 1984–.
Andrea Prichard, 29 Cashio Lane, Letchworth. 1985–.
Judy A. Pride (Reynolds), 4 Cooper Close, Lower Stondon, Beds. 1972–79.
Charlotte M. Prutton, 45 Upper Tilehouse St., Hitchin. 1986–.
Catherine Pugh, 11 Grange Close, Hitchin. 1982–.
Rachel Pugh, 66 Sefton Ave., Harrow-Weald, Middlesex. 1977–84.
Amy Purdy, 85 Chaucer Way, Hitchin. 1921–29.
Elizabeth M. Pybus (Cole), 61 Grove Rd., Hitchin. 1976–84.
Colette M. Quirk, 5 Alandale Drive, Pinner, Middlesex. Staff 1981–86.
Barbara J. Raines (Hill), 15 Pond Lane, Baldock. 1942–53.
Gillian Rauh (Fay), 1382 Winton Ave., N. Vancouver, B.C., Canada. 1947–53.
Julia S. Rawlings, 9 Oughton Close, Hitchin. 1978–84.
Tracy K. Rawlings, 62 Grovelands Ave., Hitchin. 1982–.
Catherine E. Read, 48 Manton Rd., Hitchin. 85–.
Eileen Reavley-Jenkins (McRitchie), 'Whimbrel', 45 Waveney Close, Wells-next-the-Sea, Norfolk.
    1932–42.
Judith Reed (Marston), 17 Kirstead, King's Lynn, Norfolk. 1953–56.
Gillian M. Rees (Buller), 67 Highland Rd., Kenilworth, Warwicks. 1945–50.
Margaret Rees, 6 Church View Ave., Shillington, Hitchin. Staff 1963–68.
Tracey & Amanda Reeve, 4 The Paddock, Hitchin. 1978–83 & 1985–.
Leonie & Fiona Reyne, Etonbury Farm, Stotfold Rd., Arlesey, Beds. 1984– & 1987–.
Lynn Reynolds (Fieldhouse), 31 Station Rd., Langford, Beds. 1964–69.
Patricia M. Reynolds, 16 Daywell, Hollinswood, Telford, Shropshire. 1964–71.
Amanda J. Richardson, 11 The Chilterns, Hitchin. 1981–.
Christine Richardson (Hart) & Karen Richardson, 6 Langbridge Close, Hitchin. 1957–63 & 1987–.
Janet E. Richardson (Jean Russell), Meadow Cottage, Damask Green Rd., Weston, Hitchin. 1923–32.
Joanne L. Richardson, 11 The Chilterns, Hitchin. 1982–.
Joyce M. Richardson (Follington), Reeves Hall, East Mersea, Colchester, Essex. 1936–41.
Mary H. Richardson (Wheeler), 37 Queens Rd., Royston. Staff 1984–88.
Josephine Riggs (Knight), 8 Linden Grove, Sheringham, Norfolk. 1938–45.
Christine A. Rinkel (Buxton), 79 Penn Way, Letchworth. 1963–69.
Millicent Roach (Grimes), 15 Swinburne Ave., Hitchin. 1933–38.
Alison Roberts, 11 Maytrees, Hitchin. 1981–.
Mary H. Roberts (Bates), 54 Grovelands Ave., Hitchin. 1941–46.
Zoe I. Roberts, Hitchin. 1983–87.
Cynthia J. Robinson, 'The Downs', Hitchin Rd., Letchworth. 1983–.
Susan L. Robinson (Hughes), 29 Brynswick St., Bingley, W. Yorks. 1975–77.
Margaret J. Robson (Wood), 50 Brampton Park Rd., Hitchin. 1942–47, Staff 1963–66.
Zoe M. Robson, 'Trepolpen', 8 Lindsay Ave., Hitchin. 1987–.
Susan M. Rogers (Kendall), 13 Goldsmith Rd., Friern Barnet, London N11. 1963–69.
Frances I. Rolph (Gray), 47 New Close, Knebworth. 1931–37.
Paul A. Rooke, 5 Caister Rd., Bedford. Staff 1977–.
Fiona Ross, Willow Cottages, 10 Lower Rd., Breachwood Green, Hitchin. 1984–.
Gillian M. Russell (Tebbutt), 'Lodge End', St. Ippollytts, Hitchin. 1937–47.
Hélène Russell, 24 Dacre Crescent, Kimpton, Hitchin. 1981–.
Karen L. Russell, 2 Sollershott East, Letchworth. 1984–.
Kirsty M. Russell, 119 Coleridge Close, Hitchin. 1986–.
Louisa J. M. Russell, 85 Sarsfeld Rd., London SW12 8HT.
Sarah A. Russell, Dr., 24 Elm Rd., Hale, Altrincham, Cheshire.
Susan A. Russell (Scowen), 58, Kings Hedges, Hitchin. 1970–77.
Elizabeth A. Ryan (Roberts), 39 Abbotsham Rd., Bideford, N. Devon. 1963–70.
Pauline Sadler, 83 Ninesprings Way, Hitchin. 1947–53.
Navjot K. Sahota, 1 Lancaster Ave., Hitchin. 1981–.
Ivy E. Sainsbury (Pettengell), 33 Wymondley Rd., Hitchin. 1917–24, Governor in 1950/60s.
John Sainsbury, 8 Mornington, Digswell, Welwyn. 1943–45.
Margaret F. Sale (Struthers), 'Highlands', Sandon, Buntingford. 1938–42.
Patricia M. Salmon, 40 Benslow Rise, Hitchin. 1969–72.
Peggy Salt (Garnham), 26 Pennant Crescent, Cardiff, S. Glamorgan. 1938–43.
Margot Sampson (Jefferis), Tower House, Church Rd., Winscombe, Avon. Staff 1957–64.
Rowena M. Sampson (Collins), 39 Atherstone Ave., Netherton, Peterborough, Cambs. 1968–72.
Diana Sanders (Daybell), 6 Hambridge Way, Pirton, Hitchin. 1955–61.
Penelope F. Sanderson-Bates, 6 Marjorie Hind Court, Chapelfield North, Norwich, Norfolk. 1970–77.
Lesley E. Sansom, Hitchin. 1971–78.
Margaret F. Saunders, 13 The Chilterns, Hitchin. 1937–42.

Rosemary Savage, 77 Walsworth Rd., Hitchin. 1966–73.
Mary Savill (Robertson), 22 Priory Court, Hitchin. 1926–37.
Marian D. Sayer, 245 Bedford Rd., Hitchin. 1934–39.
Emma E. A. Scarber, 40 Queenswood Drive, Hitchin. 1983–.
Katie J. Scarber, 40 Queenswood Drive, Hitchin. 1978–83.
Alexandra Scott, Pinchgut Hall, Bedford Rd., Holwell, Hitchin. 1986–.
Dinah M. Scott, 87 Barclay St., Leicester. 1973–80.
Mary E. Schooling, 11 Russels Slip, Hitchin. 1942–53.
Joanna C. Self, 9 Standhill Close, Hitchin. 1986–.
Carolyn A. Sharman (Brown), 'Orchards End', 9 Greenford Close, Orwell, Nr. Royston. 1957–63.
J. B. Sharp, 5 Maytrees, Hitchin. Staff 1984–.
Rachel E. Sharp, Winch Hill Farm, Wandon End, Nr. Luton, Beds. 1981–.
Sheila M. Shaw (Bryant), 62 Breda Drive, Belfast, N. Ireland. 1947–54.
Barbara M. Sherlock (Hewitt), 100 Bearton Rd., Hitchin. 1931–34.
Gwennet W. Shollick, 'Goldings', West Knighton, Dorchester, Dorset. 1930–47.
Carol A. Sibley, 37 Westbury Close, Hitchin. 1981–.
Eva B. Simmons (Williams), 20 Croft Court, Grammar School Walk, Hitchin. 1936–42.
Jane Simmons, Bearton Lodge, 62 Bedford Rd., Hitchin. 1954–60.
Jennifer C. Simmons, 71 Chaucer Way, Hitchin. 1985–.
Linda C. Simpkins, 'Bramela', 31 Frensham Drive, Hitchin. 1975–81.
Mr. & Mrs. E. Simpson, 16 Whitegale Close, Hitchin. Mrs. Simpson Staff 1979–.
Heidi Sims, 'Waverley', Upper Tilehouse St., Hitchin. 1975–82.
Jean Sims (Whitworth), 52 Russell Rd., Buckhurst Hill, Essex. 1954–62.
Catherine Skinner, 44 Blackhorse Lane, Hitchin. 1980–87.
Elizabeth M. Skottowe (Thomas), 10 Gloucester Rd., Ealing, London W5 4JB. 1953–61.
Barbara C. Smith (Woolley), 49 Aldebury Rd., Maidenhead, Berks. 1944–56.
Margaret E. Smith (Primett), 'Little Orchard', Kingsdown, Corsham, Wilts. 1933–40.
Maureen A. Smith (Thompson), 'Fairways', 42 Barrington Rd., Letchworth. 1950–55.
Miranda E. Smith, 26 Dacre Crescent, Kimpton, Hitchin. 1983–.
Natasha G. Smith, 26 Dacre Crescent, Kimpton, Hitchin. 1985–.
Rhoda Smith, 7 Broadmead, Hitchin. Staff 1974–.
Tracey Smitham, 2 Elm Tree Ave., Cockernhoe, Nr. Luton, Beds. 1986–.
Doreen Spanyol (Upchurch), 26 Passingham Ave., Hitchin. 1943–48.
Esther B. Speed (Brayshaw), 'Crowlink', 63 Lytton Ave., Letchworth. 1926–33.
Margaret Spiller (Percy), 'Weston', 45 Padbrook, Limpsfield, Surrey. 1933–40.
Dora Squires (Taylor), 3 Charlton Beeches, Charlton Marshall, Blandford Forum, Dorset. 1926–32.
Clare J. Staple, 'Thistle Bank', Blackhorse Lane, Hitchin.
Heather L. L. Staple, 'Thistle Bank', Blackhorse Lane, Hitchin. 1985–.
Ann E. Steel (Gentle), 3 Greenacre Mews, Leigh-on-Sea, Essex. 1975–83.
Susan J. Steel, 15 Wellingham Ave., Hitchin. 1978–85.
Catherine C. Stewart, 19 Bowmans Ave., Hitchin. 1984–.
Una Stock, 74 Stopples Lane, Hordle, Lymington, Hants. Staff 1975–84.
Louise Stocker, 65 Westwood Ave., Hitchin. 1982–.
Miriam M. Stone, Lee Abbey, Nr. Lynton, N. Devon. 1970–77.
Ruth B. Stovin, 34 Wymondley Rd., Hitchin. Staff 1947–72.
Susan P. Strain (Desborough), 'Myrtle Cottage', Curdridge Lane, Curdbridge, Southampton, Hants. 1959–66.
Lois Strangeways (Thrussell), 59 Rock Rd., Cambridge. 1931–38.
Susan Streets (Molyneux), 79 Hillcrest, Baldock. Staff 1980–.
Elaine A. Stride, 4 Boswell Drive, Ickleford, Hitchin. 1985–.
Daphne Such, 30 Blythe Hill Lane, London SE6 4UN. 1957–64.
Barbara Sudweeks, 47 Wymondley Rd., Hitchin. 1986–.
Gail Summerfield (Reffell), 82 West St., Winterton, Scunthorpe, S. Humberside. 1955–62.
Marilyn J. Summers (Kirkman), 83 Bearton Green, Hitchin. 1950–57.
Patricia A. Sutherland (Day), 15 Salcombe Way, Ruislip, Middlesex. 1952–57.
Dieuwke E. Swain, 23 Fishponds Rd., Hitchin. 1983–.
Helen R. Swain, 23 Fishponds Rd., Hitchin. 1980–87.
Joanne Swinn, 1 Browning Drive, Hitchin. 1984–.
Anne W. Sworder, 37 Gernon Rd., Letchworth. 1929–38.
Vivienne Sykes (Dilley), 4 New St., Tiddington, Stratford-upon-Avon, Warwicks. 1966–73.
Caroline J. Taylor, 2 Fouracres, Manor Park, Letchworth. 1978–83.
Juliet C. Taylor, 10 Lovell Close, Hitchin. 1982–.
Mary E. Taylor (Thurley), 10 Church Lane, Eaton Bray, Dunstable, Beds. 1929–35.
Vera A. Taylor (Johnson), 'The Trees', 25 Harborough Rd. North, Northampton. 1937–42.

Rosalind A. M. Temple, St. Catherine's College, Oxford. 1974–81.
Ruth E. Thackray (Thacker), The Vicarage, Martin Lane, Bawtry, S. Yorkshire. 1962–70.
Isobel M. Theobald (Farrow), 33 Gosmore Rd., Hitchin. 1931–41.
A. V. M. & Mrs. G. Thirlwall, 'Che Sara Sara', Gosmore Rd., Hitchin.
Monica M. Thomas (Holmes), 'Four Views', Lilley, Luton, Beds. 1943–48.
Lyndsay M. Thompson (Abbott), 78 Cowslip Hill, Letchworth. 1956–63.
Pamela E. R. Thompson, 4 Moss Green, Welwyn Garden City. 1937–42.
Sally J. Thompson, 78 Cowslip Hill, Letchworth. 1981–.
Monica A. Thorne (Cooper), 'Little Cedars', Handscombe End, Shillington, Hitchin. 1932–42.
Elizabeth Thrussell, 93 Hylands Rd., Walthamstow, London E17 4AN. 1971–78.
Louise Thrussell, 2 Whitwell Rd., St. Paul's Walden, Nr. Hitchin. 1973–79.
Elizabeth M. Thurlby (Watts), Weatherhill House, The Meadows, Breachwood Green, Hitchin. 1960–67.
Paula K. Tilley (Gant), 39 Strathmore Ave., Hitchin. 1974–81.
Gail A. Timothy (Leuty), 89 Dalton Rd., Bedworth, Warwicks. 1968–73.
Judith E. Titmus (Scott), 22 Brocket Rd., Stanborough, Welwyn Garden City. 1967–74.
Betty Titmuss (Biltcliffe), 35 Royal Oak Lane, Pirton, Hitchin. 1932–39.
Hillary C. Tooke (Metcalfe), 4 Northborne Close, Beech Lane, Reading, Berks. 1966–73.
Suzanne J. Torbett (Horsnell), 38 Dacre Rd., Hitchin. 1974–81.
Jacqui Towersey (Saunders), 33 Langton Rd., Bishops Waltham, Southampton, Hants. 1973–80.
Anna Trigell, 47 High St., Whitwell, Hitchin. 1983–87.
Muriel E. Trumper (Haywood), 49 Estridge Way, Tonbridge, Kent. 1937–42.
Doris Joan Turner (Hoffman), 4 Batchwood Gardens, St. Albans. 1930–36.
Molly J. Turner, 47 Bunyan Rd., Hitchin. 1940–47.
Pamela M. Turner (Haig), Swallow Cottage, 105 Haslemere Rd., Liphook, Hants. 1935–42.
Philippa E. Turner, 'Charlecote', Lucas Lane, Hitchin. 1984–.
Phyllis Turner (Marriott), 197 Bedford Rd., Hitchin. 1919–26.
Roberta Turner (Dumsday), 18 Fletching Rd., Charlton, London SE7. 1965–70.
Winefrede M. Turner (Jackson), Old Parsonage Farm, Brampton, Nr. Beccles, Suffolk. 1910–14.
Genevieve F. M. Usher (Murray), 'Chy-an-Brea', The Common, Cookham Dean, Berks. 1965–72.
Pamela E. Vanner (Smith), 100 Valley Rd., Codicote, Hitchin. 1937–42.
Dorothy R. Vinall (Peters), 8 Howard Close, Haynes, Bedford. 1953–57.
Nancy J. D. Waddilove, Mount Hermon, P.O. Box Ixopo, Natal, S. Africa. Staff 1957–67.
Joan Wake (Wade), 1 Clifton Rd., Henlow, Beds. 1941–49.
Audrey M. Walden Crockford (Crockford), 56 Darland Ave., Gillingham, Kent. 1942–48.
Tina Waldock, 51 Harkness Way, Hitchin. 1976–81.
Emma J. Walker, 162 Bearton Rd., Hitchin. 1986–.
Felicity A. Walker, 11 The Sycamores, Baldock. 1985–.
Jane Walker, 105 Wymondley Rd., Hitchin. 1987–.
Dawn Wallace, 20 Trevor Rd., Hitchin. 1982–87.
John D. Wallace, 11 Heath Hall, High St., Baldock. Staff 1971–.
Ian Walters, 84 High St., Ashwell.
Muriel J. Walmsley (Anderson), 205 Icknield Way, Letchworth. 1953–59.
Bridget A. Walsh, 17 Offley Hill, Offley, Hitchin. 1984–.
Pauline M. Walsh, 7 Playter Crescent, Toronto, Ontario, M4K 1SI, Canada. 1959–66.
Karen R. Waples, 2 Sandover Close, Hitchin. 1985–.
Sheila Ware (Fay), 16 Lime St., Olney, Bucks. 1949–54.
Catherine L. Warwick (Marshall), 38 Swift Close, Letchworth. 1977–84.
G. Margaret Warwick (Harrison), Hitchin Girls' School, Highbury Rd., Hitchin. Headmistress 1962–.
Rosie Waters, 105 Whitehill Rd., Hitchin. 1987–.
Deborah Watters, 10 Gosling Ave., Offley, Hitchin. 1976–83.
Brenda M. Watson (Richardson), 9 Benson Rd., Forest Hill, London SE23 3RL. 1958–65.
Joyce M. Watson (Ramsey), 56 Wade Reach, Walton-on-the-Naze, Essex. 1940–45.
Lynda M. Watts, 8 Bowling Green, Stevenage. 1985–.
Beryl Wearmouth, 10 Purwell Lane, Hitchin. Chairman of the Governors 1973–.
Betty Wearmouth (Lawrence), 10 Eastern Way, Letchworth. 1925–30.
Sheila Wearmouth (Smith), 181 Baldock Rd., Letchworth. 1963–70.
Pauline M. Weaver (Prince), 145A Kempshott Lane, Basingstoke, Hants. 1943–48.
Becky Webb, 30 Royal Oak Lane, Pirton, Hitchin. 1986–.
Elizabeth A. Webb (Betty Woolley), 25 Priory Heights, Eastbourne, E. Sussex. 1940–45.
Jean M. Webb (Austin), 117 Inwood Rd., Hounslow, Middlesex. 1957–63.
Patricia R. Webb (Wilson), 34 Franklin Gardens, Hitchin. 1948–53.
Margaret J. Weir (Fletcher), 13 Pippens, Welwyn Garden City. 1934–37.
Susanne E. Welch (Jacks), 14 High St., Pirton, Hitchin. 1948–55.

Janet Wells, 2 Gatesbield, New Rd., Windermere, Cumbria. Staff 1935–48.

Nicola J. Westbrook, 14 The Crescent, St. Ippollytts, Hitchin. 1982–.

Sarah L. Westbrook, 14 The Crescent, St. Ippollytts, Hitchin. 1985–.

Sarah E. Westell, 6 Riddy Hill Close, Hitchin. 1983–.

Monica M. Whatmore (Tucker), Palmers Lodge, Hawkenbury Rd., Tunbridge Wells, Kent. 1927–33.

Barbara Wheldon, 50 Maugham Court, Whitstable, Kent. 1921–26.

Alison J. Whitby (Walker), 2 Market Hill Cottages, Manor Lane, Clopton, Woodbridge, Suffolk. 1971–78.

Doreen S. White (Handscomb), 3 Eleanor Drive, Nepean, Ottawa, Ontario, Canada, K2E 6A3. 1931–36.

Patricia A. White (Simpson), 6 Broadcroft, Letchworth. 1953–60.

Doris Whitehead (Marriott), 'Veronica', New Rd., Wootton, Nr. Ryde, Isle of Wight. 1926–31.

Mollie Whitworth, 27 Spenser Ave., North Walsham, Norfolk. 1947–55.

Barbara A. Wilding (Thompson), 'Chy Kerensa', 6 Stuart Drive, Hitchin. 1962–69.

Julie B. Wilkes (Watson), 15 Whitegale Close, Hitchin. 1963–70.

Bridget S. Wilkins, Dr., 104A Waterloo Rd., Freemantle, Southampton. 1970–77.

Elizabeth J. Wilkins, 3 The Willows, Hitchin. Staff 1980–.

Sheila Wilkinson, 54 Broadmead, Hitchin. Staff 1975–.

Wendy Wilkinson, 61 St Michaels Rd., Hitchin. 1976–83.

Anne R. B. Williams, The Grange House, London Rd., St. Ippollytts, Hitchin. 1982–89.

Dr. & Mrs. J. R. B. Williams, The Grange House, London Rd., St. Ippollytts, Hitchin.

Jacqueline S. Williams (Roberts), 9 Bloomfield Drive, Shefford, Beds. 1967–74.

Anne, Jane, Susan & Caroline Willmott, 2 Latchmore Close, Hitchin. 1981–86, 1982–87, 1982–87 & 1984–.

Patricia A. Willmott (Hill), Cainhoe Manor, Clophill, Beds. 1939–52, Staff 1966–67, Governor in the 1970s.

Mary Wills (Garnham), 11 Marlborough Close, Welwyn. 1938–46.

Mary A. Willoughby, 9 Longmeadow Drive, Ickleford, Hitchin. 1986–.

Sarah Jane Willoughby, 9 Longmeadow Drive, Ickleford, Hitchin. 1981–.

Barbara M. Wilshere (Castle), 4 Manor Crescent, Hitchin. 1928–34.

Christine Wilson (Holland), 19 Girons Close, Hitchin. 1963–69.

Fay Wilson (Pinkstone), 4 Magdalene Close, Dunton, Nr. Biggleswade, Beds. 1958–64.

Marion J. Wilson (Lee), 'Colindale', Pirton Rd., Holwell, Hitchin. 1952–58.

Sally N. Wilson, 96 High St., Langford, Beds. 1975–80.

Anne Winch (Kirbyshire), 51 Ampthill Rd., Shefford, Beds. 1970–77.

Margaret D. Winch, 81 Ninesprings Way, Hitchin. 1938–44.

Ann B. Wingfield (Hewett), Pensilva Fen Rd., Pakenham, Bury St. Edmunds, Suffolk. 1937–42.

Sheila F. Wintle (Ridgon), Sir Williams Lane, Aylsham, Norwich, Norfolk. 1931–39.

Philippa M. J. Wood (Lumsden), 2 Pirton Rd., Holwell, Hitchin. 1963–69.

Marion H. Woodbridge (Grant), 27 West Hill, Hitchin. 1948–53.

Pamela J. Woodford (Tickett), 9 Garwood Close, Churchill Park, King's Lynn, Norfolk. 1971–78.

Sarah & Kate Woodham, 77 Wymondley Rd., Hitchin. 1983– & 1985–.

Krista Woodley, 15 Bury Lane, Codicote, Hitchin. 1986–.

Peter Woodward, 9 Pirton Rd., Hitchin. Governor 1985–.

Brynhild M. Woolley (Bucklar), 41 The Meadows, Kingstone, Nr. Uttoxeter, Staffs. 1940–45.

Mary W. Woolman (Plummer), Top Flat, 54 Vale Rd., Tonbridge, Kent. 1939–46.

Judith P. Wray (Davison), Thatched Cottage, Lower Green, Ickleford, Hitchin. 1950–57.

Lindsay G. Wright, 25 Franklin Gardens, Hitchin. 1984–.

Sally H. Wythe (Barker), The Cottage Loaf, Bakers Lane, Codicote, Hitchin. 1957–63.

Gwenda A. Yates (Brown), 51 London St., Godmanchester, Huntingdon, Cambs. 1956–62.

Jakki Yates, 15 Tilehouse St., Hitchin. 1987–.

Claire C. Youdan, 'The Cottage', High St., Guilden Morden, Nr. Royston. 1985–.

Rosalind M. M. Young, St. Martins House, Church Lane, Preston, Hitchin. 1980–87.

Nasreen Zaidi, 31 Weston Rd., Stevenage.